# Corporate Social Responsibility and Marketing Ethics

Changes in the economy and greater competition force us to adapt our business practices and to take greater account of the needs of consumers and the social problems they care about. Consumers are placing an increasing weight on the social responsibility of the organisations they choose to purchase from and associate with, and businesses must adopt corporate social responsibility (CSR) practices into their marketing strategies.

This book demonstrates the concept of CSR and how it is included as an element of value-based marketing. Using research from the Polish market, the author explores the concept of value-based marketing, how organisations are implementing CSR, and analyses the effect on consumer behaviour. It examines consumer awareness of CSR practices and the effect this has on their purchasing decisions and brand loyalty, making the argument that disregarding CSR can be detrimental to businesses success and profit.

Providing both empirical and theoretical perspectives, this book will be a useful reference for scholars and upper-level students across business disciplines including marketing, CSR, and business ethics.

**Honorata Howaniec** holds a PhD in Economics and is Assistant Professor in the Department of Marketing and Entrepreneurship, Faculty of Management and Transport, University of Bielsko-Biala (Poland). Her research interests include corporate social responsibility, value-based marketing, brand management, competitiveness and innovativeness. She is a member of the Committee for Organizational and Management Sciences of the Polish Academy of Sciences and an expert of the Polish Agency for Enterprise Development and National Center for Research and Development.

## Routledge Studies in Marketing

This series welcomes proposals for original research projects that are either single or multi-authored or an edited collection from both established and emerging scholars working on any aspect of marketing theory and practice and provides an outlet for studies dealing with elements of marketing theory, thought, pedagogy and practice.

It aims to reflect the evolving role of marketing and bring together the most innovative work across all aspects of the marketing 'mix' – from product development, consumer behaviour, marketing analysis, branding, and customer relationships, to sustainability, ethics and the new opportunities and challenges presented by digital and online marketing.

**27 Artificial Intelligence for Marketing Management**
*Edited by Park Thaichon and Sara Quach*

**28 Sustainable Marketing and Customer Value**
*Edited by Subrata Chattopadhyay, Sundeep Singh Sondhi and Arunava Dalal*

**29 Religion and Consumer Behaviour**
Influence of Religiosity and Culture on Consumption
*Edited by Gaurav Gupta, Mandakini Paruthi and Shivinder Nijjer*

**30 Corporate Social Responsibility and Marketing Ethics**
The Effects of Value-Based Marketing on Consumer Behaviour
*Honorata Howaniec*

**31 Ethnic Hospitality Marketing**
Authenticity and Quality Constructions in the Greek Food Industry
*Elena Chatzopoulou*

For more information about this series, please visit: www.routledge.com/Routledge-Studies-in-Marketing/book-series/RMKT

# Corporate Social Responsibility and Marketing Ethics

## The Effects of Value-Based Marketing on Consumer Behaviour

Honorata Howaniec

Routledge
Taylor & Francis Group
LONDON AND NEW YORK

First published 2023
by Routledge
4 Park Square, Milton Park, Abingdon, Oxon OX14 4RN

and by Routledge
605 Third Avenue, New York, NY 10158

Routledge is an imprint of the Taylor & Francis Group, an informa business



British Library Cataloguing-in-Publication Data
A catalogue record for this book is available from the British Library

ISBN: 978-1-032-32922-2 (hbk)
ISBN: 978-1-032-32923-9 (pbk)
ISBN: 978-1-003-31736-4 (ebk)

DOI: 10.4324/9781003317364

Typeset in Bembo
by codeMantra

# Contents

# Figures

# Tables

# Introduction

## Justification of the problem

In recent years, business has been criticised as the main cause of social, environmental, and even economic problems. Depletion of natural resources, environmental degradation, and growing expectations towards business have shifted interest in the functioning of the economy towards the perception and analysis of social costs, i.e. all direct and indirect losses that are incurred by the environment as a result of the functioning of economic entities. On the other hand, increasing globalisation and facilitating mobility and communication make the decisions and actions of enterprises subject to greater control of a wide range of different groups and individuals.

Confidence in business has dropped. Companies are accused of prospering at the expense of the community, not caring for the well-being of present and future generations and inhibiting social progress. It is expected not only to increase the involvement of business in solving social problems, but also to consider the social and environmental perspective in day-to-day management. The analysis of the functioning of the business confirms that a large part of the problem lies in the business itself. Enterprises still give priority to a narrow approach to value creation, i.e. they are focused on optimising short-term financial results. Any additional activities that do not bring a positive economic result in a short period of time are not viewed by the business as justified. The main problem, therefore, lies in the conflicting expectations of society and business. Society requires increased responsibility in the day-to-day operation of enterprises, while business, in turn, is interested in increasing the value of the enterprise, i.e. carrying out activities in an economically reasonable manner, thus giving a specific return to the owners.

Discussions on the contemporary role of business once again drew the attention of both theoreticians and practitioners to the ethical aspects of business operations and the concept of corporate social responsibility (CSR). While the cost-benefit analysis of CSR has long been questioned, the existing literature largely recognises the role of community involvement in adding value to an enterprise. The benefits of implementing CSR into practice are presented in various aspects, including an increase in operational efficiency (Porter,

DOI: 10.4324/9781003317364-1

Kramer 2002; Saiia et al. 2003; Brammer, Millington, 2005), an increase in employee productivity (Valentine, Fleischman 2008), profits from products (Menon, Kahn 2003), benefits on the capital market (Dhaliwal et al. 2012), or benefits in the area of risk management (Dhaliwal et al. 2011). Of course, CSR is also subject to criticism. The main accusations against CSR relate to economic aspects. It is emphasised, inter alia, that not all activities included in the CSR area have a positive impact on the company's profits, and in particular, this impact is not visible in a short period of time. The peripheral nature of CSR is also considered a weakness of the present "image" of CSR. It is alleged that CSR has been largely limited to the largest companies and public relations (PR) departments and is not a business integrating function. It is also alleged that social responsibility is incremental. CSR adopted a model typical of quality management, i.e. resulting in incremental improvements that correspond to neither the scale nor the urgency of the needs it should respond to (see Visser 2012: 3). The proposed solution to the situation thus defined is to redefine the purpose of the business from creating value for shareholders, to creating "shared value", which again combines the company's success with social progress (Porter, Kramer 2011).

Existing literature tends to emphasise the need for value creation targeted at different types of stakeholders. Research on the benefits of being responsible in business confirms the positive impact of CSR on the company's results. Despite the perceived need to create value for customers, there is no clear conceptualisation of how to create this value, consequently improving the perceived use value of the business offer. The flagship item in the field of value marketing is the book by P. Doyle (2000), in which the positive effect of creating shared value in the area of marketing is widely described and the impact of such action on the financial results of companies. However, this book does not provide knowledge on operational creating of customer value.

The book presents the concept of creating value-based marketing, considering CSR aspects, as an element that creates value for customers and other stakeholders. The aim of the work is to map the key challenges faced by value marketing and to indicate areas where the inclusion of CSR activities will provide value to customers, thus contributing to an increase in shareholder value. From the point of view of the assumptions of the work, however, it is necessary to redefine the goals of marketing activities and move from the stage of acquiring and maintaining relationships with the client to creating real value for the client. Considering social aspects, and even morality, in the marketing activities of enterprises may significantly contribute to the increase in the effectiveness of activities carried out. The basic condition, however, is that the actions taken deliver real value for customers and other stakeholders. Treating CSR as an element of PR is insufficient and does not bring the desired effects, and what is more, such conduct reduces the confidence in the marketing activities of enterprises (greenwashing).

The rationales for including broadly understood responsibility in the marketing activities of companies – in such a way that they create value for clients and other stakeholders – are the following arguments (cf. Porter, Kramer 2006):

1 The Moral Recall: Companies have a responsibility to do what is right and be good citizens.
2 The Sustainability Argument: Companies should ensure that our current needs are met without compromising future generations.
3 Business Legitimisation: Companies need permission from governments, communities, and other stakeholders to conduct business; they should also feel obligated by the social need to increase the responsibility of their activities.
4 The Reputation Argument: CSR improves the image of the company and its brand(s), contributing to the increase in the value of the enterprise; however, a reputation-based approach to CSR that focuses mainly on external audiences rarely brings strategic benefits.

## Goals and hypotheses

In view of the perceived gap in the area of value-based marketing and the proposal to consider the elements of CSR in the field of creating and delivering real value for clients and other stakeholders, it is justified to take up the problem and propose solutions that can be used in business practice.

The main goal of the work – as already indicated – is to map the key challenges faced by value-based marketing and to indicate areas in which the inclusion of CSR activities in the market activities of companies will provide value to customers, thus contributing to an increase in shareholder value.

The theoretical and cognitive goal of this work is therefore:

1 Identifying CSR elements that affect the value perceived by customers and other stakeholders of the company.
2 Identifying the mutual relations between CSR and shaping the marketing activities of companies, with particular emphasis on the potential to create value for customers and other stakeholders.
3 Defining the areas of value creation for stakeholders in the market activities of enterprises.

The methodological goal is the operationalisation of CSR areas and elements, which are perceived as elements creating value for individual stakeholders.

In connection with the objectives formulated in this way, the main hypothesis of the work was adopted, containing the assumption that considering the broadly understood social responsibility in market activities of enterprises is a value noticed by both customers and enterprises themselves, which contributes to the conscious creation of value for stakeholders as an element of the company's strategy.

The main hypothesis was assigned the following supporting hypotheses:

Ha1 Consumers who know the basic assumptions of the CSR concept positively assess the activities in the area of social responsibility undertaken by enterprises and, seeing their value, take CSR into account when making purchases.

Ha2 The perception of CSR as a value and its consideration by consumers when making purchases is conditioned by their socio-demographic features.

Ha3 Enterprises that know the basic assumptions of CSR positively evaluate the concept of CSR and apply its principles in their business activities.

Ha4 CSR awareness and acting in accordance with its principles are determined by the characteristics of enterprises.

In relation to the adopted auxiliary hypotheses, detailed statistical hypotheses were adopted, which allowed for the verification of the adopted statements. These hypotheses are presented in Chapter 5.

## Research methodology

The concept of CSR still seems to be a new concept in developing markets. Despite numerous examples provided by multinationals and large enterprises, small- and medium-sized enterprises very often have not come across this term yet. The level of knowledge of the subject among consumers is similar. Although the concept is not known to most of the people in practice, efforts were made to define the perceived value of CSR activities and their impact on the creating of value by enterprises.

The research was conducted among two groups: 800 consumers in 2011–2013 and 180 enterprises in 2013–2015, both in the Silesia and Lesser Poland voivodships. The first sample includes ordinary citizens, the so-called consumers who, when making purchases, consider CSR aspects or not. The structure of the sample partially reflects the distribution of the characteristics of the society in Poland (quota selection based on gender, place of residence, and, partially, education; Table 0.1). The second sample includes both public and private companies operating on the Polish market. The companies represent various business lines and are diversified in terms of the characteristics that describe them (Table 0.2).

In both groups, a survey with the use of a questionnaire was used. Convenient selection was used in the research (in the first group, convenient selection with an attempt to maintain the quota of the sample). In the first group, after rejecting invalid responses, 502 questionnaires were used as the basis for calculations. In the group of enterprises, the survey was conducted in the form of a structured interview. After rejecting invalid responses, 150 questionnaires were used as the basis for the calculation.

*Table 0.1* Customers – sample structure (%) (*N* = 502. Own study)

| *Gender* | *Female* | | *Male* | | |
|---|---|---|---|---|---|
| | 57,4 | | 41,2 | | |
| Age | Up to 25 years | From 26 to 35 years old | From 36 to 45 years old | From 46 to 55 years old | Over 56 years old |
| | 49.0 | 17.3 | 12.2 | 12.2 | 9.4 |
| Education | Primary/Middle school | Vocational school | High school education | A university degree | |
| | 2.4 | 9.8 | 53.6 | 32.7 | |
| Place of residence | City of over 100 thousand. residents | City from 25 to 100 thousand. residents | City to 25 thousand. residents | Village | |
| | 14.5 | 20.3 | 22.7 | 42.4 | |
| Monthly net income per family member | To 500 zlotys | From 500 to 1500 zlotys | From 1500 to 2500 zlotys | Over 2500 zlotys | |
| | 8,8 | 51,6 | 25,7 | 10,6 | |
| Status | Student | A working person | An unemployed person | Pensioner | |
| | 45.2 | 45.2 | 9.4 | 7.6 | |

*Table 0.2* Enterprises – sample structure (%) (*N* = 150. Own study)

| *Organisational position* | *Chief executive officer/ Managing Director/ Company owner* | *Chief marketing officer/ Marketing department manager* | *Sales director/ Sales manager* | *CSR specialist* | *Other* |
|---|---|---|---|---|---|
| % | 48.7 | 10.7 | 22.7 | 0.7 | 17.3 |
| **Formal status and structure of the company** | Enterprise branch | A one-company enterprise | Multi-company enterprise | Capital group | |
| % | 10.7 | 70.0 | 12.7 | 6.7 | |
| **Financial condition** | Very favourable | Favourable | Average | Difficult | |
| % | 7.3 | 57.3 | 29.3 | 6.0 | |
| **Number of brands** | One | From 2 to 3 | From 4 to 6 | 7 or more | |
| % | 52.0 | 22.7 | 14.0 | 11.3 | |

(*Continued*)

*Table 0.2* Continued

| *Organisational position* | *Chief executive officer/ Managing Director/ Company owner* | *Chief marketing officer/ Marketing department manager* | *Sales director/ Sales manager* | *CSR specialist* | *Other* |
|---|---|---|---|---|---|
| **Knowledge of the brand(s) in the market** | Leading | Well known | Rather known | Barely known | |
| % | 5.3 | 42.7 | 35.3 | 16.7 | |
| **The employment** | Below 10 people | 10–49 people | 50–249 people | More than 250 people | |
| % | 48.0 | 29.3 | 10.0 | 12.7 | |
| **Company's size** | Micro-enterprise | Small enterprise | Medium-sized enterprise | Large enterprise | |
| % | 43.3 | 34.0 | 10.0 | 12.7 | |
| **The form of company ownership** | Private | The state | Cooperative | | |
| % | 93.3 | 4.7 | 2.0 | | |
| **Ownership supervision** | Domestic | Foreign | Mixed | | |
| % | 86.0 | 6.0 | 8.0 | | |
| **Annual revenue value** | Up to 500,000 zlotys | From 500 to 2 million zlotys | From 2 million to 10 million zlotys | Above 10 million zlotys | |
| % | 60.0 | 23.3 | 4.7 | 12.0 | |
| **Business range** | Local | Regional | National | International | Global |
| % | 40.0 | 22.0 | 15.3 | 16.0 | 6.7 |
| **Time of doing business** | Less than 5 years | From 6 to 10 years old | From 11 to 20 years old | Over 20 years old | |
| % | 16.0 | 30.7 | 35.3 | 18.0 | |
| **Nature of the business** | Production | Trade | Services | Other | |
| % | 37.3 | 43.3 | 57.3 | 0.0 | |

Due to the lack of quantitative data indicating, for example, expenditure on CSR activities and revenues generated by such activities, only qualitative data was used in the study.

## Statistical analysis of data

In order to answer the research questions and test the hypotheses, statistical analyses were carried out using the Statistica ver. 13.1. (Statsoft, Inc., Tulsa,

USA). The classic threshold $\alpha = 0.05$ was considered the level of significance. The relationship between the variables, the values of which were compiled in multi-way tables, was identified using the significance test for qualitative (categorised) Pearson Chi-square variables. Fi ($\phi$) was used as a measure of the correlation between the two qualitative (categorised) variables in the $2 \times 2$ table. Its value can vary from 0 (no relationship between the variables) to 1 (complete relationship between the variables in the table). As a measure of the correlation between qualitative (categorised) variables in the table $m \times n$, where m or $n > 2$ (relationships between two nominal variables, at least one of which has more than two values), the Cramer's V coefficient was used, the value of which may vary from 0 (no relationship between the variables) to 1 (complete relationship between the variables in the table).

# 1 Corporate social responsibility

## Genesis, the role of ethics in shaping the concept

### Ethics and ethics in business: explanation of terms

Defining ethics is not easy. There are many definitions of this concept in the literature. For example, for D. Runes, ethical behaviour refers to fair or appropriate standards of behaviour between the parties in a particular situation (Runes 1964: 98). T. Beauchamp and N. Bowie define ethics as an inquiry into what is right and what is wrong, what is appropriate and what is not appropriate, and therefore it is an inquiry of what we should and should not do (Beauchamp, Bowie 1983: 3). R. De George, meanwhile, defines ethics as the science of morality, arguing that the concept of morality is the appropriate term to describe those practices and activities that are considered important from the point of view of fighting evil, the principles governing these activities, and the values that are supported or implemented by these practices and activities (De George 1982: 13–15).

Ethics (Greek: ethikos – customary, ethos – custom) arose in antiquity as a science of moral values. Plato divided the philosophy of that time into (Nogalski, Śniadecki 2001: 20–21)]:

- ontology – the science of being (Greek: óntos – being, logos – science), also called metaphysics, dealing with the nature and structure of reality and the general theory of objects,
- gnoseology – the science of cognition (Greek: gnósis, gnóseös – cognition), also known as epistemology,
- axiology – a theory of value that examines the nature of value as well as the foundations and criteria of evaluation (Greek: áksios – valuable).

Two disciplines emerged from axiology: ethics – dealing with moral values, and aesthetics – studying aesthetic values.

Referring to the encyclopedic explanation of the scope of ethics, it can be treated: first, as the totality of moral features and norms adopted in a specific community, i.e. society, class, or social group, and second, as a science of morality (New Universal Encyclopedia 1995: 280). In individual versions of business ethics, the emphasis may be on various values, but it is always about

DOI: 10.4324/9781003317364-2

realising some positive values and avoiding and eliminating negative values. Ethics that would not refer to any values and therefore would be in the so-called "axiological vacuum" would be axiologically undefined, and thus devoid of a deeper meaning (Węgrzecki 2012: 22–23).

Ethics can therefore be treated as a system of values and norms of conduct in force in a particular community or as a science of morality dealing with establishing binding norms of conduct as well as describing and explaining the actually existing morality (Potocki 2000: 150). Ethics, however, is not altruism or common sense, struggle or sacrifice, religion, or compliance with laws or contracts (cf. Sternberg 1998: 88–94). When analyzing the concept of ethics, it should be emphasised that ethics can be considered on the basis of absolute values, i.e. universal, a priori, innate, final, obvious and not requiring explanation, and instrumental, i.e. posteriori, acquired, serving to achieve a goal and requiring justification (cf. Nogalski, Śniadecki 2001: 21).

From the point of view of ethics in the broadly understood economy or business, many questions arise. The most important ones include the question of the context in which ethical conduct in business can be talked about, and the fundamental question whether the pursuit of profit can be ethical or excludes such conduct.

The first economic work in history on household management – The Economics of Xenophon (430–355 BCE), a student of Socrates – was devoted to the ethics of running a household and work organisation (New Universal Encyclopedia 1995: 597–598). The subject of ethics, including ethics of management, work, and organisation, can also be found in the writings of theologians, e.g. St. Augustine (354–430), St. Thomas Aquinas (1225–1274), as well as in the Bible, Talmud, and Quran (cf. Nogalski, Śniadecki 2001: 27). The contemporary term "business ethics" or "business ethics" was therefore and still is the subject of interest of theoreticians, but also of practitioners.

When reflecting on business ethics, it is very easy to come across the statement that the concept is internally contradictory, and the term itself is an oxymoron, i.e. a juxtaposition of words with opposite meanings. A look at an enterprise as an entity whose primary goal is to generate and multiply profits is no stranger to society. Many theoreticians and practitioners present just such a view of business, emphasising that economic activity is based on benefits and its primary goal is to provide profit to its owners (cf. Friedman 1970). However, such an approach is met with equally committed opposition, or, to put it differently, many authors present a different position (among others Porter, Kramer 2003: 85).

Moral (ethical) norms are the backbone of social life. They regulate the functioning of each community, indicating what is desired and accepted and what is not. Due to their fundamental nature, the most important of them are guaranteed by law. For breaking the less important, customary ones, there is a risk of an environmental sanction (Myśliwiec 2013: 9–13). All human activity, including economic activity in particular, is governed by moral standards. No one can only impose their own rules of conduct, because they are dependent on others, which means that they must consider their norms, or at least know them. Failure to comply with elementary principles of activity means that the company is no longer perceived as a trustworthy partner, which affects both contacts with cooperating entities and clients (Myśliwiec 2013: 12–13). According to E. Sternberg, the present times necessitate the need to pay special attention to business ethics and there are a number of reasons for this, including political, social, or demographic reasons (cf. Sternberg 1998: 43).

What is business ethics? There are many definitions in the literature. First of all, it is emphasised that it is a combination of two words: "ethics" and "business", that is, it refers to ethics applied in business. Ethics itself, however, is a philosophical approach and is not identical to its subject, i.e. moral expectations and conventional judgments. Ethics is normative inquiry, but it does not make neutral lists of specific moral practices, but organises issues within clearly defined assessments (Pratley 1998: 12–13). Business ethics, which is treated as one of the concepts of management, as well as ethics in general, focuses on human behaviour, i.e. looking for answers to the questions of whether we should take specific actions or not, whether these actions are good or bad, right or wrong, commendable or condemned, etc. In this case, we can speak of a descriptive (descriptive) ethics, which deals only with the description of what is happening in the moral sphere. We can also talk about normative (prescriptive) ethics, understood as a discipline that sets "norms" of behaviour, "recommends" appropriate behaviour, and issues instructions on what should and should not be done (Chryssides, Kaler 1999: 18–20).

Due to the subject of research, which in the case of business ethics is "morality" in the broadly understood economic sphere, business ethics is not only descriptive, as it assesses existing practices on the basis of clearly defined moral standards. Business ethics adapts the goals and methods of normative ethics, adjusting them to specific requirements related to moral problems occurring in market activity.

By deepening the definitional approach to business ethics, it can be defined as a philosophical reflection on the ethos, i.e. a set of virtues that define the scope of activities of people who make up the business world (Gasparski 1997: 17) or the application of our understanding of what is good and appropriate to the assessment of institutions, technologies, transactions, and scope of activities and work that we call business (Velazquez 1998: 1).

Business ethics must therefore base its conclusions on the analysis of actual norms and values, but its main task is not descriptive. Business ethics deals with the assessment of moral attitudes in the environment of market activity, using clearly identified moral standards, and also develops specific moral guidelines that correspond to real problems occurring in the economic sphere (Pratley 1998: 33–35). To put it differently, in business ethics, ethical reasoning applies to situations and activities specific to the broadly understood business and it is an attempt to resolve or clarify those issues that usually arise in the course of economic activities. Starting from the analysis of the nature and assumptions on which market practice is based, business ethics uses general moral principles to indicate what is right and wrong in the actions taken (Sternberg 1998: 95), and it refers both to the behaviour of individuals and as well as entire organisations.

According to W. Gasparski, the issues of business ethics relate to four levels at which economic activity is carried out. These are: basic level, i.e., the level of behaviour of people, e.g. employees, managers – a micro scale, central level, i.e., the level of organised behaviour, i.e. organisations, enterprises, corporations, etc. – a meso scale, level of the economic system on the scale of the state or groups of countries related to agreement or treaty (e.g. the European Union) – a macro scale and the level of the world economy – a global scale (Gasparski 2012: 80–83).

The ethical issues of individual actions in the above-mentioned hierarchical system of economic responsibility concern playing social roles in enterprises and in market activities undertaken by economic entities. The variety of these issues is a derivative of the variety of roles played by people in business, who are, for example, employees, sellers, managers, or owners of companies. Each of these roles is related to a set of specific problems related to rights, obligations, rewards, penalties, etc. The context of the profession performed raises ethical problems, in which the paramount rule is: do your job as best you can and do not take advantage of the weakness (physical, economic, or cultural) of people using your services (Bunge 1988: 159; Gasparski 2012: 80–81).

The meso level refers to the level of enterprises, and we can talk about all types of enterprises, including small, family-owned companies, and organisations, not only of a commercial nature, but also non-profit, and even transnational corporations. In the case of this group, the actions taken can be divided into internal, i.e. taking place in the organisation/enterprise, and external, i.e. taking place in the environment of a specific entity. Due to this division, we can also talk about internal and external stakeholders. Issues related to the meso level relate primarily to the identification of all stakeholders of an economic entity, the analysis of their interests, including possible conflicts of interest, if any, and the related social responsibility. In this case, the ethical substance of the entity is important, i.e., what the organisation or enterprise adds to the intention, intuition, and skills of the staff and what it exerts pressure on (Kaptein 1998: 58; Gasparski 2012: 82). The ethical substance of the entity, therefore, concerns the moral quality of the coordinated morale of the staff as a community, i.e. these are a kind of expectations of the organisation/enterprise directed at employees as to the incentives or brakes of ethical or unethical behaviour, and the way of stimulating and supporting them towards the behaviour desired by the subject (Kaptein 1998: 58).

We deal with the macro level in the discussed approach when the subject of interest of business ethics is particular markets, countries, or associations of countries (the above-mentioned European Union is an example). According to the theory of exchange, the social world is perceived as a system of exchange of material and non-material goods between individuals and social groups (Homans; cf. Sztompka 2016: 64–70). Contemporary society, in turn, is very often referred to as a business society, i.e. exchanges between the main elements that make up the social system (organising factors), while the society specifies exchange institutions, i.e. enterprises, organisations, banks, etc., the government that organises the legal system and the manner of its enforcement and integrating institutions, such as the church, family, school, and associations. The condition for the successful existence of a business society is to maintain the right proportions between these systems, and the issues of business ethics at this level are related to issues considered by social and political philosophy (Gasparski 2012: 82–83).

The last of these levels is the global level, which goes beyond the international exchange of goods and services and is the result of a global approach to the market as a whole. In this case, the subject of interest of business ethics is the functioning of the economy on a global scale, which is manifested in numerous regulations at this level.

In practice, however, we can talk about some differentiation in the approach to ethics in business. For example, R.T. De George distinguishes five types of business ethics involvement (De George 1995: 23–25):

1 Applying general ethical principles to the assessment of individual business cases, in this case, case studies and ethical analysis are used.
2 Metaethical considerations of the applicability of ethical concepts and concepts to issues related to the functioning of business in various forms of its organisation (e.g. moral subjectivity of an organisation).
3 The study of the moral attitudes of systems and procedures adopted and applied in economic activity, in this case, the use of critical analysis and empirical research (e.g. fairness of competition).
4 Study of business and organisational behaviour when using interdisciplinary research in the fields of anthropology, psychology, sociology, economics, organisation theory, management sciences, legal sciences, etc. (e.g. the issue of supply/value chain relationships).
5 Indicating standards, ideals, and models to follow, in this case, a case studies and interdisciplinary research are used (e.g. pro-ecological solutions).

The basic task of business ethics is therefore helping to make economic activity responsible, not only within a specific entity and with regard to everyone who is employed in it, but also in relation to the wider natural and sociocultural environment.

The differences between ethics, economics, and business ethics are presented in Table 1.1.

To sum up the considerations so far, it should be assumed that business ethics is applied ethics, it refers to philosophical ethics and other theories of morality, as well as the theory of action (praxeology) and social sciences. Through critical analysis, it provides theoretical knowledge and practical

*Table 1.1* Basic differences between ethics, economics, and business ethics (Gasparski, Lewicka-Strzałecka 2001: 35)

| *Specification* | *Ethics* | *Economics* | *Business ethics* |
|---|---|---|---|
| Objective | Human improvement | Profit or survival | Social profit or public interest |
| Field of interest | A man and interpersonal relations | Production and replacement | Social and economic interpersonal relations |
| Methods used | Reflection on oneself | Quantitative methods | Reflection and quantitative methods |
| Assessment criterion | Compliance with suitable moral rules and standards | Effectiveness, technical rules | Integral development, voluntariness |
| Constitutive concepts | Greek idea of good | Free market, tangible goods | Shared good, responsibility |
| Attitude | Kindness | Competitive fight, individualism | Fair competition or cooperation |
| The nature of the basic structure | Life | Game, instrumental action | Community, communication activity |

solutions in the form of, inter alia, programs or codes of ethics, contributing to the institutionalisation of ethics and the creation and development of corporate social responsibility (CSR; Gasparski 2012: 79). In practice, business ethics is normative ethics, i.e. it consists in formulating orders or rules of action.

## The place of business ethics in the concept of corporate social responsibility

The convergence of definitions of business ethics and CSR means that for some people these concepts may seem identical, and if not, at least convergent. However, it is not appropriate to balance these two concepts. There are at least several reasons to treat their meaning in a completely separate way, although at the same time it must be admitted that there is a strong relationship between ethics and CSR, which was especially visible in the initial, model approaches to CSR.

In one of the first attempts to define CSR, R. Eelss and C. Walton define the perception of CSR in terms of problems that arise when enterprises cast a shadow on the social sphere and ethical principles that should govern the relationship between the corporation and society (Eells and Walton 1961: 457–458). The relationship between CSR and ethics can also be seen in their later definition, which is taken as the complete definition of CSR by these authors. R. Eelss and C. Walton define CSR as concern for the needs and goals of society that go beyond the purely economic framework (Eells and Walton 1974: 247; cf. Carroll 1999: 278). A great convergence between ethics and CSR is also noticed in the model proposed by Eells, later developed by Walton (1967: 127–141). This model placed the organisation in a bipolar system, depending on its behaviour in relation to the adopted social norms. These two poles are: minimum, that is action oriented towards shareholders, and maximum, that is action in accordance with the stakeholder theory (Eells 1959: 33–41; 1960: 334–340). The discussion triggered by the publication of M. Friedman, who described CSR as a dangerous doctrine, also had a significant influence on the defining of the concept of CSR. According to M. Friedman, only actions and behaviours contributing to the maximisation of the company's profit can be considered ethically justified, and the concept of CSR undermines the foundations of a free society (Friedman 1962: 133; 1970). M. Friedman believed that the social and therefore ethical duty of the enterprise is to increase its profit, and the pursuit of any other goals is nothing other than the implementation of goals different or even contrary to those approved by the owners (Friedman 1970).

Considering ethics when defining CSR is also visible in the model proposed by M.D. Schlusberg. This author proposes a bipolar model of organisation: from an isolated, i.e. focused on profit maximisation and minimisation of social relations, to an integrated, i.e. focused on a wide range of social forms of influence (cf. Schlusberg 1969: 65–67). The relations between business ethics and CSR are most visible, however, only in the model proposed by A. Carroll (1979: 499–503) who ranked ethical responsibility as one of the elements of CSR (Figure 1.1).

A.B. Carroll presented CSR as distinguishing economic, legal, ethical, and philanthropic responsibility (Carroll 1979: 499–503; 1991: 40–41; 1993: 31).

*Figure 1.1* The Pyramid of CSR by A.B. Carroll (1991: 42)

According to A.B. Carroll, CSR is based on the economic responsibility, which together with legal accountability is required by society. The economic responsibility of enterprises should be understood as their care for profit, assuming minimisation of costs while making rational strategic decisions, maintaining appropriate employment, and developing and being competitive on the market. This is because enterprises are expected to be profitable, or at least not to bring losses. The profitability of enterprises is a necessary condition for implementing social responsibility into economic practice. Failure to meet this condition, in Carroll's opinion, would shift the discussion on CSR to the academic level only, without justifying the implementation of other types of social responsibility based on economic responsibility. The legal responsibility is nothing else than the actions of enterprises expected by the society within the limits of the law. Enterprises are required to comply with the standards and regulations in force in a particular country, including the protection of employees and consumers, and compliance with agreements which, in principle, define the "rules of the market game" accepted by the society. A. Carroll believes that the "minimum" standard for compliance with the law is not satisfactory. The level expected by the society is going beyond the limits imposed by law. However, such a procedure was included in the next, higher level of corporate responsibility (CR), which is ethical (moral) responsibility. The overriding goal of such perceived responsibility is to behave in a fair manner, which is understood as appropriate, reliable, fair, or honest behaviour. According to this approach, ethical responsibility assumes avoiding behaviours that may raise ethical doubts, and in the case of ambiguous situations, it assumes acting in accordance with social expectations. It is the incorporation of "morality" into the company's conduct. The philanthropic responsibility is at the highest level. According to Carroll, this responsibility responds to society's expectations that companies are "good citizens". This means the active involvement of economic entities in solving social problems, including devoting a part of the company's resources to society, e.g. through charity, voluntary work, etc. (Carroll 1991: 39–41; Carroll, Buchholtz 2009: 44). It should be emphasised at this point that A.B. Carroll clearly distinguishes responsibility imposed by law from economic responsibility, imposed by the market, and voluntary responsibility – on an ethical and philanthropic level. Ethical responsibility is for him the responsibility expected by society.

Indeed, in an institutional approach, an enterprise integrates two basic spheres of human life: intellectual and ethical. It is assumed, however, that the ethics of business activity is the primary norm and the basis for long-term competitiveness of the enterprise (Mroziewski 2010: 136). Ethics is a structural factor in business, and the adoption and wide application of ethical principles testifies to the fact that it gives economic activity a good meaning (cf. Malara 2006: 270). The approach to business ethics and its relationship with CSR differs depending on the assumptions made. For example, E. Sternberg postulated running "clean business", which should be honest, but does not have to fulfil obligations towards society. As she emphasised, business ethics not only does not oppose business, but effectively and concretely supports the maximisation of long-term value for the customer. E. Sternberg, contrary to M. Friedman, does not focus on profit maximisation, but on the maximisation of ownership value (Sternberg 1998: 21–22, 33). P. Drucker, meanwhile, argued that there are no grounds for creating a separate line of ethical reflection for the business sphere (Drucker 2010: 227–249). In his opinion, CSR should be practiced in such a way as to transform social problems and needs into business opportunities (Drucker 1984: 53–63). According to P. Drucker, such an approach to CSR may not only increase the profits of the organisation, but also reduce social costs (Drucker 1984a: 17–28).

The development of the concept of social responsibility is undoubtedly related to the shaping of the approach to the values considered the most important in human life and the desired way of dealing with others. Starting from the rule of reciprocity, propagated as the basis of the Christian faith, but also Buddhism, Judaism, and Islam, through E. Kant's categorical imperative, utilitarianism propagated in the 18th century, indicating that utility is a measure of fair conduct, J. Rawls' theory of justice, the Aristotelian moral philosophy renewed by A. MacIntyre, known as the virtue ethics and the Kohlberg's theory of moral development, we have reached contemporary expectations towards other entities, and we do not limit them only to other people, but we also formulate these expectations for entities such as enterprises and organisations in general. We require broadly understood responsibility for future generations (cf. Murphy 1999: 108–116). The ethical concepts that had a significant impact on the development of the CSR concept are presented in Table 1.2.

Evidently, the formation of contemporary requirements that society formulates with regard to enterprises has a long way to go. Their basis is the so-called the golden ethical rule, meaning "do not do to another what is displeasing to you". This principle appeared in the foundations of many religions, but it can also be found in Confucian dialogues, the works of Aristotle, Plato, and Seneca. We consider it decent to treat others the way we would like to be treated ourselves. We expect the same from business. It would be appropriate for society to simply treat the environment as a responsible partner for enterprises, excluding the excessive exploitation of any (i.e. both natural and human) resources. A man above all measure is a value and it is a value that should be perceived in this way when we use his work, as well as when we provide him with all goods or services. Concern for man, or a kind of honesty towards the species, is in fact concern for the value of future generations. Guaranteeing people's basic rights, but also the right to happiness, is an investment in the quality of humanity. Therefore, enterprises cannot forget about it when creating working conditions or formulating their offer. They should also be prudent in the exploitation of natural goods. Today's consumption should not deprive future generations of access to resources.

*Table 1.2* The main philosophical foundations of CSR (based on Żemigała 2016: 229)

| *Philosophical basis* | *Origin* | *Explanation* |
|---|---|---|
| The golden rule | Ancient philosophy and religious philosophical systems | The principle of treating others as one wants to be treated; a kind of reciprocity principle that can be found in Judaism, Buddhism, Christianity or Islam (Flew 1984: 134; Kietliński et al. 2005: 15–16). |
| Categorical imperative | Immanuel Kant (1724–1804) | Proceeding according to such rules that we want them to become universally binding law. In case of doubt, the categorical imperative makes it easier to make an ethically right choice, based on three criteria: the possibility of reversal (it is about checking whether one's own actions do not harm others, as this can lead to harm to ourselves), universal acceptance (it is about checking whether every person will behave in the same way under particular circumstances) and respect for people (a man cannot be treated in an instrumental way to achieve a goal, but is an end in itself) (Kant 2013: 19; Skiba 2013: 197–198). |
| Utilitarianism | Jeremy Bentham (1748–1832), John S. Mill (1806–1873) | The main goal in life is to maximise benefit (the result of cost-benefit calculation). The utility itself was defined differently by J. Bentham, who argued that personal benefits would lead to benefits for the general public, while the main personal benefit and, at the same time, the ultimate goal of an individual's actions was their own pleasure or avoiding pain (this is the so-called hedonistic utilitarianism). J. Mill approached utility differently, assuming that the utility of society should be the overriding goal of an individual's actions. In his considerations, he went beyond the category of pleasure, claiming that the ultimate goal of actions is happiness, that is, a more permanent state of human well-being (Pratley 1998: 189–201; Chryssides, Kaler 1999: 98–104). |

(*Continued*)

*Table 1.2* Continued

| *Philosophical basis* | *Origin* | *Explanation* |
|---|---|---|
| A theory of justice | John Rawls (1921–2002) | The impartial reconciliation of freedom, equality and efficiency. Ensuring freedom while caring for the less well-off (Rawls 2009: 107). J. Rawls formulated two principles of justice: (1) everyone should have the right to the greatest possible freedom, which should be compatible with the freedom of others; (2) social and economic inequalities should be distributed for the benefit of those who are most disadvantaged; every individual should have the right to opportunities and an equal chance as other individuals of similar ability (Chryssides, Kaler 1999: 225 and 190). |
| Virtue ethics | Among others: Socrates, Plato, Aristotle, but also Alasdair MacIntyre (born 1929) | Virtue as the basis for the durability of all practices that create traditions (Gałkowski 2004: 1–17). In such an approach, virtue is understood as an acquired feature, thanks to which internal goals for action – practices (e.g. related to improvement) can be achieved. The ethics of A. MacIntyre's virtue is also linked to justice, courage and honesty (Pratley 1998: 304–313). |
| The theory of moral development | Lawrence Kohlberg (1927–1987) | Man passes through the next levels of moral development, perfecting a sensitivity with the ability to make decisions (Trevino 1992: 445–459). Moral development begins with obedience to authority and punishment or focus on rewards and benefits, and ends at the level of universal ethical principles (Klimczak 2006: 30–34). |

However, identifying business ethics with CSR is not appropriate for several reasons. Business ethics, despite its normative nature, is a philosophical approach, and the main area of its interest is, as already indicated, "morality" in broadly understood business. Meanwhile, CSR is a management concept that is embedded in various ethical theories, but does not require their in-depth knowledge or analysis, as it focuses on the specificity of the organisation's functioning. The most important difference between business ethics and CSR is that CSR has a wide range of tools that can be used in management practice, while business ethics focuses more on theoretical reflection (Żemigała 2016: 228). Moreover, the ethics of CSR performs a corrective function, its aim is to change or limit economic rationalisation in areas where the market does not work perfectly or at least sufficiently. Moreover, CSR is a voluntary concept. Despite the expectations, in order to increase the social involvement of not only business entities, but also others, CSR is not a concept required by law, i.e. mandatory, it is not even required by common law. Enterprises themselves decide not only about their social involvement, but also about the level or type (direction) of this involvement. It is also important that CSR is a concept used in the practice of business. This means, inter alia, that it is based on the motive of maximising the value of the enterprise. Business ethics, meanwhile, is a philosophical approach that refers to the category of good and value (cf. Pratley 1998: 18–28).

## The origin of corporate social responsibility: from philanthropy to the concept of social involvement

CSR, also called as, inter alia, corporate conscience, corporate citizenship, sustainable responsible business, or responsible business, is now the standard that we expect in the operation of enterprises, regardless of their scale of operation (Howaniec 2016b: 33). However, the concept of CSR is not new. Discussions on the role and obligations of business towards society, which formed the basis of the present concept of CSR, have been conducted at least since the end of the 19th century.[1] References to CSR can be found, among others in academic works from the 1980s and 1990s, for example: L. Preston and J. Post (1975), R. Ackerman and R. Bauer (1976), W. Frederick (1978), A. Carroll (1979), R. Freeman (1984), S. Wartick and P. Cochran (1985), R. Miles (1987), D. Wood (1991).

However, when discussing the process of CSR evolution, several research paths can be distinguished. The first is a universal path presenting the approach to CSR from the perspective of business ethics and philosophy, law and institutional economics, started in the 1930s, currently focused on building internal ethical infrastructure. The second is a comparative path, often referred to as CR, derived from the first works of P. Drucker (1974), and continued to some extent by M. Porter (1980, 1987). And the last – the third one – is the basic path, referring to the principles of sustainable development, started in the 1950s (2013: 18).

Searching for the beginning of the concept of responsible business, many authors refer to philanthropy (cf. Carroll 1979: 500, Griffin 2004: 118–119). The Greek term philanthrōpia means charity, kindness, while philánthrōpos means "loving humanity". Thus, philanthropy is defined as the activity of persons or institutions consisting in disinterested financial or material assistance to those in need.

The philanthropic activity of entrepreneurs in Europe developed for good in the second half of the 19th century, mainly inspired by positivist ideas (Leś

2001). Well-known philanthropists operating, for example, in Poland were, among others, A.I. Lubomirski, J. Falkowski, and L.S. Kronenberg. Entrepreneurs supported, among others development of vocational education, co-created social facilities for employees, including factory housing estates, health care, supported culture and art, and made donations to charity.

There are more known examples of philanthropic activity on the American market, where for nobility was valued, among others, A. Carnegie (steel magnate), who, along with others, supported public libraries and the construction of housing for the poorest, and donated money to schools and many other institutions working for the community. A. Carnegie is also known for his article The Gospel of Wealth and is considered the author of the first version of the CSR doctrine (Carnegie 1889). According to Carnegie, it consisted of two principles: charity and stewardship (Post et al. 1996: 41–43; Stoner et al. 1998: 112). The principle of charity is based on some kind of commitment from the rich to provide services to those in need. In line with this principle, on the initiative and with the support of enterprises, inter alia, apartments, churches, schools, libraries, medical aid, or legal advice was provided (cf. Post et al. 1996: 41–42). The second principle – the principle of trust – is based on the belief that rich people manage goods on behalf of others and therefore should use wealth in a socially acceptable manner and in accordance with the so-called in the public interest. Entrepreneurs, by controlling resources, the use of which may have a significant impact on many people, become a kind of trustees of society, which means that by taking up economic activity, they simultaneously take on specific obligations. Therefore, it is socially justified to expect responsibility for the use of these resources in a good way not only for owners or shareholders, but also from the point of view of the good of society as a whole (Post et al. 1996: 41–43).

According to A. Carnegie, the wealth accumulated by entrepreneurs should be "distributed" in order to improve the conditions and for the development of mankind. According to the tycoon, rich people themselves become a value, but only when they spend the accumulated resources for the good of mankind (Carnegie 1889). Such views at the end of the 19th century were accompanied by political activities. The United States government, meeting the expectations of the American society, passed a number of laws, the main purpose of which was to ban unacceptable business practices, and which defined the relations between economic circles, the state, and society. For the first time, it was indicated that large enterprises have a role to play in society that goes beyond maximising the profit for capital owners (cf. Rybak 2004: 16).

According to this approach, enterprises should in their activities consider not only the interests of individual groups directly related to them, but should consider the interests of the entire society, including groups that are indirectly related to the enterprise. This approach has been, and still is, represented by many authors. For example, R. Bauer, representing the early views on the issues of social responsibility, believed that it manifests itself in the serious treatment by organisations of the influence that their activities have on society (Carroll, Buchholtz 2003: 30). Also, for R. Eells and C. Walton, CSR is that part of the company's activity that has a direct reference to the social consequences of the company's operation or ethical principles that should regulate the relationship between the corporation and society (Carroll 1991: 39). In such an approach, CSR is nothing else than an obligation to care for social welfare, especially when it could be violated as a result of the activity of enterprises (Baran 2010: 176).

The presented approaches confirm the social acceptance of the principle of stewardship, which seems to be also understood by contemporary businessmen (Rybak 2004: 15). A large part of the society agrees with the thesis that entrepreneurs have resources, which has or may have a significant impact on the overall welfare of society, both now and in the future. Therefore, it is entrepreneurs who are responsible for using all resources, including natural ones, in a socially justifiable way. The implementation of the obligations assumed in this way should be beneficial not only for the company, but also for the society, and in the long term (Post et al. 1996: 41–42). One of the precursors of social responsibility is J. Clark, who in 1916 argued that it was necessary to transform the economy from the inherited "economy of irresponsibility" to the "economy of responsibility", which should be incorporated into business ethics. J. Clark also pointed out that responsibility exceeding the applicable law is not only an ideal, but a fact (Clark 1916: 210, 227). He emphasised that despite the necessity to introduce collective responsibility, it is necessary to be aware of individual responsibility, the shaping of which is equally important (Clark 1916: 216–217).

As can be seen in the presented approaches, CSR is clearly presented as an obligation to care for social welfare, especially if it were to be violated by the negative consequences of the company's activities. An important role in this process is assigned to the managerial staff, who should consciously neutralise the effects of the company's negative impact on the environment and act not only in the interest of the enterprise, but also considering the broadly understood social interest.

The discussion undertaken by A. Berle and E. Dodd made a significant contribution to the development of the CSR concept. A. Berle, in defense of shareholders (owners), believed that it is justified for the law to strictly control decisions made by managers who had a wide range of responsibilities, significantly exceeding the interests of shareholders (Berle 1931, 1932). E. Dodd had a different view. He believed similarly that the only group to which managers had obligations were shareholders, but that, in his opinion, managers should be free to decide how different groups and individuals would benefit from the activities of companies (Dodd 1932; cf. Wells 2002: 78).

One of the most important books that determined the present shape of the CSR concept is the book by A. Berle and G. Means (1932), in which the authors formulated a modern, for those times, corporate vision, creating the foundations of the stakeholder theory. A. Berle and G. Means emphasised that a corporation, being a part of society, should serve not only its owners or shareholders, but also the whole society (Berle, Means 1932).

The works of E. Mayo (1933) and C. Barnard (1938) also indicated the need for a broader look at the need for managers to consider many aspects of the functioning of enterprises, including the increasingly broadly defined responsibility. These works were part of the Great Depression of the 1930s and the increased activity of governments in trying to neutralise its effects. Significant for the development of this concept was also the introduction, under the New Deal policy of F. Roosevelt, of a great program of economic reforms carried out in the United States in the years 1933–1936. These reforms regulated, inter alia, monetary policy, subjected large companies to state control, they tried to improve industry, agriculture, transport, trade, and labour relations (New Universal Encyclopedia 1995: 442). The regulations included, inter alia, the stock exchange through appropriate legal regulations (Securities Act of 1933) and the establishment of the Securities and Exchange Commission, the purpose of which was to regulate the stock market and prevent abuse related to the reporting and sale of securities (Kennedy 1999: 367).

The debate on CSR returned in the 1960s, when the concept was experiencing a kind of renaissance. One of the authors popularising CSR at that time was A. Berle, who wrote about the need to be responsible also towards other stakeholders than stockholders, justifying it with the profit generated for the last ones (Berle 1954; cf. Rok 2013: 23–24). A significant contribution to the development of the concept is made by the work of H. Bowen, who considered as obvious the broadly understood business obligation to consider social consequences and take responsibility for decisions made in this context. Bowen applied social responsibility to the obligations of managers who, when choosing a strategy, should make decisions and actions desired from the point of view of the goals and values of society (Bowen 1953: 6). Research on CSR was also conducted by M. Heald, who analysed the development of the CSR concept in the years 1900–1960. The author stated that already in the mid-1950s the recognition of the social dimension of business responsibility was common and it became an element of thinking about business development (Heald 1970).

With theses presented in such a way agreed, inter alia, P. Drucker, who believed that what should really distinguish a manager is primarily responsibility (Drucker 1954). In his opinion, the development of management meant that a manager must be more than a "technocrat" and his mastery of management skills, tools, and techniques is no longer sufficient. Contemporary management is not free from culture and is treated, as part of the natural world, as a social function (Drucker 1986: 10, 18). According to Drucker, each organisation exists because of the society and within a specific community. This is why it is considered due to the impact it has on the environment and is obliged to be responsible for its actions. For P. Drucker, it is obvious that managers must consider social responsibility, they must rethink the values, beliefs, or obligations towards society (Drucker 1986: 18). P. Drucker, however, reduced CSR to the responsibility of managers. In his opinion, it is the management staff who should be required to act in such a way that everything that is really in the public interest becomes the company's own interest (Drucker 1986: 18; 1994: 418). According to Drucker, the CSR concept no longer asks what are the constraints in the economic sphere or what business should do for those who are under its influence, but requires that business take responsibility for social problems and issues, social and political goals and become a guardian conscience of society (Drucker 1986: 220).

The development of the CSR concept in the 1960s and 1970s was accompanied by mass pro-ecological movements and numerous changes in the law. Organisations demanding increased care for the natural environment not only forced a change in the regulations in this respect, but the consequence of these actions was also an increase in the care for the principles of occupational health and safety (CED 1971). Environmental protection and safety were one of the main directions of social interest in the consequences of the activities of enterprises at that time. This interest was additionally deepened by such publications as Silent Spring (Carson 1962) on the impact of pesticides on the natural environment and the quality of food produced. A strong pro-ecological movement led, among others, to education and activation of organisations interested in building an alternative society and an alternative economy, defined today as the social economy or social entrepreneurship (2013: 29–30). From the point of view of the development of the CSR concept, however, the trend that emerged at the end of the 1960s was much more pronounced, thanks to, inter alia, people like T.H. Smith (later president of the Social Investment Forum) or A. Tepper Marlin (founder of the Council of Economic Priorities, who later presented the first standard of social responsibility SA8000). General Motors (GM) also played an important role in the development of the CSR concept, in particular a GM Campaign, under which, among others, was created a kind of forum, which consisted of representatives of the supervisory board, trade unions, and Campaign GM activists, and its task was to assess the social effects of GM's activities (Rok 2013: 30). This forum has become a kind of prototype of the currently used stakeholder panels (multistakeholder panels). The GM Campaign was held during the Earth Day celebration in 1970 and was received by some economists and entrepreneurs as an attempt to "socialize" the business (Rok 2013: 31).

A significant publication from the point of view of the discussion on CSR is an article by M. Friedman, in which the author referred to economics, ethics, and even common sense, proving at the same time that CSR is a dangerous and subversive idea (Friedman 1970). The idea formulated in the title of the article was quickly picked up, emphasising that the sole purpose of the enterprise is profit ("The business of business is business"). However, M. Friedman was mainly opposed to the unjustified extension of the competences of managers whose decisions could expose the company and its owners to losses. He believed that the primary responsibility of managers who are employees of business owners is responsibility towards those owners. This responsibility, in turn, should essentially consist in carrying out the business according to their wishes, that is, in making as much money as possible. Of course, respecting the basic principles contained not only in the law, but also those of an ethical nature, but not exposing the company to unjustified behaviour or costs (Friedman 1970: 17).

The approach presented by Friedman was widely discussed and is also often referred to in current CSR studies. However, it is difficult to completely disagree with the presented point of view. Similar voices can be found in other works, incl. A. Berle (1931; 1932). One of the authors who agreed with M. Friedman was also P. Drucker. In his opinion, enterprises are economic units and it is economic goals that are the ones they should stick to. According to P. Drucker, there is a risk that CSR will weaken the economic efficiency of enterprises, which will affect the entire society. And an even more real threat is the unauthorised extension of the power of managers to areas where they do not have such power (Drucker 1986: 227). A certain convergence with the point of view of M. Friedman can also be seen in the definition of K. Davis and R. Blomstrom, who believe that enterprises (or more precisely their management) should care primarily about their own interest, i.e. multiplying their profit, and then in their activities, they should consider the protection and multiplication of social welfare (Davis, Blomstrom 1975: 6). P. Drucker admits, however, that social impact and social responsibility are not a fashion, but areas in which business, and not only, must rethink its role, set goals and implement them (Drucker 1986: 227). He also emphasised that business should "transform" its social responsibility into business opportunities. For P. Drucker, CSR consists in transforming a social problem into economic benefits and opportunities, productive capacity, human resources competences, into well-paid jobs, and ultimately into wealth (Drucker 1984: 62).

An important contribution to the definition of the concept of CSR is the model of social enterprise performance proposed by A. Carroll (1979; 1991). This author distinguished four types of responsibility, i.e. economic, legal, ethical, and philanthropic responsibility, while the main responsibility for him is also economic responsibility, i.e. care for the company's profit. A. Carroll emphasises, however, that this should be related to a certain rationality of decisions in other areas.

Consumer movements, which in the 1960s became an element of civic awareness and the changing perception of the role of business in society, were also important for the development of CSR. Economic growth is no longer perceived as a good in itself that generates economic and social progress. Side effects accompanying business activity have been noticed, such as degradation of the natural environment, monopolisation of markets, development of excessive consumption, unfair competition, or lowering the quality of human life (cf. Klimczak 1999: 103; Piontek 2002: 41–42). This resulted in a decline in confidence in business. Large transnational companies were suspected, inter alia, for the use of unfair business practices, non-compliance with international standards regarding human rights or environmental standards, which was confirmed by numerous scandals from that time period. This led, inter alia, to change the awareness of managers, forcing them to become interested in CSR (Lewicka-Strzałecka 2006: 127). The expectations of the American society towards large companies played a significant role in this respect, which in their opinion – being a "common good", like others – are obliged to play the role of a "corporate citizen" (De George 1993: 189; cf. Rybak 2004: 17).

As can be seen, CSR has been a subject of interest for both theoreticians and practitioners since the end of the 19th century. The topic of the role of business in shaping social welfare is important, and the progressive economic development and the change in business functions (e.g. by assigning it to social functions) make us expect active inclusion of enterprises in social life. In the development of the CSR concept, at least several consecutive periods can be distinguished, which determined the areas of CSR research, and also influenced the perception of CSR (Table 1.3).

The 1990s of the last century include social debate on CSR after the disclosure of irregularities in the financial statements of companies such as Enron[2] or WorldCom[3] (Lyke, Jickling 2002: 2; Li 2010: 37). The creative accounting of the above-mentioned companies not only led to their bankruptcy, but also became an example of extremely unethical behaviour by managers. More attention is also paid to the role of business in the social field. It is emphasised, inter alia, the destructive impact of business on traditional family values, the preservation of which, together with the dignity of a person, Pope John Paul II (John Paul II 1981: 13–15). Increased interest in the unit can also be observed in the documents of the European Union. Created i.e. Community Charter of Fundamental Social Rights of Workers (1989), numerous resolutions, such as European Parliament resolution of 6 February 2013 on CSR: accountable, transparent, and responsible business behaviour and sustainable growth (EC 2013a), European Parliament resolution of 6 February 2013 on CSR: promoting society's interests and a route to sustainable and inclusive recovery (EC 2013b), and CSR is defined as a tool allowing to ensure

*Table 1.3* Searching for the subject of research in the area of CSR (see Rok 2013: 28)

| *The main issues* | *Principal authors* |
|---|---|
| The social duty of wealthy people, philanthropy and trust. | Carnegie (1889) |
| The economy of responsibility. | Clark (1916) |
| Responsibilities of managers towards shareholders and other stakeholders. | Dodd (1932), Berle (1932) |
| CSR as the best way to overcome market failure in the social area, CSR determined by social expectations. | Bowen (1953) |
| Constant consideration of the impact of business decisions on society in managerial work. | Drucker (1955) |

long-term trust of employees and consumers (EC 2010: 20). The broadly understood responsibility of the company has also been clearly emphasised in the so-called The Principles for Business, adopted in 1994 by the Caux Round Table (cf. Węgrzecki 2012: 27).

In 2000, on the initiative of United Nations Secretary-General Kofi Annan, an initiative called the UN Global Compact was adopted, which became the basis for subsequent CSR arrangements and regulations. According to the UN Global Compact program, announced at the World Economic Summit in Davos (supplemented in 2004), the company should follow the relevant principles in the following areas (UN Global Compact 2020):

I Human Rights

Principle 1: Businesses should support and respect the protection of internationally proclaimed human rights; and

Principle 2: make sure that they are not complicit in human rights abuses.

II Labour

Principle 3: Businesses should uphold the freedom of association and the effective recognition of the right to collective bargaining;

Principle 4: the elimination of all forms of forced and compulsory labour;

Principle 5: the effective abolition of child labour; and

Principle 6: the elimination of discrimination in respect of employment and occupation.

III Environment

Principle 7: Businesses should support a precautionary approach to environmental challenges;

Principle 8: undertake initiatives to promote greater environmental responsibility; and

Principle 9: encourage the development and diffusion of environmentally friendly technologies.

IV Anti-corruption

Principle 10. Businesses should work against corruption in all its forms, including extortion and bribery.

The following factors contributed to the deepening of interest in CSR on the part of customers and other stakeholders: years of crisis (2007–2008). The relatively high interest in the concept of CSR in the last two decades has resulted in the fact that this concept is widely known and adopted by business (Zu, Song 2008: 5, 7–14), and in society it is referred to the process in which the organisation expresses and develops their "corporate culture" and social awareness (Khan et al. 2012: 41).

Despite criticism from opponents of expanding CR, who justify that such an approach to business is inappropriate, the concept of CSR has entered the canon of management sciences. Moreover, the constant changes to which

CSR is subject and a lively discussion on the economic justification of taking actions in the field of CSR only confirm the importance of the issues raised. Industrial development as we know from the last century is inadequate in relation to the current problems and needs of society. Changing their expectations in relation to the sphere of business causes the necessity to change the current rules of conducting the market game and considering social responsibility as a necessary condition for achieving success on the market in today's competitive conditions. Enterprises can no longer limit themselves only to the achievement of economic goals, as such perception of business by entrepreneurs is negatively perceived by both customers and other business stakeholders.

**Google LCC**

Google LLC is an American multinational technology company that focuses on artificial intelligence, search engine technology, online advertising, cloud computing, computer software, quantum computing, e-commerce, and consumer electronics. It is one of the most valuable brands in the world due to its market dominance, data collection, and technological advantages in the field of artificial intelligence, its value in 2021 was estimated at $191,215 million (Brand Finance 2021). In 2015, Google was reorganised as a wholly owned subsidiary of Alphabet Inc. Google is Alphabet's largest subsidiary and holding company for Alphabet's Internet properties and interests.

One of the activities of the Google LLC is its philanthropic activities. In 2004, Google formed the philanthropic Google.org, with a start-up fund of $1 billion. It is not a typical not-for-profit organisation, but "for-profit philanthropy" (Rana 2008). The mission of the organisation is to create awareness about climate change, global public health, and global poverty. One of its first projects was to develop a viable plug-in hybrid electric vehicle that can attain 100 miles per gallon. Google.org supports the development of smart electric vehicle-to-grid (V2G) (Daim et al. 2016).

In March 2007, in partnership with the Mathematical Sciences Research Institute (MSRI), Google hosted the first Julia Robinson Mathematics Festival at its headquarters in Mountain View. In 2011, Google donated 1 million euros to International Mathematical Olympiad to support the next five annual International Mathematical Olympiads (2011–2015) (Pantano et al. 2022).

In 2008, Google announced its "Project 10100" in which they asked people to submit ideas that could change the world. Thousands of people from over 170 countries submitted over 150,000 ideas. After two years of silence, Google unveiled the project's winners, donating a total of 10 million dollars to ideas ranging from non-profit organisations promoting education to a website that intends to make all legal documents public and make them available online (Google 2008; Nagar et al. 2016).

In July 2012, Google launched a "Legalize Love" campaign in support of gay rights.

In response to the humanitarian crisis following the Russian invasion of Ukraine, Google announced a donation of $15 million to support Ukrainian citizens (Zmuda 2022). The company also decided to transform its office in Warsaw into a refugee assistance centre.

## Development of the social responsibility of business in Poland

Poland is not a country without a history of ethical business. From the second half of the nineteenth century, social activity of companies and their owners developed in Poland, taking the form of emergency aid – financial or material, or in the form of extensive social programs. At the beginning of the 20th century, the direction of philanthropic activities began to change and was identified with social support understood as a kind of help "provided to individuals and groups mainly in order to mobilise their strength, potential and resources, which they retained so that they could cope with their own problems" (Sikorska-Kowalska 2010: 55). Many good examples of corporate social involvement come from the interwar period. At that time, enterprises financed not only kindergartens or libraries, but also often satisfied the housing needs of the society (cf. Łapa, Gruszecka-Tieśluk 2018: 42–78). However, the political system of the People's Poland inhibited and even ruled out this kind of involvement. The return to the market economy took place only after the political changes in 1990.

The time of returning to the entrepreneurial culture in Poland is the time of the most difficult economic and political changes (1990–1993), which often require entrepreneurs to fight for existence. Profitability was much more important to managers than the way in which it was obtained. A significant number of entrepreneurs assumed that running a business has little in common with the principles of ethics and social responsibility. It was also very popular to think that activities that are not expressly prohibited by law are allowed. At the same time, cases of corruption in business, bad treatment of employees, cheating clients, economic crimes, or unclear relations between business and politics were of course publicised. It was not, however, the atmosphere of an open dialogue on CSR (cf. Bartkowiak 2011: 18). In economic practice, ethical problems were common: instrumental and oppressive approach to people, dehumanisation of management, and manipulation aimed at increasing the benefits of people in authority in organisations

(Sułkowski 2013: 56). The Polish economy is still referred to as the "young" market economy. The period of the communist regime, which determined e.g. the way the private sector is perceived by Polish society, influenced at the same time the nature of Polish entrepreneurship and expectations towards business. High unemployment, inflation, and widespread corruption in the early 1990s meant that entrepreneurship was associated with dishonesty and acting outside or on the border of the law. For example, the saying that "the first million has to be stolen" was common. All this has significantly lowered social trust in enterprises and entrepreneurs.

The development of CSR in Poland began to be visible in the first decade of the 21st century. Poland's accession to the European Union on 1 May 2004 was of great importance for the development of CSR in Poland. Poland began to actively participate in shaping and implementing CSR solutions promoted by the European Commission, and detailed reports on the analysis of individual stages of CSR development in Poland were also started (Rok 2013: 59). The main driving forces for the development of CSR in Poland, however, were the expectations of transnational corporations, trade partners, and industry organisations from European Union Member States towards the Polish enterprise sector due to its growing participation in the European market (UNDP 2007: 20). Another factor introducing moral order in the Polish economy was foreign capital. It was Western corporations that were able to compensate for market failures, bringing about a compromise between the conflicting interests of various parties. Thus, from the stage of "ignoring" the need for social involvement of enterprises, despite academic debates on this area also taking place in Poland and numerous publications in the field of ethics and CSR, Poland has gone through the stage of reluctance and justification of the abstract nature of such an approach for business implementation, the stage of showing off with interest CSR and undertaking activities in this area, until more and more conscious incorporation of social responsibility into the practice of enterprises. Despite some noticeable imperfections in the business approach to CSR, more and more companies not only declared their social involvement, but enterprises took a number of actions that confirmed the growing maturity of their approach in this area. CSR was also more and more often perceived as an element of shaping strategies implemented by enterprises, i.e. it was used as an element of promotion or personnel policy of companies. Public institutions also had a large share in the implementation of CSR into business practice. The priority areas in Poland were initially counteracting social exclusion, social education, promoting entrepreneurial attitudes and high-quality work places (UNDP 2007: 20–21). The first stages of CSR development in Poland are presented in Table 1.4.

Recently, there has been a significant development of CSR in both theoretical and practical aspects. Enterprises are not only aware of the essence of the concept, but also consciously engage in activities for the benefit of society and the environment. Initially, this involvement was most often implemented through sponsorship or charity, but today they are more and more advanced

*Table 1.4* Initial stages of CSR development in Poland (UNDP 2007: 22)

| *Stage* | *Characteristic* |
|---|---|
| 1997–2000 | A stage of silence and a complete lack of interest in CSR. |
| 2000–2002 | A stage of reluctance and opposition from business leaders and journalists who believe that the free market is a panacea for all problems. |
| 2002–2004 | Expression of interest in CSR and public declarations of recognising the role of ethics and social responsibility of every self-respecting company. |
| 2004–2005 | Undertaking specific, although partial projects, covering selected, significant areas of company operation. |
| 2006–still | An attempt to combine CSR with other strategies implemented in companies – communication, personal, marketing or corporate governance strategy (in the case of large companies). |

social programs (Howaniec 2014). The attitude of Poles towards CSR is also changing.

The academic community has played and continues to play an important role in promoting social responsibility in the economic sphere and building awareness among Polish society. Many universities introduced CSR subjects into their study programs, many also conduct postgraduate studies in this area, which allows to supplement the knowledge of people who graduated before the economic changes (Bobola 2016: 264–271). There are also many organisations in Poland that promote the idea of CSR and, through education and promotion, affect both the business sector and society. The most important of them include: The Responsible Business Forum (RBF), which is the largest non-governmental organisation dealing with CSR in Poland, the Academy for the Development of Philanthropy in Poland, and the Foundation for Social Communication. Support is also provided by numerous business ethics centres and international institutions, such as, for example, the United Nations Development Agenda. Polish governmental bodies have also been established to promote the essence of social responsibility.

The first initiative promoting CSR principles on a large scale in Poland was the Global Compact initiative (2001), in which entrepreneurs, the Polish government, and non-governmental organisations took part. The result of this meeting was the appointment of a Steering Committee whose task was to promote CSR among enterprises. There are also many social initiatives to popularise CSR in Poland. The initiatives promoting and at the same time verifying the social commitment of enterprises in Poland include, among others the Ranking of Responsible Companies conducted by RBF since 2007, the Fair Play Enterprise competition which has been organised since 1998, the Philanthropy Leaders competition, etc. (cf. Makuch 2010: 15–28).

In 2009, the Warsaw Stock Exchange also launched the RESPECT Index – the first index of responsible companies in Poland.

The reason attributed to the lower-than-expected interest of business in Poland in CSR principles is the economic situation of Polish companies. Assuming that the introduction of CSR principles requires, in the first stage, incurring certain initial costs, the worse financial condition of Polish companies in relation to the capabilities of foreign companies makes this task difficult. Introducing the code to the company, adopting an appropriate strategy, employing a CSR specialist, preparing annual reports, and in particular obtaining appropriate certificates is costly (Filek 2008: 67–68). It is difficult to argue with the occurrence of additional costs in enterprises that implement CSR principles. They just are. However, specifying costs as a justification for not taking CSR activities is not supported by any of the presented studies on CSR in Poland. Therefore, it is necessary to verify why CSR in Polish practice is still the domain of large enterprises, mainly with foreign capital, and what prevents the small and medium-sized enterprise sector in particular from including CSR in its market activities.

## Notes

1 Strictly philosophical discussions on morality and ethics in the areas we consider business and earning money today were not included.

2 Founded in 1985, Enron has been recognised as one of the world's leading and more innovative supply companies for electricity, natural gas, communications and the paper industry. Before it went bankrupt, its annual revenues grew from about $9 billion in 1995 to over $100 billion in 2000. In late 2001, it was revealed that the company's financial situation was confirmed by institutionalised, systematic and creatively planned accounting frauds. Enron shares fell from $90 per share in mid-2000 to less than $1 per share in late 2001. The company filed for bankruptcy on 2 December 2001 (Li 2010: 37).

3 WorldCom, the American telecommunications giant, was founded in 1983 as the operator of Long Distance Discount Services Inc. (LDDS). Intensive development of the company, incl. the acquisition of MCI in 1998 made it the second largest long-haul operator with revenues of $39.2 billion in 2001 ranking it 42nd on the list of America's largest Fortune 500 companies. Faced with financial problems related primarily to the industry recession, WorldCom has manipulated the accounting records. After the media disclosure of the abuses, the company filed for bankruptcy (2002). Ultimately, the company emerged from bankruptcy and was purchased for $7.6 billion in 2005 by Verizon Communications. However, it is an example of unethical behaviour of managers (Lyke, Jickling, 2002: 2).

# 2 The essence of corporate social responsibility

## Contemporary understanding of business social responsibility

From the very beginning, a broad definition of the essence of corporate social responsibility (CSR) allowed for an individual interpretation of this concept and great freedom in its formulation. Despite some differences in approaches, all concerned agree that CSR cannot be equated with legal compliance. Of course, additional questions often arise in this area, namely: (1) Do enterprises have moral and social obligations? (2) Should companies voluntarily involve their resources in, for example, environmental protection, culture, or local community development (Reinhardt et al. 2008: 16–23)?

For many, the answer to such questions includes the essence of CSR. Well, to talk about being socially responsible not only must be in accordance with the law, but also go beyond this compliance by investing in "human capital", the environment, and relations with all interested parties (EC 2001: 6). CSR is engaging in activities that seem to promote social welfare and go beyond the interests of companies and legal requirements (McWilliams, Siegel 2001: 117). However, CSR should not be equated with the participation of enterprises in campaigns and charitable activities. CSR is a much broader concept. It is responsibility for the development of society by anticipating future plans of socio-economic "justice" and awareness of responsibility for the welfare of society in the future (Khan et al. 2012: 41).

The main emphasis of considerations on CSR has long been placed on justifying its rightness (Ackerman, Bauer 1976). The actual behaviour of companies was not analysed, assuming only their declaration in this area as proceedings. Meanwhile, it is the actual behaviour of enterprises that is important (Ackerman, Bauer 1976: 7). Research on the real business conduct was carried out by, among others, S. Sethi (1975: 58–64). The change in the approach of the research community to social responsibility contributed to shifting the debate from the discussion of whether the idea of CSR is right or not to the issues of the actual behaviour of enterprises (Rybak 2004: 35). As a consequence, the CSR doctrine was replaced by, among others, the concept of corporate social responsiveness (CSR2), and then the concept of

DOI: 10.4324/9781003317364-3

corporate social performance (CSP – CSR3) (Pinkston, Carroll 1996: 200; Rybak 2004: 35). CSR2 refers to the company's ability to respond to social pressure (Frederick 1994: 154). Meanwhile, in the concept of social contribution, the emphasis is on appropriate behavioural patterns and mechanisms, structures, and procedures that enable the enterprise to respond appropriately to the demands and expectations of society that lead to "social improvement" (Frederick 1994: 154–158). Despite the introduction of these concepts to the literature on the subject, they are not commonly used. Most authors still use the term CSR. However, a change in the approach to defining CSR can be noticed, which is visible, among others, in publications in this area and in European Union documents. In 2001, the European Commission (EC) emphasised the increased awareness of enterprises which, in its opinion, perceive the direct economic value resulting from or related to CSR. For the EC, this was the reason why enterprises could contribute to the achievement of social and environmental goals by introducing CSR as a strategic investment in the basic business strategy, management instruments, and activities (EC 2001: 4). In 2011, however, the EC significantly shortened the definition of CSR, describing it as the responsibility of enterprises for their impact on society (EC 2011: 6).

The definition proposed by the EC is very general and seems to shift the burden of responsibility of companies, giving priority and even exclusivity to society. Of course, such defined social responsibility does not exclude caring for positive relations with other stakeholders, especially when it ultimately brings benefits to the society. In part of the definition of CSR, however, the concept of stakeholders appears directly, most often in two variants, the definitions refer to their importance for the overall development of the company, or they list individual direct or indirect interest groups. For example, J. Post, L. Preston, and S. Sachs believe that according to the concept of CSR, an enterprise is perceived as an organisation serving the interests of a wide group of entities that constitute it (Post et al. 2002: 11). The stakeholders of the enterprise are also indicated in the definition of CSR by W. Halal, for whom they are partners who cooperate with the enterprise, creating both social and economic value (Halal 2001: 27–42). For example, the group of recipients was indicated in great detail by, for example, L. Zbiegień-Maciąg, according to which CSR is the company's moral responsibility and obligations to be accountable to the society for its activities, in particular to owners, internal customers – employees as well as shareholders and representatives of local authorities, pressure groups, ecological and consumer movements, suppliers, cooperators, and state administration (cf. Zbiegień-Maciąg 1991: 48–49). The importance of stakeholders is also indicated by the EC definition from 2001, according to which CSR is a concept of running a business, in which enterprises voluntarily consider social and environmental aspects in their strategies and activities and in contacts with stakeholders (EC 2001: 6).

Summing up the definitions presented in this way, it could be said that the role of business is not only to generate profits, but it is the service in the understanding of the obligation to meet the expectations of the enterprise's environment and consists in balancing the interests of the groups that function in it. In addition to achieving business goals, a company should consider social and environmental goals in its strategy (Howaniec 2016: 34).

In CSR research and theory building, however, CSR has been viewed from different perspectives, such as social performance (Carroll 1979; Swanson 1995), stakeholder management (Freeman 1984; Donaldson, Preston 1995; Lozano 2002), corporate governance (Freeman, Evan 1990), business ethics (Solomon 1993), responsibility (Elkington 1998; Valor 2005), corporate citizenship (CC; Waddock 2000; Zadek 2001), or even from the perspective of the so-called social contract (Donaldson, Dunfee 2002). However, a certain evolution of the approach to CSR is noticeable, which is more and more often defined as the broadly understood responsibility for society, considering not only the present time, but also its welfare in the future.

The indication of care for the broadly understood social welfare can be seen both in contemporary definitions and in those at the beginning of the formulation of the CSR concept. Such perception of social responsibility assumes that under the so-called protection of social welfare, enterprises should not undertake socially harmful activities, even if they bring a profit. On the other hand, they are obliged to take actions aimed at preventing and eliminating negative social effects, to which they contributed by operating on the market. According to many authors, enterprises should create social welfare by engaging in various types of projects for the country (Carroll 1993: 31–32). Social responsibility is also seen as a set of obligations of a company to protect and strengthen the society in which it operates (Griffin 1998: 144). Similarly, CSR is defined by K. Kietliński, V. Reyes, and T. Oleksyn, for whom CSR is something more than just bringing profits to shareholders (owners). According to these authors, the concept of CSR defines the way in which business decisions and actions of enterprises affect all individuals and entities that deal with them, both inside and outside the organisation (Kietliński et al. 2005: 132). M. Rybak also points out the concern for broadly understood welfare (Rybak 2004: 28).

The change that has taken place in the definition of CSR also applies to entities that are required to apply it. Initially, the interest in CSR focused solely on economic entities operating for profit, hence the commonly used term to describe the social involvement of enterprises was the term: "corporate social responsibility". In recent years, the need for a broadly understood practice considering the good of society has also been extended to other entities. Society, business, business environment units, and other entities have noticed the impact of all other entities on society and the broadly understood development and social welfare in the long term. The view that CSR applies to all organisations has been developed as the impact on the sustainable development of various types of organisations, in particular non-business organisations, has been noticed and realised by them themselves (ISO 2012: 17). Increasingly, the term "social responsibility" has been used, which does not limit the involvement in question only to the business sphere. Finally, it is now more correct to use the term "social responsibility of market entities", which indicates a wide range of entities actively operating in the market economy, which, regardless of their nature – commercial or non-commercial – are obliged to take actions considering the present and future good of society.

The evolution of the definition of CSR, despite the fact that the current framework is varied and not always consistent (Jones 1980; Carroll 1999; Windsor 2001), also changed the perceived scope of the required involvement of broadly understood market entities. Initially, society's expectations towards entrepreneurs were satisfied through their participation in social life in the form of donations and charity. Then came the issues of working conditions and integrity in operating practices. Human rights, the environment, consumer protection, and anti-fraud and anti-corruption have been added as they gained importance. This evolution of social expectations was a response to various difficulties faced by society. When these difficulties were transformed into specific social problems, society expected that various types of organisations, including economic ones, would become the engine of change and progress (mainly due to their size, financial resources, and the possibility of exerting influence) (Pinkston, Carroll 1996: 199). As the years passed, social problems grew in number and scope. Hence, among others extending the scope of CSR. Since social responsibility is to respond to the needs of society reported at a given time, it is necessary to adjust its scope to the expectations formulated by them.

Changes in the perception of social responsibility also changed the commonly accepted models. This applies, inter alia, to the model of A. Carroll. The changes that have taken place in economic practice have resulted in a narrowing of the gap between economic and ethical responsibility, and the ethical sphere itself has gained greater importance with a simultaneous decline in companies' involvement in philanthropic responsibility (Pinkston, Carroll 1996: 205). In the first decade of the 21st century, the four-level pyramid model was replaced by a model consisting of three main areas of responsibility (a three-domain model of CSR), to which the authors included economic, legal, and ethical responsibility (Schwartz, Carroll 2003: 508). A separate sphere of philanthropic responsibility has been abandoned, assuming that in the proposed model this responsibility would be perceived as part of ethical and/or economic responsibility (Figure 2.1). As a result, seven partial domains, the so-called spheres of responsibility we created (Schwartz, Carroll 2003: 513–520):

1 purely economical – the overriding goal of the activities undertaken in the enterprise is to maximise profits, each activity of the enterprise is aimed at direct or indirect economic benefits, with the simultaneous failure to comply with the law or only the necessary compliance, where the actions of the enterprise are considered amoral or unethical;

2 purely legal – the overriding goal of the company's activities is their compliance with the law, but these activities are not ethical or economically justified;
3 purely ethical – the overriding goal of activities undertaken by the enterprise is compliance with moral principles, while these "purely" ethical activities do not have direct or indirect economic or legal character;
4 economic/ethical – actions are taken by the enterprise due to economic and ethical conditions, and most often basic compliance with the law is maintained, because illegal actions are considered unethical;
5 economic/legal – actions are taken by the enterprise due to economic and legal conditions, while disregarding ethical aspects (such a situation may take place when searching for legal loopholes and using them for economic benefit), such actions are most often taken considering the basic ethical criteria;
6 legal/ethical – actions are taken by the enterprise due to legal and ethical requirements, and not for economic reasons, although most often they indirectly provide economic benefits to the enterprise;
7 economic/legal/ethical – actions are taken by the company considering economic, legal, and ethical conditions, i.e. management, according to which the management strives to ensure profitability, but only within the framework of compliance with the law and sensitivity to ethical standards (cf. Carroll 1987: 10).

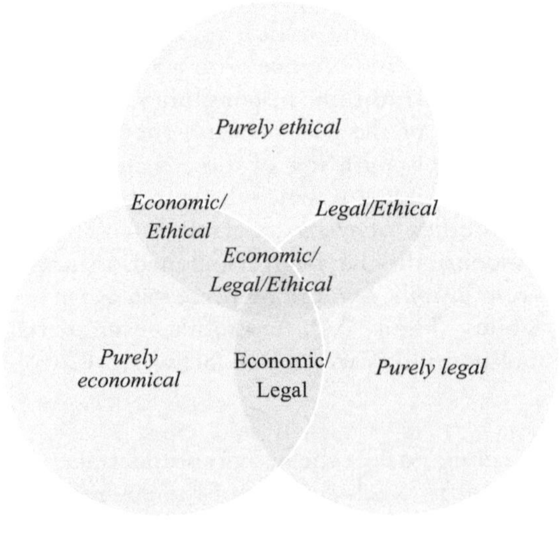


*Figure 2.1* The three-domain model of corporate social responsibility (Schwartz, Carroll 2003: 509)

A popular CSR model is also that of M. Porter and M. Kramer (2006: 78–92). When building it, the authors adopted the following assumptions:

1 Society and business need each other, and neither can function without the other. This interdependence means that the basis of business decisions and corporate social policy should be shared value, and enterprises should incorporate a social perspective into their strategy.
2 Enterprises influence society through their activities in the value chain, e.g. employment practices, emission of pollutants, pro-environmental activities, and society influences the sphere of business. These two types of impact are inside-out linkages, i.e. the organisation affects the social environment through positive or negative consequences for society and outside-in linkages, i.e. the social environment affects the organisation.
3 Enterprises must prioritise and select social problems that are related to their activities, i.e. those that have a significant impact not only on the company's operations, but on its competitiveness. Most important in this process is to determine if the identified problem provides an opportunity to create shared value, i.e. a significant benefit for society and a valuable benefit for the enterprise itself.
4 Enterprises should establish an action program in which social and economic benefits can be achieved simultaneously. This program must include a responsive and strategic CSR.

M. Porter and M. Kramer warn companies against irrational consideration of social issues. Some of the problems are important from the point of view of society, but solving them is not important for the industry or the company itself. They do not allow for the achievement of a common value for the company and society, and therefore will never be the basis for improving the company's competitiveness, leaving the inside-out and outside-in impact at a low level. According to Porter and Kramer, the CSR concept: (1) must pay off (profit maximisation motive), (2) benefits must be significant and long-term (strategic approach), (3) should bring a significant improvement in the competitive position (competition strategy), and (4) benefits should be mutual, i.e. for business and society (Porter, Kramer 2011: 62–77). The concept of shared value presented by them initiated the development of the term CSV (creating shared value), i.e. the creation of a shared value.

Despite clearly set goals for the social involvement of all entities operating in the market, the area that is constantly discussed is the required level of CSR. Returning to the ethical issues, or more precisely the prohibitions and orders, many practitioners and theorists ask the question whether a socially responsible organisation that does no harm can be considered as socially responsible, or whether it is necessary to engage in doing "good things". The literature on the subject distinguishes in this respect a passive and active approach to social responsibility. The passive approach is about avoiding harm, which in practice means that enterprises or other entities refrain from taking harmful and socially undesirable activities. Meanwhile, the active approach is the assumed elimination of negative effects, the source of which was the conducted activity, including the activity carried out in the past, as well as the prevention of such effects in the current activity of the enterprise (cf. Rybak 2004: 28). Proponents of such a division argue that the cause-effect sequence leading to a negative state can be presented either as a sequence of successive events or as a sequence of actions that were not taken for various reasons (Des Jardis, McCall 1985: 44). The ethics of responsibility considers not only the effects of our actions, but also the effects of inaction.

In conclusion, although CSR has been the subject of academic studies for over 50 years, the concept of social responsibility is very broad and complex, and there is no single standard or system covering all its aspects. Moreover, recently there has been a noticeable change in the approach to CSR, which has been attempted to present here. The ethical context, which was dominant a few years ago, is beginning to give way to the analysis of the effectiveness of CSR application in practice. One can also notice the transition of the analysis from the macro level to the micro level, or even a change in the scope of CSR (cf. Carroll, Shabana 2010). All this makes a further discussion on the social role of not only business but all entities operating on the market justified. It is not appropriate to limit social responsibility solely to the economic sphere. Responsibility for society and its present and future welfare is borne not only by enterprises of an economic nature, i.e. production, service, or trade, but also by all entities that, through their actions, influence the shape of the functioning of society as a whole.

## Stakeholders and their place in the social model of the enterprise

The term stakeholder as it stands today first appeared in 1963 in an in-house study of the Stanford Research Institute. The study emphasised that stockholders and shareholders, or more precisely shareholders, are not the only ones that should be considered in management. The groups important for the organisation include shareholders, employees, customers, suppliers, lenders, and the society, and the concept of stakeholders has been defined as groups without whose support the organisation would cease to exist (Freeman et al. 2010: 30–31).

The term stakeholder comes from the English word stake, which means something that has meaning or value for a person, cause, or action. The word stake can also mean participation in something, stake, or interest. Stakeholders are therefore defined as any entities that have shares, rights, or other interests related to some enterprise/organisation and their operation.

The breakthrough that influenced the grounding of the concept of stakeholders in management science and the way of thinking of managers was the publication of R. Freeman, for which a stakeholder in the organisation is any group or person that can affect the achievement of the organisation's goals or feel the impact of the organisation's activities on itself (Freeman 1984: 46). The proposed theory focuses on the analysis of stakeholders, relations between the enterprise and its stakeholders, and the mechanisms of shaping them (Freeman 1984: 33). The departure from focusing solely on ownership groups was to lead to better results of organisational activities of enterprises in an increasingly complicated and turbulent environment (Freeman 1984: 249). The definition of R. Freeman's stakeholders is very broad and does not "close" the number of groups that may be them. Moreover, according to this definition, the indicated "impact" may be one-way. For Freeman, there are no implications or necessity for the stakeholder-enterprise interaction. A much narrower definition is provided by M. Clarkson, who limits the definition of a stakeholder to the necessity of risk and loss that he would incur as a result of the company's activity. For Clarkson, without the element of risk, there are no stakes, and therefore no stakeholder (Clarkson 1994: 5). T. Donaldson and L. Preston take a similar position, pointing to the need to clearly distinguish between the groups that affect the company and the interested parties. Some entities operating in the environment of the enterprise may be both (e.g. investors), as they have both influence and a "stake", i.e. they are real stakeholders of the enterprise. However, there are parties identified as stakeholders, even though they are not, because they either have no influence on the enterprise (e.g. job applicants) or – even if they have such an influence (e.g. media) – do not have any shares (cf. Donaldson, Preston 1995: 86). This approach narrows down the scope of stakeholders to those with legitimate claims, regardless of their strength of influence on the firm or the legitimacy of their relationship with the firm (cf. Mitchell et al. 1997: 856–857).

The definitions of R. Freeman and M. Clarkson present essentially extreme approaches to explaining the essence of stakeholders. As the discussion on the proposed theory developed, many other terms appeared, which were an attempt to define the concept (Mitchell et al. 1997: 858). This summary is presented in Table 2.1.

Numerous approaches to defining stakeholders and a discussion on the legitimacy of including them in the enterprise management process, in addition to positions supporting the rightness of such an approach (e.g. Donaldson, Preston 1995; Freeman, Philips 2002; Post et al. 2002) or against (e.g. Ansoff 1965: 34), enriched the literature with further attempts to distinguish: (1) groups influencing the enterprise and (2) ways of their classification. For example, R. Freeman and D. Reed proposed to divide the stakeholders into two groups (Freeman, Reed 1983: 91–92):

1 stakeholders in a broader perspective – any identifiable group or person that may affect the achievement of the organisation's goals or whose achievement of the organisation's objectives is influenced by (public interest groups, protesting groups, government agencies, competitors, trade associations, trade unions, such as also employees, customers and other similar stakeholders, as well as shareholders);

*Table 2.1* Chronological review of stakeholder definitions (1963–1995) (Mitchell et al. 1997: 858)

| *Source* | *Stake* |
|---|---|
| *Stanford Note*, 1963 | "those groups without whose support the organization would cease to exist" |
| Rhenman, 1964 | "are depending on the firm in order to achieve their personal goals and on whom the firm is depending for its existence" |
| Ahlstedt, Jahnukainen, 1971 | Groups which, driven by their own interests and goals, participate in the activities of the company, and therefore depend on the company and the company also depends on them |
| Freeman and Reed, 1983 | Broad approach: "can affect the achievement of an organization's objectives or who is affected by the achievement of an organization's objectives"<br>narrow approach: "on which the organization is dependent for its continued survival" |
| Freeman, 1984 | "can affect or is affected by the achievement of the organization's objectives" |
| Freeman, Gilbert, 1987 | "can affect or is affected by a business" |
| Cornell, Shapiro, 1987 | "claimants" who have "contracts" |
| Evan, Freeman, 1988 | "have a stake in or claim on the firm" |
| Evan, Freeman, 1988 | "benefit from or are harmed by, and whose rights are violated or respected by, corporate actions" |
| Bowie, 1988 | "without whose support the organization would cease to exist" |
| Alkhafaji, 1989 | "groups to whom the corporation is responsible" |
| Carroll, 1989 | "asserts to have one or more of these kinds of stakes" – "ranging from an interest to a right (legal or moral) to ownership or legal title to the company's assets or property" |
| Freeman and Evan, 1990 | contract holders |
| Thompson et al., 1991 | in "relationship with an organization" |
| Savage et al., 1991 | "have an interest in the actions of an organization and $_4$ the ability to influence it" |
| Hill, Jones, 1992 | "constituents who have a legitimate claim on the firm$_4$ established through the existence of an exchange relationship" who supply "the firm with critical resources (contributions) and in exchange each expects its interests to be satisfied (by inducements)" |
| Brenner, 1993 | "having some legitimate, non-trivial relationship with an organization [such as] exchange transactions, action impacts, and moral responsibilities" |
| Carroll, 1993 | "asserts to have one or more of the kinds of stakes in business"– may be affected or affect $_4$ |
| Freeman, 1994 | Participants in "the human process of joint value creation" |
| Wicks et al., 1994 | "interact with and give meaning and definition to the corporation" |

| | |
|---|---|
| Langtry, 1994 | the firm is significantly responsible for their well-being, or they hold a moral or legal claim on the firm |
| Starik, 1994 | "can and are making their actual stakes known"-"are or might be influenced by, or are or potentially are influencers of, some organization" |
| Clarkson, 1994 | "bear some form of risk as a result of having invested some form of capital, human or financial, something of value, in a firm" or "are placed at risk as a result of a firm's activities" |
| Clarkson, 1995 | "have, or claim, ownership, rights, or interests in a corporation and its activities" |
| Näsi, 1995 | "interact with the firm and thus make its operation possible" |
| Brenner, 1995 | "are or which could impact or be impacted by the firm/organization" |
| Donaldson and Preston, 1995 | "persons or groups with legitimate interests in procedural and/or substantive aspects of corporate activity" |

2 stakeholders in a narrower perspective – any identifiable group or person on which the survival of the organisation depends (including employees, customers, major suppliers, key government agencies, financial institutions, and shareholders).

The same authors also proposed the division of stakeholders according to their influence on the organisation. In this configuration, the authors distinguished (Freeman, Reed 1983: 93–95):

1 stakeholders with a formal or legal force of influence (shareholders and stockholders, management, or, under certain conditions, minorities with legally guaranteed interests),
2 stakeholders with economic power of influence, i.e. having the ability to influence market decisions (customers, competitors, suppliers, all kinds of associations having such an impact),
3 stakeholders with the political power of influence, i.e. having the ability to influence through the use of political mechanisms (entities representing consumer interests, government, local governments, and trade associations).

Another classification distinguishes two groups of stakeholders: primary stakeholders, which include consumers, employees, suppliers, financiers, and local communities, and secondary stakeholders, i.e. competitors, government, consumer associations, media, and special interest groups (Freeman et al. 2010: 30–31).

The basis for the division of stakeholders may also be:

- the location of the stakeholders,
- the degree of connection with the organisation,
- the nature of the relationship between the stakeholder and the organisation,
- the type of stake involved in the organisation (Table 2.2).

The classification of stakeholders may also be based on the division of the CSR area of interest, according to which it is distinguished (cf. Majkut, Wójcik 2015: 27–30):

1. market area – includes customers, competitors, and business partners;
2. workplace – responsibility towards employees, and more broadly, responsibility for human resources, health and safety at work, and managing changes (EC 2001: 7); responsibility in the workplace is also honesty towards co-owners or investors.
3. society, including the local community.
4. environment.

Despite the large divergence of the approaches presented, there are certain common elements in them. The parties interested in the activities of enterprises certainly include customers, investors (shareholders), employees, suppliers, media, public administration (government), and the local community (Howaniec, Waszkielewicz 2007: 261). Each of these groups has specific expectations towards the enterprise, which affect the quality of the relationship between them and the enterprise. For example, for investors, the most important aspect of cooperation with a company is the return on invested capital. However, this does not mean that they are only interested in profit, both in the short and long term. Important aspects for this group are also, among others: certainty of investment, the value of the company's brand (brands) and the company's position on the market. Employees look at the company differently, for them the most important are working conditions, including content and working time, material working environment or social and living activity of the enterprise, and the system of motivation implemented in the enterprise. The expectations of individual groups towards the enterprise are presented in Table 2.3.

In today's world, links with stakeholders are an essential asset that a company needs to compete in the market. Thanks to these relationships, trust is born, which is helpful in the decision-making process by the company and in the use of emerging opportunities (Smith, Lensen 2009: 35). Especially in the era of globalisation, the attention of enterprises should focus on ensuring efficiency and development in the long term, e.g. through the innovation of products and processes, and the way to this is considering the interests of all stakeholders (Rybak 2004: 85). A responsible enterprise is one that cares for the interests of its employees and the local community, cares for the

*Table 2.2* Classifications of the company's stakeholders – selected examples (based on: Rybak 2004: 43–48; Bukowska 2008: 90–99; Paliwoda-Matiolańska 2014: 60; Świerk 2016: 31–32)

| *The criterion of the division of stakeholders* | *Stakeholder classification* |
|---|---|
| Stakeholders' place of presence | Internal stakeholders (insiders) – entities that control the activities of the organisation due to ownership (shareholders) or due to their position in the organisation (board members, managers, employees).<br>External stakeholders (outsiders) – entities outside the organisation that are interested in the activities of the organisation (customers, suppliers, etc.). |
| The degree of connection with the organisation | First degree stakeholders – natural or legal persons entering into formal contracts or agreements with the organisation. Without their involvement, the company cannot survive (e.g. shareholders, employees, customers, suppliers, investors, and the public sector: government and local communities).<br>Second-degree stakeholders – individuals or groups of people that can exert an influence on the organisation or be influenced by it, who do not conduct any transactions with it, so the functioning of the organisation is not dependent on them (e.g. the media). |
| The nature of the relationship between the stakeholder and the organisation | Substantial stakeholders – these are all those who are within the enterprise, who, thanks to their work inputs, competences and skills, knowledge, and their capital, contribute to the enterprise (employees, shareholders, owners).<br>Contract stakeholders – derive directly from the company's operations; their relationship with the enterprise is a formal contract (customers, cooperators, suppliers, competitors).<br>Contextual stakeholders – they play a fundamental role in achieving good name and acceptance by the company for its activities; entities that defend common goods and show concern for common goods, e.g. the environment, peace, security, freedom, justice (various communities: from local through state to global, as well as social and government institutions). |
| The type of stake involved in the organisation | Ownership stake (dependence) – applies to a situation where the value of the organisation has a direct impact on the welfare of stakeholders (e.g. shareholders).<br>Economic stake (dependence) – the stakeholder is economically dependent on the organisation, without having any ownership rights (e.g. employees receiving remuneration, state institutions, and organisations for which the organisation incurs expenses, including taxes).<br>Social stake – stakeholders are not directly related to the organisation, but are interested in making it act socially responsible (e.g. local community).<br>Silent stakeholder (the so-called mute) – a stakeholder who is not able to directly convey his expectations (e.g. the natural environment). |

*Table 2.3* Stakeholders' needs in relation to business (based on: European Commission 2001: 8–15; Howaniec, Waszkielewicz 2007: 261; Howaniec 2017: 152)

| *Stakeholders* | *Needs* |
|---|---|
| Investors (shareholders) | They expect a return on their invested capital. |
| Employees | They focus on working conditions; their expectations relate to employment conditions, remuneration, and appreciation. |
| Customers | They perceive the company through the prism of its market activities, brands, products, services, prices, promotions, advertisements, etc.; they expect safe, reliable products, reliable communication, and facilitation of the purchasing process. |
| Suppliers | They expect reliability in cooperation and the possibility of joint business development; they are interested in long-term cooperation, order reliability, and timely payments. |
| Public administration (government) | They see the company as an entity that creates jobs and pays taxes. |
| Local community | Expects the company to act responsibly, not only in terms of running a business, but also social and charity, including contributing to the development of the local economy. |
| Media | They evaluate the company through the prism of social interest and the actions of the management staff. |

environment in which it operates, which means running a business based on building lasting, transparent relationships with all interested parties.

## Economic responsibility and creating shared value

The discussion on the legitimacy of considering social goals in the current activities of enterprises and other market entities concerns, inter alia, justification of the costs incurred for this purpose. Chapter 1 presents the points of view presented in the literature by those researchers who opposed the idea of incurring non-economically justified costs in the enterprise, claiming that the overriding goal of the enterprise is profit and profitability in the long term. Despite the loud opposition to the inclusion of social functions in business practice and agreement on some of the allegations made against CSR, the concept of CSR not only has not ceased to be relevant, but we can even speak of its renaissance. Nowadays, however, more and more talk about the social involvement (also social engagement, social commitment, or social participation) of enterprises and the creation of common value.

CSV is a term proposed by M. Porter and M. Kramer (2006). These authors argue that the interdependence between business and society implies the need to consider common value when making all business decisions in such a way that both business decisions and social policy are consistent with the principle of common value. In practice, this means incorporating the social perspective into the current operations of the company, i.e. including it in the process of planning, organising, leading, and controlling.

Each company operates in the conditions of competition, which significantly affects its ability to implement the strategy, especially in the long term. Social conditions constitute a key part of this context, and thus the competitiveness of enterprises may more and more often be determined by the extent to which enterprises consider social and environmental aspects in their strategies and activities. Meanwhile, CSR is very often not perceived in a strategic way. Despite the development of the approach to CSR, enterprises still do not see social involvement as an opportunity to increase their competitiveness, but only treat it as an addition to their basic activities, most often of a promotional nature. However, external conditions encourage a different approach to social responsibility in practice. CSR should be treated as part of a core business strategy that allows to increase innovation and lead to a competitive advantage (Porter, Kramer 2006). The way in which society influences business (and not the other way around) justifies solving social problems as a basic business strategy and even philanthropy activities can improve the competitiveness of enterprises (Porter, Kramer 2002). Similar conclusions can be found, among others, in R. Williams and J. Barret (2000), F. Simon (1995), and B. Seiffert, S. Morris, and B. Bartkus (2003).

CSV enables society to progress faster, ensuring faster development of companies, which ultimately contributes to the increase in prosperity in general. The ability to create economic value by creating social value is one of the most powerful growth drivers in the global economy. However, this approach is a new way of understanding customers, productivity and the impact of external factors on the company's success (Porter, Kramer 2011: 75). Similar conclusions are found in the report prepared with the participation of the UN Global Compact. Interviews with company directors from around the world indicate that business sees a future era of sustainable development, which will require the creation of more sustainable economies and societies, but also a change in the approach to the competitiveness of enterprises (Lacy et al. 2010: 55). Economic success, and at the same time creating social value, is not only a responsibility, but also the opportunity to rethink the way in which a business should be conducted, in line with sustainable economic growth (Bockstette, Stamp 2011: 1).

The CSV concept proposed by M. Porter and M. Kramer is perceived by them as an evolution of CSR. And it's hard to disagree with this approach. CSR, which consists in doing good, is not desired by business, which most often accuses the concept of social responsibility of its lack of correlation with financial results. Meanwhile, the appropriate selection of support can be a benefit both for the enterprise and for the society. However, it is important to choose the area of support that is consistent with the company's industry, its knowledge, and experience, so that the support must also be a value for the company itself. This value can be manifested in improving relations with the company's target customers, increasing knowledge about the market needs, developing research in the area of business activity, etc. In this way, the appropriate selection of the support area may become the basis for the growth of the company's competitiveness and contribute to the synergistic (increased by the social value noticed by customers) maximisation of revenues from the market. Such perception of the value of social involvement, however, excludes looking for areas of support in the most publicised social problems. This decision should be a strategic decision, dictated by the future development and financial goals of the company. The main differences between the concept of CSR and CSV presented by Porter and Kramer are presented in Table 2.4.

The concept of shared value also appeared in the guidelines of the European Union. In 2011, the EC: (1) presented a new definition of CSR as the responsibility of enterprises for their impact on society, (2) noted that the prerequisite for fulfiling this obligation is compliance with the applicable legislation and collective agreements concluded between social partners, (3) indicated that in order to fully comply with their social responsibility, enterprises should implement social, environmental, ethical, human rights, and consumer protection aspects in their business activities and core strategy, in close cooperation with stakeholders, and (4) defined the objectives of the business activities undertaken, indicating that it is: (a) maximising the creation of common value for the owners/shareholders of the company and for other stakeholders and the whole society, and (b) identifying, preventing, and mitigating any possible negative effects of the company's operation (EC 2011a: 6). The EC also encouraged enterprises to adopt a long-term, strategic approach to CSR and to explore the possibilities of developing innovative products, services, and business models that contribute to social welfare and lead to higher quality and productivity (EC 2011: 6).

The CSV is therefore an intermediate solution between creating business value and creating social value. Enterprises, instead of perceiving business and society as spheres with different goals, should perceive the enormous potential of the economic sphere, which can contribute to social progress. Assuming a two-way relationship between business and society, enterprises need to understand that they need healthy and well-functioning societies in order to function and develop efficiently. Increasingly, therefore, they should seek to create "shared value" by integrating social considerations into their core business strategies, delivering benefits to society, and improving their competitiveness (Figure 2.2).

Such an understanding of business obligations is consistent with the approach presented by W. Gasparski, for whom economic activity must conform to the 3E rule, i.e. effective, economic, and ethical (Gasparski 2004a: 135–136). Gasparski emphasises that activities in the field of business ethics do not consist in replacing the economic goal with social and environmental goals, but in the harmonisation of goals, that is, considering ethics in the company's day-to-day operations.

*Table 2.4* CSR and CSV – basic differences (Porter, Kramer 2011a: 16)

| *CSR (Corporate Social Responsibility)* | *CSV (Creating Shared Value)* |
|---|---|
| Values: doing good | Values: economic and social benefits in relation to costs. |
| Civic feeling, philanthropy, sustainable development | Joint creation of value for companies and communities. |
| Discretionary or in response to external pressure | Integrated with competitiveness. |
| Separated from profit maximisation | Integrated with profit maximisation. |
| The agenda is determined by external reports and personal preferences | The agenda is company specific and internally generated. |
| Impact limited by CSR program and budget | Adjusts the entire budget of the company. |

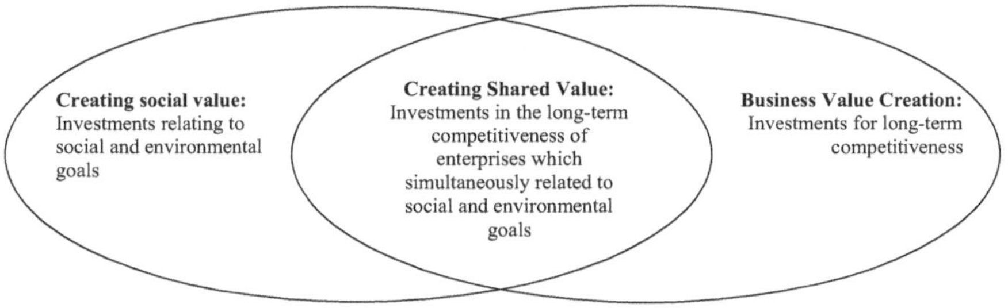


*Figure 2.2* CSV scope (Bockstette, Stamp 2011: 4)

A major contribution to today's perception of CSR and the creation of shared value were also the assumptions presented by J. Elkington, who proposed the concept of The Triple Bottom Line, i.e. an accounting system covering three dimensions of enterprise performance: social, environmental, and financial. This system differed from the commonly used reporting framework in that it included environmental and social measures that were difficult to assign and measure (Elkington 1994). The dimensions proposed by him are now commonly known as the 3P (Three P's Balance) formula, where the following P mean: "Profit", "Planet", and "People". According to the 3P principle, enterprises should not focus their attention only on economic values, but also on ecological and social values, keeping the balance between profit and public interest.

## Business commitment to the environment

One of the areas which, in the opinion of the society, should be "taken care of" by broadly understood business is the natural environment. Ecological responsibility is recognised both in the internal and external dimensions of CSR (Howaniec, Waszkielewicz 2007: 261). In the internal dimension, it includes managing the company's impact on the environment and natural resources. In the external dimension, meanwhile, it is explicitly concerned with the care for the broadly understood natural environment. Some authors also believe that it is an element of shaping relations with the local community. Certainly, ecological responsibility should not be related only to limiting the negative impact of a company on the natural environment. Responsibility in this area relates more to environmental risk management and covers not only protection but also revitalisation of the natural environment (Chodyński 2011: 227–228).

An element of the considerations on ecological responsibility is the discourse in which the issue of whether the natural environment is legitimate to influence the enterprise and whether it can be assigned the status of a stakeholder is raised. Opponents of recognising the natural environment as one of the stakeholders emphasise that this status is associated with a certain level of moral references, meanwhile, the natural environment does not have its own mentality and has no needs in the human sense. Needs on behalf of the natural environment are reported by environmentalists (cf. Chodyński 2011: 239, 242).

This point of view was strongly opposed by some authors. For example, N. Haigh and A. Griffiths not only recognise the natural environment as a business stakeholder but also assign it the role of the primary stakeholder. For these authors, the natural environment has all the attributes, i.e. power, legitimacy, and strength, which, in accordance with the framework indicated by R. Mitchell and others, identify stakeholders (Mitchel et al. 1997: 865–867), including the additional closeness element incorporated by C. Driscoll and M. Starik (2004: 63–66). N. Haigh and A. Griffiths approached the status of the natural environment as one of the stakeholders not from an ethical point of view, but from the point of view of its strategic impact on infrastructure, resources, and markets (Haigh, Griffiths 2009: 351–356). For these authors: (1) the natural environment has an economic share in organisations, (2) there is no need for a moral obligation between organisations and the natural environment from a strategic point of view, (3) the lack of will and other human attributes of the environment is not a problem, and (4) the condition formulated by M. Freeman (1984) that the stakeholder "affects or is affected by" is met (Haigh, Griffiths 2009: 356–357).

C. Driscoll and M. Starik were also unequivocal in treating the natural environment as a stakeholder. It is obvious for these authors that economic entities interact both with the ecological system on a global scale and with the environment on a local scale. The economic sphere influences, changes, and/or interferes with the complexity and interrelationships occurring in the natural environment. This impact may be direct – obvious, direct, visible, tangible, and similar spatially and temporally impact on the natural environment, e.g. the impact of pesticides on the contamination of water reservoirs and watercourses, or indirect – subtler, less visible, less tangible, and less similar spatially and temporarily, often of a global nature (Driscoll, Starik 2004: 66).

Discroll and Starik also argued that the stakeholder attributes determined, inter alia, by R. Mitchell, B. Agle, and D. Wood are largely anchored in a social paradigm limited by too narrow economic rationality and traditional political influences. Meanwhile, the change in the conditions of competition, dictated by the global nature of the economy, means that the concept of stakeholders must also be broadened. Stakeholder theory that focuses solely on stakeholder transactions and economics-based databases ignores ecosystem transactions that organisations need to survive (Driscoll, Starik 2004: 67).

M. Porter and van der Linde (1995) or S. Hart and S. Sharma (2004) also indicate the necessity to consider the natural environment in companies' strategies. Some authors claim that even if the obligations towards the environment were considered as obligations towards future generations, companies should include it in their strategies and actions (cf. Jackson 1999: 163–173, 190–195). The author also agrees with this approach, treating the natural environment as the main stakeholder in the economic sphere. The natural environment has an impact on the economy, for example through the climate, water resources, natural resources, and the "stake", which is the state of the environment, which changes due to urbanisation and the impact of industry. Meeting these conditions qualifies it as a real stakeholder of enterprises.

The interdependence of the economic sphere and the environment is clear and cannot be ignored in the day-to-day activities of enterprises. T. Dyllick and K. Hockerts, describing the relationship between business, society, and nature, introduced the concepts of eco-efficiency, socio-efficiency, eco-effectiveness, and socio-effectiveness (Dyllick, Hockerts 2002: 138). Ecological efficiency (eco-efficiency) is the provision of goods and services at competitive prices that meet reported needs and ensure the quality of life, while gradually reducing the impact on the environment and reducing the amount of resources throughout the product life cycle. Social efficiency (socio-efficiency) assumes the minimisation of negative social effects or the maximisation of positive effects and describes the relationship between the added value of the company and its social impact (Dyllick, Hockerts 2002: 138). This definition is extended by A. Chodyński, for whom socio-efficiency means activities related to the processes of building relationships of a relational nature, shaping marketing orientation and quality (including service quality), building trust, cooperation, strategic planning, and governance (cf. Chodyński 2011: 230, 234). Ecological effectiveness (eco-effectiveness), in turn, presupposes an effective impact on the natural environment, manifested by a positive impact on its condition. For Chodyński, it means restoring the state of the natural environment, both to technical aspects and to having the necessary resources (sufficiency) (Chodyński 2011: 231). The last of the concepts introduced – social effectiveness – relates to the social commitment of enterprises. Ecological responsibility was finally adopted as an element of social commitment of companies and is treated as part of the business model that today guarantees competitiveness at the level imposed by the market. Models considering aspects of environmental protection were presented, among others, by B. Cohen, B. Smith, and R. Mitchell (2008) and G. O'Neill Jr, J. Hershauer, and J. Golden (2006).

Increased ecological awareness of the society, tightening legal regulations, and higher care for the image have resulted in increased interest in environmental protection also in practice. Companies seem to notice the benefits of caring for the environment and undertake a number of initiatives important from the point of view of ecology. The activities undertaken by enterprises significantly exceed the implementation of the Environmental Management System compliant with the PN-EN ISO 14001 standard.

Economic practice also provides us with many negative examples, and unfortunately not only those in which can be seen the achievement of goals related to improving the company's image. The actions taken by BP after the explosion of the Deepwater Horizon oil rig in the Gulf of Mexico were an example of total ignorance of environmental problems and their own negative impact on them. The accident was dubbed an "unprecedented environmental catastrophe", but also had severe consequences for BP. It resulted, inter alia, in a significant drop in the value of the company's shares, multi-billion in damages, and public pressure led to the creation by BP of a recovery fund worth 20 billion dollars (Harlow et al. 2011: 82).

**The Coca-Cola Company**

The Coca-Cola Company (TCCC) is an American multinational beverage corporation, best known as the producer of Coca-Cola. The company's stock is listed on the NYSE and is part of the DJIA and the S&P 500 and S&P 100 indexes.

TCCC undertakes many actions in the area of CSR. One of the projects is the World Without Waste, which was launched in 2018. The project has three main goals:

1 Make 100% of their packaging worldwide recyclable by 2025 – and use at least 50% recycled content in their packaging by 2030 (PROJECT);
2 Collect and recycle a bottle or can for each one they sell by 2030 (COLLECT);
3 Bring people together to support a healthy, debris-free environment (PARTNER).

The company's achievements in the area of waste reduction (TCCC 2020: 27):

- In total, 16 markets offer beverages packaged in 100% recycled PET (rPET) bottles. Water brands in Austria, Belgium, Ireland, Peru, the Philippines, Switzerland, South Africa, and Uruguay, among others, are making water bottles entirely from recycled plastic;

- TCCC, together with Changchun Meihe Science and Technology, developed a technology for producing PlantBottle bottles that contain 30% plant-based material. According to estimates, the use of this bottle allows the avoidance of over 650,000 metric tons of CO2 emissions – which corresponds to the burning of about 1.5 million barrels of oil;
- In Brazil, all 2-litre bottles across Trademark Coca-Cola, Fanta, and Sprite brands are sold in refillable "universal bottles" that are the same shape, size, and colour, which increases the efficiency of collection, cleaning, and filling. The reusable bottles are replacing 200 million regular bottles each year. In addition to Brazil, in over 25 countries, refillables make up half or more of their sales, and in more than 50 countries, refillables currently represent 25% or more of the sales portfolio, including Germany, Chile, Colombia, Peru, Pakistan, Kenya, the Philippines, and Tanzania;
- Introduced refillable microchip cups that work with Coca-Cola Freestyle on select cruise lines, amusement parks, and universities, causing around 15 million drinks a day (5.5 billion per year) to spill from around 52,000 units Coca-Cola Freestyle in the US and other countries.

TCCC conducts activities in many areas indicated in CSR, one of its activities is responsible marketing. TCCC is committed to responsible marketing of its products. Their marketing policy clearly states that they will respect the role of parents and caregivers by not marketing directly to children under 13, which in practice means, inter alia, that:

- do not advertise on any media directly targeting children under the age of 13, including programs, print media, websites, social media, movies, and SMS/email marketing;
- do not design their marketing communications in a way that directly appeals to children under the age of 13;
- do not show pictures of their products consumed by children under the age of 13 without the presence of an adult;
- do not show any children who are, or appear to be, under the age of 5.

They also describe TCCC's Global School Beverage Policy. In line with this policy, TCCC does not advertise commercially in primary schools. Their system supports educational programs for children under the age of 13 in local communities around the world, but any brand presence in children's programs simply means and recognises financial support/sponsorship and is not for advertising purposes (TCCC 2022).

## "Good citizenship" and commitments to the local community

The concept of the company as a good citizen (CC) was born in the 1990s. This concept is related to the concept of CSR and is treated as a response by practitioners to social expectations (Matten et al. 2003: 111; cf. Nakonieczna 2008: 68).

The necessity of being a "good citizen" was indicated by A. Carroll in the pyramid of social responsibility proposed in 1991, in which the author linked philanthropic responsibility with being a "good citizen" (Carroll 1991: 39–41). According to this approach, it meant the involvement of enterprises in solving social problems, including devoting a part of resources to the benefit of society, e.g. through charity, volunteering, etc. R. De George also wrote about good citizenship (De George 1993: 189).

Treating business entities as "good citizens" was and is popular especially in the United States, where the enterprise is treated on an equal footing with other citizens, having specific rights as well as obligations towards the state and society. According to the assumptions of the concept of good citizenship, each enterprise is obliged to contribute not only to the welfare of society, which relates to the sphere of "possession", but also to the improvement of the quality of life of society in a holistic manner, i.e. broadly understood well-being, which relates to the mental sphere (emotional and mental) and bliss, which in turn relates to the sphere of feelings or the spiritual sphere (Borys 2015: 9–10). The enterprise should demonstrate a civic attitude and contribute to the common good.

As can be seen from the above definitions, CC does not differ significantly in its scope from the concept of CSR or the theory of stakeholders in a significant way. These concepts also expect the enterprise to care for the broadly understood, present, and future social welfare. Some researchers treat the concept of CC only as a new name to define the scope of CSR, which, however, has the advantage that in its content it "does not admonish" the business, pointing to shortcomings in the field of ethics or social responsibility. For H. Van Luijk, the conclusion of both the concepts of "business ethics" and "corporate social responsibility" is that "ethics" or "responsibility" are concepts that are absent in business, and even worse, that are contrary to business (Van Luijk 2001; after: Matten et al. 2003: 111). On the other hand, "citizenship" has a different connotation to business. It emphasises the fact of "place in society" alongside other "citizens" with whom the corporation forms a community. It is alleged here economic practice that, rather than accepting academics and critics to become more responsible, corporations simply decided to establish their own agenda based on being a "good citizen" (Matten et al. 2003: 111). There is also a second approach, according to which CC is treated as an element of CSR. In this case, the term is used to describe the philanthropic roles and responsibilities that the company voluntarily undertakes for the benefit of the local community. The most common activities of companies are financial support in various forms, material support, or employee volunteering. Such an understanding of good citizenship is consistent with the approach proposed by A. Carroll, which is treated as a prototype of the concept of CC (cf. Carroll 1991: 39–41). Similarly, CC is defined by, for example, I. Maignan and O. Ferrell (2000: 294).

It is noted, however, that Carroll defined this type of responsibility as something additional, optional, discretionary, beyond what is required of a business, not dictated by any moral imperative, and therefore less important than the other three categories of responsibility he indicated (Matten et al. 2003: 112). Such an interpretation of the idea of good citizenship causes that companies perceive CC as an element of their own interest and take such actions that are in line with their long-term profitability. This approach gave rise to the term "social investment" undertaken to build social capital (Waddock 2000: 326–327) or reputational capital of an enterprise (Fombrun et al. 2000: 86–87). Social investments are understood, among others, as investing in the activities of non-profit organisations, such as voluntary and social organisations or social enterprises, whereby such investment is not only to create the social value of a given activity, but also to bring a specific return for the investor.

This approach has both supporters and opponents. N. Smith refers to the concept of CC as "the new corporate philanthropy" (Smith 1994). It is defined in a similar way by D. Saiia (2001). Meanwhile, for some authors, CC is an innovation in relation to the concept of CSR, and the element of novelty that distinguishes it from CSR is that, according to the concept of CC, business perceives itself as part of the public culture and does not treat social involvement as an external matter, as is the case of the CSR concept (cf. Matten et al. 2003: 113).

There is also a third interpretation of the concept of CC, presented by D. Matten and A. Crane, according to which CC is nothing more than a reconceptualisation of the relationship between the state and society and enterprises, related to the entry of business into the sphere so far served by public authorities (Matten, Crane 2005: 170–174). The need to redefine the social contract is indicated, inter alia, by J. Filek, according to whom the contemporary approach to business has changed, which is perceived as an active participant in social life, and the justification for such a change is, inter alia, progressing globalisation, changing the system of forces governing society, in particular in the context of economic forces and economic power (Filek 2009: 25, 31–38). Therefore, some of the authors speak of CC as requiring "internalization" of the sense of public good (Reilly, Kyj 1994: 42) or commitment to the creation of the common good (Jeurissen 2004: 89).

Regardless of the way CC is defined, the key importance in this concept is cooperation with the community, and in particular with the local communities in which the company operates. However, such details can already be found in the definitions of CSR. For example, the World Business Council for Sustainable Development (WBCSD) defines CSR as the company's continuous commitment to ethical behaviour and contributing to economic development, while improving the quality of life of employees and their families, as well as the local community and general public (WBCSD 1999: 3). It is similar to the definition of M. Ness, for whom CSR is a strategic decision, according to which the organisation fulfils its obligation to society, for example through sponsorship, involvement of local communities, paying attention to environmental issues, and responsible advertising (Ness 1992: 38).

The concept of good citizenship is not very popular in Europe, especially in Central Europe. Enterprises engage in the development of local communities more because of good-neighbourly relations than because of the need to fulfil their obligations towards society. As a result, indigenous enterprises from this area do not feel the need, calling it a bit lofty – to do good, and the activities in the area of sponsorship or charity activities undertaken by them indicate a large randomness of the area and entities towards which the support is directed. Of course, it cannot be said that companies in Europe or Central Europe are not interested in actively supporting environmental and cultural activities or activities undertaken for the benefit of local communities. A lot of good examples are provided by transnational companies that transfer behaviour from other markets. The next group is companies that cooperate with companies from other markets, e.g. they are suppliers and transfer the acquired experience or good practices. The least interested are small enterprises operating on the local or regional market, with respect to which consumers do not express any expectations as to their increased social involvement. In this case, their involvement is most often limited to one-off sponsorship or charity activities.

**Facebook Inc.**

Facebook is an online social media and social networking service owned by American company Meta Platforms. Founded in 2004 by Mark Zuckerberg with fellow Harvard College students and roommates Eduardo Saverin, Andrew McCollum, Dustin Moskovitz, and Chris Hughes. Other Meta Platforms brands include: Instagram, Messenger, WhatsApp, Oculus, Mapillary, Workplace, Portal, and Diem. In 2021, the brand itself was valued at over $81,476 million and was ranked 7th in the ranking of the most valuable brands (Brand Finance 2021).

Facebook has been heavily criticised for issues such as user privacy, such as the Cambridge Analytica data scandal, which led to a record $5 billion penalty imposed on Facebook by the Federal Trade Commission (FTC) in July 2019 (Hu 2020), political manipulation (such as in the 2016 US elections (Assibong et al. 2020) and mass surveillance (Srinivasan 2019).

Some of the activities undertaken in the area of CSR:

- $40 million in grant funding to Black businesses most impacted by COVID-19;
- $200 billion in pledged growth donations to Sub-Saharan Africa, the Association of Southeast Asian Nations (ASEAN), and Latin America over the next five years through Meta partnerships and digital access infrastructure;
- support for women in the form of training and mentoring so that they can develop their activities on the Facebook platform through the #SheMeansBusiness program.

However, in the area of the environment, they have set themselves the most ambitious goals. As of 2020, their global business has achieved zero net emissions and is supported by 100% renewable energy. Their next goal is, among others, achieving zero net emissions across the value chain by 2030 and aiming for a positive global water yield by 2030, meaning they want to recover more water than they consume. To achieve this:

- meta restored 2.3 million cubic meters of water in 2021 (while they used 2.6 million cubic meters in their entire activity);
- as of 2021, they had contracts in place for more than 7,500 megawatts (MW) of renewable energy.

Meta prepares its Sustainable Development Reports taking into account, inter alia, of the Global Reporting Initiative (GRI) guidelines (Meta 2021).

## Cultural engagement as an element of social involvement

Supporting the arts and culture sector was not originally mentioned as part of CSR. For the first time, this sphere was mentioned as one of the areas of socially responsible activities undertaken by enterprises in the publication Business and Society, Public Strategy, Public Policy, Ethics in 1988 (Frederick et al. 1988: 33). After this publication, references to supporting culture and art as part of corporate social involvement began to appear much more often in the literature. Moreover, issues related to supporting culture are treated as the fourth pillar of sustainable development (e.g. CIDA 1997; Hawkes 2001; Nurse 2006). There are also the concepts of Corporate Cultural Responsibility (CCR) or Corporate Cultural Involvement (CCI).

The nature and scope of cultural responsibility of enterprises are difficult to define. For some authors, cultural responsibility means setting a modern, developed form of artistic and cultural sponsorship. For others, the cultural involvement of companies consists in collecting art collections, supporting employees in the area of culture, sponsoring art and culture, and patronage activities (Kohl 2007: 343). Unfortunately, not everyone agrees with this approach to CCR. In the opinion of some authors, CCR goes beyond focusing on art or philanthropic activities. These authors, as they themselves say, want to avoid too narrow a conceptualisation of potential cultural influences and responsibilities. Such a broad description can be found, for example, in the academic works of F. Maon and A. Lingreen. In their opinion, CCR refers to the extent to which a corporation voluntarily develops its business in a way that recognises and ensures the conscious consideration, respect, and defense of the value and belief systems underlying the plurality of behaviours and practices that represent existing cultures in different contexts (Maon, Lingreen 2014: 760; cf. Howaniec, Wróblewski 2018: 157).

Such a broad definition of culture as an area of support within CSR is justified for at least two reasons. First, culture is defined very broadly in general. For example, for R. Willams there are at least four different definitions of culture (Williams 1981: 11–13):

1 culture as a developed state of mind, i.e. culture contained in a "person", "cultured person",
2 culture as development processes, i.e. culture included in "cultural interests", "cultural activities",
3 culture as the means of these processes, i.e. culture as "art" and "intellectual works",
4 culture as a "whole lifestyle", "semantic system" through which the social order is transmitted, recreated, lived, and examined.

The second reason explaining the legitimacy of such a broad definition of culture is considering it as an element of the sustainable development of society and CSR. In this case, it is justified to go beyond the perception of culture solely as "art", "heritage", and "cultural identity" and focus on the whole way of material, intellectual and spiritual life, in other words, the achievements of civilisation embodied in culture (anthropological approach to culture). Obviously, adopting such a scope of culture raises further questions regarding the relationship between such a broadly understood culture and economic, environmental, and social responsibility of business.

Cultural responsibility has been considered, inter alia, in the guidelines of the International Organization for Standardization ISO 26000 (2010) on social responsibility. This was a pioneering but very clear signal of the formal inclusion of cultural issues in CSR policy. This standard call, inter alia, to promote cultural activity as well as respect and values for local communities, culture, cultural traditions, and the heritage of the environment in which enterprises operate. The value of respect for cultural diversity and tolerance as an element of respect for human dignity was previously emphasised by, inter alia, UNESCO (UNESCO 2002: 4).

Should culture be an element of corporate social involvement? More and more often it is emphasised that most of the activities undertaken by enterprises in the area of the so-called CSR are about the natural environment. It is very often difficult to talk about social involvement in such a case, as the goal of organisations is to be in compliance with environmental regulations, not only national ones, if their activities go beyond the borders of the country. Scientific works, on the other hand, very often focus on the analysis of the impact of stakeholders on the company's operations or the study of their mutual relations, and not the impact of the organisation on the environment. Meanwhile, economic entities not only change the environment, but even create it, including the broadly understood culture (Barley 2007: 214).

Progressing globalisation is blurring the differences between markets, and the world seems to be gradually moving towards one, large, global market. These processes are associated not only with the homogenisation of consumer behaviour, but also, inter alia, cultural behaviour (cf. Baughn and Buchanan 2001). The search for economic efficiency may eventually lead to the synchronisation of cultural processes around the world. There is talk of the phenomenon of "McDonaldization", that is, the uniformisation of social life, the schematisation of all human behaviour, and the standardisation of products and services offered to them (Ritzer 1997: 46–73). However, this state of affairs was not only influenced by American companies (e.g. Coca-Cola, McDonald, Apple, and Walt Disney). European companies (e.g. Benetton, Tesco, and Zara) and multinational corporations also had a large share in this process. Any blurring of differences can be assessed both positively and negatively. The positives include, among others increasing the availability and comparability of goods and services, it is easier for us to meet our needs (24-hour economy, 7 days a week, 365 days a year), and individuals (people) are treated the same. Unfortunately, the progressing market integration negatively affects the preservation of local culture and values, leading to cultural standardisation (e.g. Klein 2000). This is because supranational entities do not influence the society only through the products or services they offer, which very often are carriers of specific values, symbolic meanings that go beyond the functional utility of products or services (Belk 1988: 160; Clarke et al. 2002: 29; Berger, Heath 2007: 132), but also through marketing activities, applied business models, including employment strategy, etc. All these activities affect not only the behaviour of people as consumers in the market, but also the values and cultural patterns they perceive, shape their personal and social identity. Thus, the design, production and marketing of products and services is also a culture-forming process in which ideas, values, norms, and beliefs are symbolically expressed in the environment in order to create new cultural and semantic forms (Low 1988: 187).

All these arguments support the legitimacy of including culture as an area of potential CSR support. The development of industry and the change in the conditions of competition define modern civilisation, constituting a significant contribution to the overall social coexistence. The protection of knowledge, beliefs, art, customs, etc. is part of the process of protecting the cultural heritage of mankind. Leaving it only to institutions established by public authorities is unjustified. Enterprises influence the broadly understood culture and every aspect of their support for culture, also in the so-called narrow view is desirable. The economic sphere not only can contribute to the preservation of the entire spiritual and material heritage of society, but also can influence the habits acquired by a person as a member of this society. In the second aspect, educating citizens in the desired areas may contribute to reducing or eliminating social problems (e.g. reducing poverty, the number of cases of disease), improving the well-being of individuals, and ultimately leading to changes in the social structure. For example, a frequent goal of CSR activities of brewing companies is to promote moderate and responsible alcohol consumption (e.g. SABMiller). Undertaking such programs, which are aimed at reaching all consumers of brands sold by their owners, in this case by producers of beer or other alcoholic beverages, is much more effective than undertaking similar actions at the national level.

## Benefits of social involvement

There are many reasons that motivate companies to become socially involved. First, they may be altruistic intentions, meaning that companies believe that their efforts are good for the wider public, and through social commitment they become good citizens themselves. In such cases, these entities are very often not interested in the wide media hype that publicises their actions. Sometimes, however, the real motives of undertaken social activities are completely different. It is the attempt to "improve the image" or even "cover up" inappropriate content that is the real reason for the social involvement of companies. In this case, the main goal is to reassure the stakeholders, and the activity undertaken is another cost of business activity. For example, Maspex's gesture of donating to living insurgents was not an expression of goodwill and social commitment of the company, but a form of compensation for the insult committed by the company on the company's official Instagram account. While promoting the Tiger brand (energy drink), on 1 August 2018, on the 73rd anniversary of the Warsaw Uprising, the company placed a graphic with an extended middle finger and the words "Screw what was. Important, what will be!". Unfortunately, this time the intended promotion of the brand brought unintended effects and caused widespread media outrage (Maspex 2017).

The unclear reasons for taking actions in the field of CSR were noted, among others, by M. Porter and M. Kramer. These authors indicate that the common cause of corporate social involvement is only the desire to improve the image in the eyes of stakeholders. As an example, they provide information from CSR reports, which in most cases (64% of the analysed 250 reports from 2005) do not present a coherent framework for actions taken, not to mention a strategic approach to social responsibility, but are a collection of funny stories about uncoordinated initiatives companies. The authors also criticise the way of presenting the achieved indicators. For example, philanthropic initiatives are described in terms of donated amounts or hours spent by volunteers, but almost never in terms of impact (Porter and Kramer 2006: 81). The risk of losing financial benefits means that the most common corporate response is neither strategic nor operational, but cosmetic. Entities undertake public relations (PR) activities or launch media campaigns aimed solely at improving the CSR report and the company's image (Porter, Kramer 2006: 80). While the definition itself assumes that the social commitment of enterprises allows for the creation of social and economic value (Halal 2001: 27–42), adopting image improvement as the main goal of CSR activities is assessed as low. CSR should not be only a cosmetic effort of a company aimed at responding to social expectations (Porter, Kramer 2006: 82). Approaching CSR solely from the perspective of reputation is treated as a misunderstanding of the essence of corporate social commitment. CSR is presented in theory as a central business issue that has a significant impact on most operations undertaken in a company (Carlisle, Faulkner 2005; Ayuso et al. 2006; Porter, Kramer 2006). So how to shape activities in the field of social responsibility and what are the benefits of social involvement?

B. Husted and J. Salazar distinguished three motives for applying CSR in a company, namely, altruism, forced egoism, and strategic use of CSR. Altruism is viewed in a typical way, which, according to the authors, occurs when companies are genuinely interested in social responsibility without looking at the profit and loss account. The situation in which the enterprise is forced, either by law or by other external factors, such as, for example, public opinion, is called forced egoism. For authors, it is simply investing in social products for the sake of survival or growth. The lack of any form of coercion means that investments are not undertaken. The third path that they distinguished and rated the highest was the strategic use of CSR to obtain long-term benefits for the company. This definition is consistent with the understanding of CSV, i.e. the creation of common value, which is a value not only for society, but also for the enterprise. In this case, social investments are undertaken due to the expected strategic benefits for the company (cf. Husted, Salazar 2006: 76–86).

Considering the benefits of social involvement of companies in a holistic manner, i.e. without indicating the reason why the company has decided to be socially responsible, the most common ones are internal benefits, i.e. direct benefits (for the company), more often of a material nature, and external benefits, i.e. indirect benefits – social, more often of an intangible nature.

The internal benefits that the company receives as a result of implementing CSR include (cf. Rok 2004: 54):

1 Increased investor interest. Financial institutions/investors are more interested in cooperation with companies that care for social acceptance

and a positive image, build good relations with the environment, as well as care for the transparency of their activities. For many investors, a company's financial credibility depends on its social credibility.

2 Increasing consumer loyalty. Customers are becoming more and more aware and socially involved, which means that they often pay attention not only to the quality and price of the product, but also to its "eco-friendliness" and the producer's social commitment.
3 Increase of competitiveness. A positive image of the company: (1) increases the trust of customers, which translates into their higher interest in the company's offer, (2) improves cooperation with business partners, which facilitates running a business and, consequently, improves the ability to compete.
4 Improving the organisational culture and image among the company's employees. The company's social involvement changes the behaviour and reactions of individuals and social groups in the enterprise. Employees have a better perception of the company that cares for them and is focused on solving important and important social problems from their point of view. Such a changed perception influences their attitudes, assessments, and even the ways of solving problems of the organisation.
5 Obtaining the image of a good employer and access to better employees. Employees of companies implementing CSR principles identify with their enterprise to a greater extent, they are satisfied and loyal, which means that socially responsible organisations have a greater chance of retaining the best staff, as well as an effective recruitment process (an employer who is socially engaged and cares about employees is better perceived on the labour market).

Meanwhile, the external benefits of implementing CSR include (cf. Rok 2004, 54):

1 Improving the relationship between the economic entity and the local community. Conducting a socially responsible business allows to win the favour of residents, authorities, and local institutions, thanks to which the enterprise is perceived as a social good, and the local community, including local decision-makers, favour its development.
2 Active participation in shaping the welfare of society. Socially responsible enterprises contribute, inter alia, to publicise social problems, but also to solve them, by actively participating in this process, through charity activities, volunteer programs, etc. Thanks to the development of ethical codes or conducting training in ethics, companies also attach greater importance to the observance of basic human rights.
3 Education of the society. Socially involved companies contribute to the increase of public knowledge through publicising social problems: directly (e.g. through publications, properly prepared advertisements)

or indirectly (e.g. through the involvement of employees in individual actions). Their educational value also lies in creating attitudes of social responsibility among employees and the local community.

4 Improving the condition of the natural environment. The social commitment of companies means at least compliance with regulations, also in the field of environmental protection. Thus, socially committed enterprises not only show concern for the natural environment within the limits of the imposed law, but often take actions that go well beyond these requirements, thus contributing to reducing the level of pollution and improving the condition of the natural environment.
5 Increasing social trust in the company. Socially engaged enterprises publish reports in which they not only describe their activities,[1] but also provide financial information. Practice shows cases where companies voluntarily provide additional information to make their activities "transparent" to stakeholders. For example, The Extractive Industries Transparency Initiative, which 19 large oil, gas, and mining companies joined in 2006, took steps to discourage corruption, i.e. they agreed to full, public disclosure, and verification of all corporate payments to governments in the countries in which they operate. These companies have not only proved to be honest, but the action taken prevents corrupt governments from undermining social benefits and selecting companies that win contracts by providing a financial gain (Porter, Kramer 2006: 85).

A company perceived as socially responsible, associated with charity, or more – with concern for social welfare – gains a certain amount of trust in the society's opinion. As W. Grudzewski et al. write, trust occurs in conditions of uncertainty and risk, but it is a positive concept. By putting trust in someone or something (in this case in company), we expect positive, desired results (Grudzewski et al. 2009: 18–19). The company's stakeholders, when making decisions related to it, regardless of whether we are talking about consumers making purchasing decisions, investors wondering "whether to invest", or local authorities extending a business license, always act in a situation of "incomplete" knowledge, and therefore risk. The trust we place in the company is in this case an element supporting decisions, even if its influence is unconscious, and we will call this factor irrational.

According to the literature, the main elements of trust include: risk, belief, competences, kindness, probability, ability, responsibility, having goodwill, honesty, fairness, credibility, predictability, reliability, and dependence (Grudzewski et al. 2009: 18–19). The opinion about the company affects at least belief, kindness, and having goodwill, and the decisions of the interested parties will be shaped differently in the case of an entity that has social trust, and differently in relation to an entity that does not have such trust.

The topic of the benefits of being a socially responsible enterprise is more and more widely discussed and researched. Moreover, the number of studies confirming the wide range of benefits that may occur in connection with the social commitment of companies is increasing (incl. Turban, Greening 1997; Fombrun et al. 2000; Sen, Bhattacharya 2001; Lichtenstein et al. 2004; Sen et al. 2006; Du et al. 2007). Research conducted in developed countries shows not only the growing awareness of CSR among consumers (Bhattacharya, Sen 2004: 9–24) but also considering the efforts of enterprises in this area when making purchases (Sen, Bhattacharya 2001: 225–244; Becker-Olsen et al. 2006: 46–53; Ellen et al. 2006: 147–157). The positive relationship between companies' involvement in philanthropic activities and purchase decisions was indicated, among others, by D. Lichtenstein, M. Drumwright, and B. Braig (2004). In turn, C. Bhattacharya and S. Sen emphasised the positive impact of CSR on shaping loyalty and long-term relationships with customers (Bhattacharya and Sen 2003). Corporate social involvement can transform the company's existing customers into brand ambassadors. Such consumers become psychologically connected with the company and its products, and not only provide positive information about the brand/company, but often care for it, motivating them to achieve goals, and are even capable of additional activity for the company (Du et al. 2007: 227–228).

Of course, the economic benefits of CSR are not limited to the consumer domain. The link between Corporate Social Performance (CSP) and Corporate Financial Performance (CFP) is also of interest. For example, the Institute of Business Ethics in London showed that companies with a code of ethics generated much more economic added value (EVA)[2] and market value (MVA), were characterised by much lower volatility of the P/E (Price Earnings Ratio) throughout the year, and also achieved 18% higher profits/turnover than companies without codes. The obtained results confirmed that companies that act ethically achieve better results in terms of finance and other indicators than those that do not (Webley, More 2003: 10).[3] In another case, the results of research on the ratio of financed and social benefits are inconclusive (Margolis, Walsh 2003: 268–305).

A significant benefit of CSR is also the impact on other stakeholders, including employees and investors. Research conducted by S. Sen, C. Bhattacharya, and D. Korschun proves that the awareness of CSR not only positively influences consumers, who declare greater willingness to buy products of companies perceived as socially responsible, but also influences greater willingness to invest by investors and employment in them by potential employees (Sen et al. 2006: 164). J. Low and P. Kalafut have similar observations, they believe that not only consumers, but also contractors have greater trust in socially responsible companies, they are willing to change the supplier into a socially committed, if only the product features were comparable (Low, Kalafut 2004: 99). Interesting results are also presented by J. Brown and P. Dacin, who do not see the positive impact of associations related to CSR on the perception of product attributes, but clearly indicate that there is a positive relationship between the awareness of CSR activities undertaken and consumers' reactions to new products. Their results, however, point to something more interesting. While positive associations related with CSR can improve product ratings, it has been clearly shown that negative associations in this area have a harmful effect on overall product ratings (Brown, Dacin 1997: 79–80). This means that companies that do not care about the image of a socially responsible company may suffer negative consequences, including in the sales area. In extreme cases, however, it may even become a kind of ostracism. Consumers strive to boycott (and on a large scale) companies that break the basic principles of social coexistence (Snider et al. 2003: 175–187).

An example of the stigmatisation of companies characterised by a lack of social responsibility was the prizes awarded by Public Eye on Davos – a movement created at the summit of the World Economic Forum in Davos, which in 2005–2015 awarded prizes to the most socially irresponsible companies. These awards were given just before the World Economic Forum.[4]

## Criticise of business social responsibility: between moral order and economy. Greenwashing as an effect of popularisation of the concept of social responsibility of business

Since antiquity, the part of business that was associated with earning money (Latin: chrematisike) was treated as contemptible. It was first publicly condemned by Aristotle, elevating economics (Latin: oikonomikos), which was then understood as the art of running a household (Środa 1999: XI). Excessive drive to accumulate wealth was not perceived as a virtue and was put in contradiction with the theory of the so-called the golden mean, indicating moderation as an attribute of proper, harmonious human development (Arystoteles 1996: 1107a).

This approach to accumulating wealth was deepened by cynics, for whom virtue was the highest good, and for whom everything else – according to their beliefs – should be indifferent to man. The lifestyle they adopted was underlining the proclaimed focus on ethical issues. Cynics, often giving away goods, left themselves a chiton,[5] a stick, and a characteristic wanderer's bag for small items. They ate on anything, drank cold water, and lived in random shelters.

This focus on ethics also appeared in other philosophical directions. This was most evident in Stoicism, which had a significant impact on the development of Christianity, and in fact also on medieval philosophy. The primacy of virtue, the achievement of which could be hindered by "bad drives", as well as the drive to become wealthy, strengthened the perception of earning money as something wrong or even wicked (Reale 2004: 396–406). Additionally, parables in the Old Testament, such as The Story of Lazarus and the Rich Man, or the cult of the lives of saints such as St. Francis of Assisi, do not create a good climate for both gainful employment and wealth. The common understanding of the messages directed by the Church and the official condemnation of usury led to aversion towards rich people, and all kinds of entrepreneurship had a pejorative tone. It was associated with greed, down-to-earthiness, which was not appropriate for the well-born or educated. A similar approach can be found in the Christian current where neither wealth nor the efforts leading to it have improved. In the Holy Scriptures, we find many exhortations criticising the pursuit of material goods, as well as the possession of them, for example: "Then he said to them, 'Watch out! Be on your guard against all kinds of greed; life does not consist in an abundance of possessions.'" [Bible, Lk 12 :15], "It is easier for a camel to go through the eye of a needle than for someone who is rich to enter the kingdom of God." [Bible, Mk: 10:25]

Ultimately, some authors question the view about the need to introduce ethical standards into economic life, which could be regulated automatically (the so-called invisible hand of the market) or by ensuring full economic rationality for economic activities (it would be guaranteed by homo oeconomicus) (Węgrzecki 2012: 23). There are also those who do not want to combine business with morality, even pointing out that in business everyone consciously behaves unethically and it is socially justified (Jackson 1999: 62–63, 67–68).

The theory of stakeholders and the introduction of the concept of CSR as a canon of business conduct evoked and still evoke objections from many circles. The CSR concept is attributed to, inter alia, appropriating an area of interest that concerned business ethics (cf. Gasparski 2004: 39–49). Still, the discussed objection is the thesis put forward by M. Friedman that the main goal of business is business and the owners' sharing of profits approach is neither economically nor socially justified (Friedman 1970, cf. chap. 1).

The accusation against enterprises declaring social commitment is spending money on CSR programs as a tactical ploy in response to pressure from environmental organisations, local communities, and other interested groups (Smith, Lenssen 2009: 24). These charities, non-governmental organisations, and other elements of the so-called civil society are called winners in this process. It is they who are credited with stimulating the demand for socially responsible enterprises by encouraging, inter alia, investors, consumers, and employees to take advantage of their potential to negatively influence companies that do not share the propagated values (The Economist: 1).

CSR is also perceived as a separate, well-developing industry. There are new professions (CSR specialists), companies specialising in CSR consulting, CSR audits, and companies specialising in CSR certification. Regardless of judging from the noble idea of improving the welfare of society, not only through direct actions for its benefit, but also indirect ones, i.e. actions for the benefit of the natural environment or culture, we get in practice a developed system of CSR certification and reporting, which is often assessed very negative.

It is accused of social reports that they do not reflect the actual activities of the organisation to the extent that they have been implemented, but are a conscious attempt to communicate positive information undertaken in environmental or social areas (e.g. Bowen, Aragon-Correa 2014: 107). The lack of requirements as to the truthfulness of the disclosed data, the qualitative nature of the information, the early stage of development of CSR reporting, and the complexity of this type of reporting mean that, first, there are doubts as to the credibility of these reports, and second, these reports resemble activities in the field of PR than CSR reporting (cf. Mazurowska 2014). This phenomenon is called a greenwashing.

Greenwashing, like other terms, has many definitions. For W. Laufer, for example, greenwashing is the creation of (informational) disorder, facade, or posturing. This "clutter" is where a company analyses documents very carefully and strictly restricts the information it makes available to regulators. A facade is an activity that uses "substituted" or "set" units or entities to challenge the importance of the problem or highlight the uncertainties associated with the problem. The last term was defined by W. Laufer as attempts to influence legislation in order to achieve specific benefits (Laufer 2003: 257).

T. Lyon and J. Maxwell do not agree with such a broad definition of the concept of greenwashing. They believe that the distinctions indicated by W. Laufer are useful, but these activities are too broad to be called a single phenomenon (Lyon, Maxwell 2004). These authors propose a different definition, according to which greenwashing is a selective disclosure of positive information about the company's environmental performance, without fully disclosing negative information (Lyon, Maxwell 2006: 31–32).

Unfortunately, it is true that companies very often outsource the preparation of CSR reports to people from the PR or corporate relations department (Hąbek 2015: 30–31) and the reports only present positive information, beneficial to the company's image, provided in a characteristic "marketing" manner. The main purpose of reports prepared in this way is for companies to present their products and processes in a way that gives the impression that they are environmentally friendly and socially responsible.

Greenwashing activities include: (Hąbek 2015: 31):

- providing false information about the product in relation to its environmental impact,
- suggesting that the product is ecological and pro-social, based on selected attributes, disregarding all contradictory issues,
- pointing to ecological facts that have nothing to do with the real state,
- reducing costs under the guise of caring for the natural environment,
- failure to provide evidence supporting the pro-social or ecological character of the product,
- deliberate use of general and/or imprecise phrases in reports that may be poorly or misunderstood by the readers,
- illegal or unjustified use of ecological labels, certificates of social responsibility, and others,
- using exaggerated, suggestive images or providing false data convincing that the product is environmentally friendly, safe, etc.

- failure to consider the actual impact of the product on the environment throughout its life cycle,
- deliberate omission of important information about the production process and its consequences (for the environment, community, and employees) that could negatively affect the image of the product.

Some researchers emphasise that companies are not really interested in social responsibility and many of them treat CSR marginally, focusing solely on convincing stakeholders that the company is doing something good (Smith, Lenssen 2009: 25). Sometimes may even talk about creating vague concepts indirectly related to the issues of CSR and taking sham actions aimed at "camouflaging" reprehensible practices of enterprises (Lewicka-Strzałecka 2006).

The way to increase the credibility of reports on CSR is, inter alia (CGA-Canada 2005: 86):

1 stakeholder engagement – establishing a dialogue with stakeholders in order to learn about their expectations (what information is important to them) and concerns about the content of the report, which will increase stakeholder trust in the organisation,
2 corporate governance – improving corporate governance through greater independence of management boards and auditors and/or the creation and disclosure of codes and policies related to sustainable development reporting and CSR activities,
3 internal audit – implementation of appropriate procedures and internal controls to ensure the proper functioning of management and reporting systems in the company (to be sure that these systems accurately capture and transmit information),
4 independent statements – independent statements or assessments of external experts or specific stakeholder groups, confirming the truthfulness of the information contained in the report,
5 third-party assurance audit – an independent opinion on the effectiveness of internal systems and processes and/or data contained in the CSR report,
6 comprehensive reporting and disclosure of "bad" information – disclosing trends in a report or presenting results based on performance against goals or external benchmarks, regardless of whether the results are good or not, and reporting bad information increases the credibility of the report and improves its transparency;
7 compliance of the report with GRI (Global Reporting Initiative) guidelines – preparation of reports in accordance with GRI guidelines requires the management or the general manager to declare that the report presents a balanced and reasonable presentation of the economic, environmental, and social performance of the organisation.

One of the goals of corporate social involvement is to gain and strengthen the image of a responsible company, which is a kind of insurance policy in the event of unforeseen image "mishaps". E. Sternberg, writing about the costs of unethicality, indicates that one of the ways of measuring the value of business for economic activities is the damage that its lack can cause (Sternberg 1998: 37). While many studies do not confirm the direct, positive impact of CSR on consumer decisions, the results obtained very often indicate the existence of significant relationships between the negative perception of a company in the area of CSR and the behaviour of its stakeholders (Brown, Dacin 1997: 79–80). Failure to perceive, ignore, and not respond to ethical problems may lead to specific burdens, not only of a legal but also financial nature. A company that today does not attach importance to being responsible is exposed not only to the loss of the effects of part of its work, for example in the area of promotion, but ethical scandals usually have a negative impact on the company's image, which can lead to the loss of reputation of company and even lead to the instability of the market position. When unethical practices are revealed, it very often has catastrophic consequences (e.g. the case of Enron or WorldCom described in Chapter 1). Ethically questionable companies risk the loyalty of their customers, the loss of employees, suppliers, and even cooperators. Customers disagree and increasingly disapprove of unethical behaviour. However, it is particularly important for cooperators who will perceive such a company as unstable, whose negative actions may affect their image and will be reluctant to be associated with such a company for a longer period of time (cf. Sternberg 1998: 37).

## Notes

1 Social reports are non-financial reports. Providing non-financial information is voluntary. In Poland for example, the only legal provision regulating reporting on non-financial activities is the Accounting Act, which obliges capital companies, limited joint-stock partnerships, mutual insurance companies, mutual reinsurance companies, cooperatives, state enterprises, that together with the annual financial statements, the entities prepare a report on activities containing "Declaration on non-financial information" [Journal of Laws No. 1994, No 121, item 591. Art. 49b]. Article 49b was attached to the Accounting Act with the amendment of 15 December 2016 and has been in force since 26 January 2017.

2 EVA (Economic Value Added) – economic added value, or economic profit. A factor that shows whether a company creates value for its owners. An increase in goodwill is understood as a situation in which the rate of return on invested capital is higher than the cost of its acquisition. EVA formula: $EVA = z * (1-t) - k * K$ i.e. operating profit after tax minus weighted average cost of capital multiplied by total invested capital (Jaruga et al. 2010: 431).

3 The research was carried out in the years 1997–2001. The sample consisted of 41 to 86 enterprises for which complete and comparable company data for 1997–2001 was available. The surveyed companies were divided into two groups: those who have had codes of ethics/behaviour / rules for five years or more and those who have clearly stated that they do not apply/have them.

4 Public Eye Award (2005–2015) – is an award granted to the worst companies that break ethical values and social norms. In 2015, the award went to Chevron, but among the infamous winners were: Gazprom and Gap (2014), Shell and Goldman Sachs (2013), Vale and Barclays (2012), Neste Oil and AngloGold Ashanti (2011), Roche, Royal Bank of Canada and UN Global Compact (2010), Newmont Mining Corporation and BKW FMB Energie AG (2009), Areva and Glencore (2008), Bridgestone and Novartis (2007), Chevron, Citigroup and The Walt Disney Company (2006), Dow, Shell, Wal-Mart and KPMG (2005) [Public Eye on Davos 2018].
5 Chiton – a linen or woollen robe fastened over the shoulders, worn in ancient Greece.

# 3 Social responsibility and value-based marketing

## A place of value-based marketing within marketing concepts

The marketing concept can be understood as a management philosophy that is based on the acceptance of the need for customer orientation, i.e. it assumes that the company recognises the needs and desires of the target market and adapts to them by delivering the desired satisfaction more effectively and efficiently than the competition. The aim of the company's marketing concept in this approach should be customer satisfaction and its inclusion in all activities undertaken by the company. This does not mean, however, that every activity of the organisation must be absolutely subordinated to the satisfaction of the target recipient. The undertaken actions should consider the broadly understood good of the customer in the long term. Such activities of the company may, however, not provide satisfaction to the customer at a given time, who, for example, would prefer simpler, cheaper solutions or otherwise imagined the aesthetics of the product. Examples of such solutions are changes in the product, packaging, promotion, etc. considering the impact on human health or the environment. Despite the acceptance of existing solutions by customers (including the price of the product), companies decide to make changes aimed at the so-called higher good, i.e. responsibility for the customer's well-being.

There are some discrepancies in the literature as to the dating of the origins of the marketing concept. Various authors are also credited with developing the concept of marketing-mix. It is commonly believed, however, that the first one who writes about the "mix" in marketing was J. Culliton (1948), who, when examining the costs of marketing activities, used the term "mixer of ingredients" to describe people (marketers) who creatively created the marketing-mix (Borden 1964: 2). Initially, however, there was no unanimity as to the elements that would create this marketing "mix". The most synthetic proposal compared to others was presented by N. Borden, who proposed a complicated model based on 12 different factors (Borden 1964: 4). The continuation and consistent use of the term "marketing mix" by Borden contributed to the popularisation of this concept in the 1950s, and the term

DOI: 10.4324/9781003317364-4

itself gained universal acceptance. The publication of E. McCarthy, who presented the concept of 4P, was a significant contribution to the development of the marketing-mix concept, including the following marketing components: product, price, distribution, and promotion (McCarthy 1960).

The way of defining the marketing concept has varied over the years. The approach to the definition of marketing has also changed. The American Marketing Association (AMA) verified its definition several times (Table 3.1). Ultimately, it was assumed that marketing is activities, a set of institutions and processes for creating, communicating, delivering, and exchanging offers that have value for consumers, customers, partners, and the whole society (Gundlach 2007: 243–244).

Of course, it cannot be said that there is a uniform marketing concept. Practical dissemination of marketing in all industries has led to the development of the concept of marketing, which has definitely differed in individual decades. The popularised 4P concept was subject to modifications. In 1981, B. Booms and M. Bitner extended the traditional four-component mix to 7P, adding: participants (people), which according to the proposed concept meant staff and customers, environmental factors and physical evidence as so-called physical evidence, and a process (Booms, Bitner 1981). This model was particularly popular on the service market and was a response to the reported shortcomings of the traditional 4P blend.

*Table 3.1* Selected definitions of marketing by the American Marketing Association (AMA 2018; cf. Gundlach 2007: 243–244)

| *Year* | *Definition of marketing* |
|---|---|
| **1935** | Marketing is the performance of business activities that direct the flow of goods and services from producers to consumers. |
| **1960** | The performance of business activities that direct the flow of goods and services from producers to consumers. |
| **1985** | The process of planning and executing the conception, pricing, promotion, and distribution of ideas, goods, and services to create exchanges that satisfy individual and organisational goals. |
| **2004** | Marketing is an organisational function and a set of processes for creating, communicating and delivering value to customers and for managing customer relationships in ways that benefit the organisation and its stakeholders. |
| **2007** | Marketing is the activity, set of institutions, and processes for creating, communicating, delivering, and exchanging offerings that have value for customers, clients, marketers, and society at large. |
| **2013** | Marketing is the activity, set of institutions, and processes for creating, communicating, delivering, and exchanging offerings that have value for customers, clients, partners, and society at large. |
| **2017** | Marketing is the activity, set of institutions, and processes for creating, communicating, delivering, and exchanging offerings that have value for customers, clients, partners, and society at large. |

The results of subsequent studies, as well as the inconveniences reported by business practice, resulted in the emergence of a research trend, we call it "revisionist", which assumes the need to find a new operational marketing paradigm, which, by exceeding traditional 4Ps, will define marketing levers more precisely. The main argument against 4P is that the model is internally oriented and does not pay enough attention to customer relations and consequently does not lead to customer orientation (e.g. Grönroos 1994: 349–350; Möller 2006: 441–442). This opinion is shared by, among others, E. Constantinides (2002, 2006), K. Möller (2006), and D. Popovic (2006).

More and more often it is emphasised that the traditional 4P is partially giving way to the 4C concept, in which, in place of the current 4P, the following are distinguished: customer needs and wants, cost to the customer, communication, and the convenience. The 4C set is a look at the implementation of marketing from the point of view of the customer's perspective, i.e., as some authors emphasise, it means the transformation of marketing-mix of sellers into a marketing-mix for the buyer. The product that the customer buys should constitute value for him. The price should be treated as a cost that the buyer is bound to bear. Instead of traditional, one-way promotion, the client expects dialogue, two-way communication. And the sale itself (distribution), in turn, should be offered on terms that are friendly to the buyer, ensuring the comfort and convenience of purchasing (Otto 2004: 11–12).

The most important turning points in the evolution of marketing management theory were the expansion of the marketing concept in the 1970s, the emphasis on the exchange transaction in the 1980s, and the development of relationship marketing and overall quality management in the 1990s (Yudelson 1999: 60). Change in the conditions of competition resulting, inter alia, from the emergence of information and communication technologies as part of 21st-century marketing has triggered the development of consumer behaviour and the evolution from mass consumer markets of the 1960s towards increasingly global, segmented, personalised markets where innovation, customisation, relationship building, and networking have become issues of significant importance (Kotler et al. 2001; Constantinides 2006: 410–411).

An important factor in the development of the marketing concept was also the increased interest in green marketing. The idea appeared only in the late 1980s, although the beginnings of the concept could already be seen in the 1970s (Peattie, Crane 2005: 358). Green marketing is also known as ecological marketing, eco-marketing, environmental marketing, or ecologically responsible marketing and applies to products that are considered safe for the environment.

Early work on green marketing spoke of a rapid increase in green consumerism, which in practice was meant to shift consumption to greener products (Prothero 1990). It was also indicated, inter alia, to increased environmental awareness of consumers, growing interest in organic products, or a clear willingness to pay higher prices for green features (Roper Organization 1990). Some studies confirmed the growing interest in green marketing among enterprises (Vandermerwe, Oliff 1990). However, practice seems to contradict this. Green marketing is still seen as an interesting form of market strategy implementation and is still the subject of research, but it is difficult to see a clear trend of considering the environmental performance of products when purchasing, due to their limited availability. Y. Chen treats green marketing as an element of brand value and writes about green image, satisfaction, and trust (Chen 2010). A. Lewandowska, J. Witczak, and P. Kurczewski, in turn, propose the use of the approach of thinking in terms of the life cycle to improve activities in the field of green marketing (Lewandowska et al. 2017). Considering the concept of green marketing by enterprises is certainly well assessed by consumers and proves their increased responsibility. However, this trend is not dominant. The vast majority of products offered have nothing to do with ecology and a responsible approach to the customer.

The development of the marketing concept is also clearly visible in terms of tools and goals that marketing has set for itself. From this perspective, the following stages of marketing development are very often distinguished:

- mass marketing,
- segmentation-based marketing,
- relationship marketing,
- value-based marketing.

Mass marketing (undifferentiated marketing) meant treating customers as a homogeneous group and consisted in offering one product for the entire market. The basis for adapting to the requirements and expectations of customers was the profile of a typical consumer, and the main goals of such a strategy are to reduce costs as a result of mass production, mass distribution, and mass promotion, which most often translated into the possibility of offering competitive prices and achieving a relatively high margin. In undifferentiated marketing so, a company treats the market as an aggregate, focusing on what is common in the needs of people rather than on what is different. It tries to design a product and a marketing program that appeal to the broadest number of buyers. The firm practicing undifferentiated marketing typically develops a (mix) aimed at the broadest segment of the market (Kotler 1967: 57–58). However, talking about the mass market is already an anachronism. The departure from such understood market strategy is indicated, among others, by P. Kotler (1989: 47).

The development of research on consumer behaviour led to the emergence of segmentation-based marketing in the late 1960s and early 1970s (Kotler 1989: 121). This approach, also known as differentiated marketing, consists in distinguishing homogeneous groups of consumers, with different reactions to the product and individual marketing tools, and targeting them with various marketing activities. The basis for adjusting the offer are therefore the characteristics and requirements of individual consumer groups, and the purpose of this approach is to notice the diversity of consumers and take it into account when designing marketing tools and influencing the market. Depending on the set strategic goals and financial possibilities, enterprises could decide on the number of serviced segments (concentrated marketing strategy), thus limiting the scope of the serviced market, expenses, and the number of competitors. Differentiated marketing is widely used by producers of consumer goods and services. In the area of services, the legitimacy of using the segmentation and differentiation strategy was indicated, inter alia, by C. Fryar, emphasising that personal customer relations and service quality are important elements of marketing in this area (Fryar 1991).

The evolution of marketing has led to the identification of a new approach to the implementation of market activities of enterprises, which was relationship marketing. Relationship marketing, also known as personalised or individual marketing, consists in recognising and servicing selected customers with whom the company builds strong economic and social relationships based on trust. This means, inter alia, establishing direct contact with the customer for whom individual marketing activities are planned, while the company not only meets the customer's expectations, but plans its development together with the customer, adjusting its own production and market programs. The aim of the marketing concept implemented in this way is to increase customer loyalty and the value of transactions in the long term, while reducing the costs of promotion and service. This concept had and still has many supporters. Relationship marketing was promoted by, among others, C. Grönroos (1994a), J. Sheth and A. Parvatiyar (1995), S. Vargo and R. Lusch (2004), and J. Otto (2004). It was emphasised that the complex network environment of market contractors means that the concept of relationship marketing seems to be the most complete and the most promising for the management of organisations (Żabiński 2002: 48).

Value-based marketing, the last of the indicated main trends in marketing, consists in considering the broadly understood, subjective environment of the company, i.e. shareholders and stakeholders, and a responsible approach to all these groups by creating the desired value in the market service strategy. The aim of this approach is to gain and maintain loyalty through broad concern for the needs, development, and environment of the customer (Howaniec, Waszkielewicz 2013).

However, the concept of value-based marketing is still considered "fresh", and the conducted research will either confirm or reject the validity of the assumptions of researchers promoting it as a "new value" in marketing. Due to the subject of this monograph, this concept is discussed in the following chapters of the book.

## Responsibility of enterprise and value-based marketing. Marketing ethics as an element of companies' liability

Considering ethics in the company's operations, the satisfaction of all stakeholders is often sought, which drives actions that can be approved by all interested parties. Such actions, however, may be superficial and shallow, and not focused on solving a specific, strategic problem for the company. P. Drucker assesses such behaviour very critically, writing that business ethics may as well be called ethical chic, and not true ethics, and also be regarded to a large extent as a product of the press and television, and not of philosophy and morality (Drucker 1997: 296).

An important question regarding the moral responsibility of enterprises is the question of whether enterprises should be liable, and if so, how this responsibility should look like (see Chapter 1). One can also wonder whether the responsibility of the enterprise is on the shoulders of a separate moral entity, which is the enterprise, and whether it is something different from the collective responsibility of individual, co-creating people, or whether the actions of the enterprise are the sum of actions of individual persons and nothing more (Pratley 1998: 112).

Some authors, following the individualist philosophy, according to which the human individual is considered the highest good, claim that in the case of responsibility one can only speak of individual responsibility. Only individuals can be held responsible and companies can never be held accountable for their actions. According to the individualistic philosophy, only people can play the role of moral subjects; therefore, enterprises cannot bear moral responsibility for any of their actions (cf. Valasquez 1983, 2003). In this view, moral judgements about the company are treated as a metaphor that actually means moral judgements of individual company employees (Pratley 1998: 113).

Although such an approach seems to be quite radical, it is difficult to completely disagree with his supporters. M. Velasquez emphasises individual responsibility, trying to prove that the corporation operates only through its employees and managers and that all activities of the organisation are undertaken by the members of the organisation and therefore these members are in fact responsible for what the organisation does, and therefore they should be punished in the event of abuses (Valasquez 2003: 535). Even supporters of assigning responsibility to an enterprise as a standalone entity agree with this justification. In their opinion, managers should bear moral responsibility also in a situation when they consciously and voluntarily act in accordance with the immoral or harmful company policy (Pratley 1998: 113).

However, individualistic philosophy and such perception of the role of business in society have many opponents. One of them is W. Hoffman, who emphasised that such perception of responsibility does not consider the fact that collective entities (both enterprises and other entities of any nature) undertake actions that cannot actually be reduced to the sum of individual actions and explain as such. The entirety of a collective organisation is more than the sum of its parts, because the units that make up the collective (whose activities are essential for its functioning) are organised around goals, directions, strategies, missions, policies, and statutes that give the organisation its identity and define its functions in detail. People functioning in a specific organisation undertake activities for a common goal in accordance with collective guidelines (Hoffman 1986: 233).

Hoffman's position is a kind of bridge between individualist and collectivist philosophy. According to the collective approach, the main emphasis is on the organisation, ethicality of its long-term goals, strategies, procedures, and control mechanisms. It assumes individual responsibility of the enterprise, i.e. the enterprise as an entity is responsible for all actions taken. This approach also met with opposition. While it has been recognised that collective societies have always existed and people are willing to cooperate to achieve common goals, such collective perception of responsibility, according to opponents of this approach, closes the way to the inside of the organisation, i.e. employees who knowingly make decisions that are unfavourable to the organisation or society (cf. Pratley 1998, 114).

For Hoffman, seeing an enterprise as some kind of moral organism is anthropomorphism at its worst, creating a situation in which individual interest and autonomy can be dominated by the good of the organisation (Hoffman 1986: 234). The solution is an intermediate option that would remove the shortcomings of the individualistic and collectivist approach to corporate responsibility. According to W. Hofman, it is necessary to create an organisational culture based on morality, and the author talks about two components, i.e. moral organisational culture and moral autonomy of an individual. The basic value of a culture created in this way should be morality, which will give meaning, identity, and internal integrity to the entire organisational collective, but must also appreciate and promote the moral autonomy of its members (Hoffman 1986: 241).

Despite logical evidence that not only the employees of the organisation are responsible for the actions taken, but also the enterprise is an entity that should be held accountable, which means that its goals and strategies should be at least in line with generally accepted social norms, the concept of responsibility of broadly understood entities market arouses objections, both among theoreticians and practitioners of management. Particular reluctance can be seen when referring to morality. Moving on to moral aspects when planning and implementing business activities, in particular with regard to products, processes, or additional activities of the company, including marketing activities, is not an everyday reality. P. Pratley explains the omnipresent aversion to moral discourse on three grounds. First, there is an opinion that putting things in this way is undesirable and confrontational, and that it leads to cyclical self-blame. Second, moral discourse is seen as a threat to performance. Referring to morality takes distracting forms (praising, blaming, and ideological profiling) and is considered simplifying, inflexible, not categorical, and vague. And third, moral discourse is seen as a threat to image and efficiency, claiming it to be too esoteric and idealistic, even rigorous (Pratley 1998: 126–127). However, the author does not cite research to confirm such claims. However, he notices certain threats related to the lack of moral discourse in shaping economic practice. They are (cf. Pratley 1998: 128–131):

1 creating moral amnesia – managers are only moved by moral obligations, but they find no way to openly refer to such justification in the day-to-day operation of the enterprise (Bird, Waters 1989: 80);
2 improper narrowing of the concept of morality – managers do not allow for asking questions of a moral nature, arguing that the issues referred to in the company are feasibility, practicality, and impersonal balancing of costs and benefits. Due to this position, decisions are made by appropriate managers and directors without public debate, unfortunately often with a simultaneous gross failure to comply with moral standards (Bird, Waters 1989: 81);
3 moral stress for an individual manager – the lack of moral discourse deepens the moral stress of managers who cannot freely articulate their point of view in this area and often make decisions that, in their opinion, are simply justified by the needs and acceptance of customers;
4 disregard for moral abuses – organisational silence regarding moral issues makes it difficult for members to raise questions and discuss specific issues (Bird, Waters 1989: 82);
5 diminished authority of moral standards – due to the fact that people do not commit themselves to the realisation of moral goals, these goals are no longer relevant to the business community.

For Pratley, the basic moral responsibility of an enterprise is threefold. First, it is producing goods and providing services that are functional and safe for every consumer. Second, it is a concern for the natural environment and the depletion of natural resources. And third, the primary moral responsibility of an enterprise relates to the quality of the enterprise itself as a moral community (Pratley 1998: 133).

The company should consider moral aspects in its activities, and this is in the scope of all undertaken activities. It is not appropriate to assign responsibility only to employees or limit morals to marketing activities. An economic entity should plan activities in such a way that they provide consumers and society with value, and the discussed responsibility should be considered at every stage of the company's activity. Moral discourse and considering broadly understood responsibility allow for the implementation of the social function, which is attributed to the enterprise, as well as for more effective implementation of its basic activity.

Considering the company's responsibility in the area of marketing activities, one can also refer to the existing philosophical theories explaining and justifying individual ways of proceeding.

For example, the contractual theory assumes that liability is the result of mutual obligations assumed by the partners in a contract. Both partners are considered fully responsible for their obligations and able to take care of their own interests (Pratley 1998: 142). This approach is in line with the transactional ethics formulated by H. Luijk, in which moral interactions are perceived as a defense of private interests, and negotiations are undertaken each time a conflict of interest arises (Table 3.2). This approach can be used, inter alia, in typical commercial situations in which both parties are successful, i.e. all participants in the transaction can benefit from the agreed arrangements (win-to-win situation).

Moreover, it is possible to claim the responsibility of the enterprise according to the theory of social costs. According to this approach, in all cases, manufacturers should bear the financial consequences of the damage caused by the use of the products they manufacture, including in the event of gross usage errors on the part of the customer. Such an approach, however, leads to abuses not only by customers, but also the risk of assigning the blame to the wrong party (e.g. in the case of accidents with several causes or a series of unfortunate circumstances, it is easy to identify the manufacturer to whom the fault is most likely to be attributed) (Pratley 1998: 148–149).

Due to the evolution of management, the company's obligations are not viewed only from the point of view of social costs, but through the prism of social obligations, i.e. actions taken on behalf of and for the benefit of society.

According to the social orientation, the task of modern enterprises is not only to earn money, but also to achieve certain social goals. This orientation does not negate the economic function of the enterprise, but does not

*Table 3.2* Shaping the responsibility of the enterprise in accordance with the theory of contracts (Pratley 1998: 143)

| *Position* | *Contents* |
|---|---|
| **Creed** | Beware, client! |
| **Assumed obligations of the manufacturer/ supplier** | Provide consumers with a product/good that complies with the terms of the sales contract. This includes contractual obligations in terms of design quality, workmanship, and delivery – nothing more. |
| **Assumed balance of power** | Both sides are equal, everyone knows what he is doing in "entering" the business. |
| **Scope of application** | Such relationships between firms and other types of commercial cooperation are contractual relationships based on the following assumptions: (a) both parties can be expected to have the same expertise in the quality of the products or services they purchase, and (b) each party has effective means of punishing an opponent for breach of contract terms, especially in relation to possible market pressures. |
| **Dangers and drawbacks** | Product malfunction that may cause injury or damage not specified in the contract is at the buyer's risk. |
| **The main use** | In typical procurement transactions. In the vast majority of everyday grocery and clothing purchases (typical low risk needs). |

consider it exclusive. Managers have obligations to shareholders who entrust them with their money, but also to society, which enables the functioning of the enterprise, gives it a legal status as a separate entity, and allows the use of natural resources (Lewicka-Strzałecka 1999: 42).

The need for consumer protection was first noticed in the United States.[1] This is where the first legal regulations appeared, the purpose of which was precisely to protect consumers. It was assumed that they are the only group that is not effectively organised and whose point of view is most often ignored. It's hard to disagree with this approach. The consumer is not a partner knowingly and voluntarily participating in the exchange process. The consumer-business relationship is asymmetrical due to the lack of information, financial and technical balance between the parties (cf. Lewicka-Strzałecka 2012: 259–260).

The term marketing ethics, like other terms, has several definitions. For L. Gasparski, marketing ethics is understood as the general name of the ethos characteristic of economic activity, i.e. the actual values and norms governing the behaviour of people involved in this type of activity (Gasparski 2012: 64). This concept is perceived slightly differently by P. Murphy and his team, for whom marketing ethics is systematic research on how moral standards are applied in marketing decisions, behaviours, and institutions (Murphy et al. 2005: XVII). The definition of marketing ethics by S. Vitell can be considered similar, for which it is a study of the nature and moral foundations of judgements, standards, and rules of conduct in marketing decisions and situations (Vitell 1986: 4).

Many ethical issues related to marketing seem to be under constant debate. Misleading advertising as to whether unsafe and harmful products have been and continue to be the subject of debate. However, scientific discussions on marketing ethics changed the subject of their interest, mainly due to changes in the perceived problems in the area of ethics in marketing. In the 1960s and 1970s, the main topics of research into marketing ethics were marketing research and basic issues of marketing strategy such as purchasing and the 4P concept. Theoretical and consumer-related issues were much less addressed. These studies were usually of normative nature, i.e. they contained recommendations and guidelines indicating the appropriate procedures (Hunt, Vitell 1986: 6). In the following years, the interest shifted to the development of theoretical models of ethical decisions of marketers (Ferrell, Gresham 1985; Hunt, Vitell 1986). The subject of the research was also the process of making decisions regarding ethics in marketing (among others Murphy 1999). The development of new technologies, which significantly influenced the implementation of current marketing activities, caused the shift of research to new ethical problems (Abela, Murphy 2008: 39). Contemporary research on the ethicality of market activities concerns, inter alia, e-commerce (Kracher, Corritore 2004), or online shopping (Marcoux 2003).

B. Schlegelmilch and M. Öberseder, making a broad review of publications in the field of marketing ethics, identified the following areas of research on the "ethicality of marketing" (Schlegelmilch, Öberseder 2010: 2–3):

1 Product ethical issues: product safety, product quality, product design, packaging, labelling, and ethical products.
2 Price ethical issues: price fairness, pricing, price discrimination, and misleading prices.
3 Ethical issues related to distribution: exclusive distribution rights, channel control, and unauthorised discounts.
4 Promotion ethics: advertising ethics, product placement, direct marketing, and sales promotion.
5 Sales ethics: sellers' ethical conflicts, ethical values, and salesperson behaviour.
6 Issues of collective ethical decision-making: corporate ethical decision-making, ethical values and ethical conduct of managers, CSR, and marketing.
7 Codes and norms: theory of marketing ethics, ethical norms, and ethical codes.
8 Ethical issues related to consumers: ethical decision making by consumers, ethical values , and perceptions of consumer ethics.
9 Ethical issues regarding vulnerable consumers: ethical aspects of marketing decisions regarding children, the elderly and the poor.
10 International and intercultural marketing ethics: unethical behaviour of multinational corporations, international comparisons, incl. topics such as corporate ethical decision making and consumer ethical decision making.
11 Ethical issues related to marketing research: ethical responsibility and running of marketing research companies, ethical responsibility of clients of research companies, e.g. beautification of results, protection of privacy, etc.
12 Ethical issues related to marketing education: integrating ethical issues with other areas in marketing education.
13 Ethical issues related to social marketing: concept and definition of social marketing, ethical dimension of social marketing, social responsibility of marketing managers, socially engaged marketing.
14 Ethical issues related to eco-marketing: social responsibility and eco-marketing costs.
15 Ethical issues related to the law: the relationship between law and ethics in the field of marketing.
16 Ethical issues related to the Internet: online privacy protection, image theft, and internet auctions.
17 Religion-related issues: the influence of religion and religious values on marketing ethics.

In practice, the elimination or even reduction of unethical behaviour in the area of corporate marketing requires many actions. These activities can take place in two ways and consist of (Garbarski 2012: 72):

- counteracting unethical behaviour,
- shaping ethical behaviour.

The most common methods of counteracting unethical behaviour are (cf. Garbarski 2012: 72):

- legal regulations of activity,
- activities of specially established state institutions (e.g. the Office of Competition and Consumer Protection),
- social control exercised, for example, by the media or consumer organisations (e.g. the Consumer Federation, the Consumers Association),
- creation and voluntary acceptance of ethical codes of associations and organisations,
- creation and compliance with ethical codes by individual enterprises (corporations).

In order to shape positive behaviours, sets of rules favouring ethical behaviour are formulated. With regard to marketing activities, these collections should include (Garbarski 2012: 76):

- the principle of consumer and producer liberty – decisions made by producers and consumers should be made in conditions of relative liberty,
- the principle of limiting potential damage – legislative interference limiting the producer or consumer is to protect against transactions that bring harm or risk,
- the principle of satisfying basic needs – marketing activities of companies traditionally aimed at better-off customers should also support economic and political activities towards weaker ones,
- the principle of economic efficiency – competition in the market supports the free movement of goods, freedom of information and contributes to the effective satisfaction of needs,
- the principle of innovation – encouraging real product innovations and their differentiation in order to meet the needs of different groups of buyers,
- the principle of educating and informing consumers – treating consumer education as an investment increasing the satisfaction and welfare of this group,
- the principle of consumer protection – making it possible to properly evaluate products, protecting the natural environment, and protecting against unfair commercial practices.

However, when considering the degree to which ethics is considered in the marketing activities of enterprises, several levels of their involvement can be distinguished. The first level of ethical activities in the area of marketing is to fulfil one's obligations, but at the lowest cost. Such an approach very often results in operating on the border of the law, and the level of commitment to ethics is negligible. The second level is considering the applicable regulations, which in practice means compliance with all legal acts, but in this case, it is assumed that the organisation does not limit itself to voluntarily considering all codes that very often go beyond legal regulations (e.g. the Advertising Code of Ethics), but is interested in creating a positive image of the company by undertaking socially justified activity. The highest level of commitment to ethics, the third level, is the ethical commitment of the company that allows the creation of a kind of moral spirit (cf. Hollensen 2003: 712–713). Figure 3.1 presents a graphical view of companies' different approaches to ethics.

The last level of ethical commitment of enterprises is compliance with the code of ethics, which should relate to such areas as (Hollensen 2003: 713):

- organisational issues (competition, strategic alliances, local organisations, etc.),
- economic issues (sources of financing activities, taxes, pricing, etc.),
- employee issues (remuneration, security, employment rights, non-discrimination policy, training, collective disputes, etc.),
- customer relations (product quality, advertising, etc.),
- industry relationships (technology transfer, research and development, infrastructure development, organisational stability, etc.),
- political relations (respecting the law, anti-corruption measures, environmental protection, etc.).

This perception of ethical commitment is very broad and close to the concept of CSR. In the proposed areas of the code of ethics, Hollensen indicates

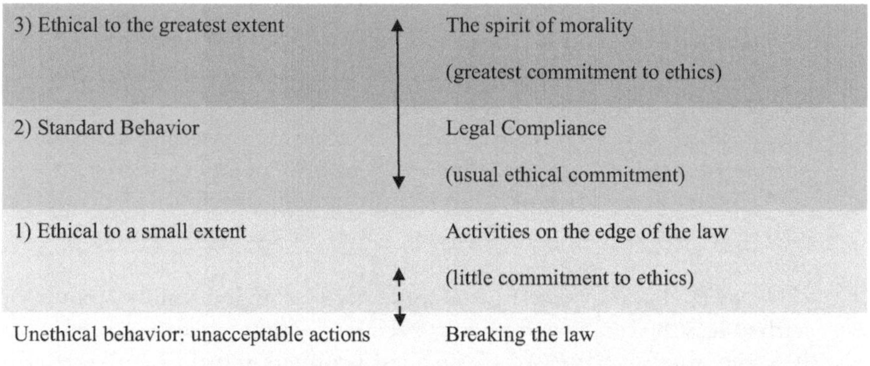


*Figure 3.1* Levels of ethical behaviour (Hollensen 2003: 712)

not only responsible behaviour in relation to the goals and activities of the enterprise, i.e. the proper implementation of the economic function of the enterprise, but also its stakeholders.

The existence of certain norms, values, codes, and rules of conduct, unfortunately, does not mean that they are automatically respected. Enterprises are not generally guided by ethical standards, and the reasons for violating ethical principles include, inter alia, the temptation to avoid some costs, simplify the activity, or even simple convenience and carelessness (cf. Garbarski 2012: 66). We can particularly often notice abuses in this area in the marketing activities of enterprises.

Breaking the ethical principles in the long term, however, causes many negative effects, including, in particular, deterioration of the company's image, loss of customer and supplier trust, and loss of credibility. As a consequence, the effectiveness and efficiency of the company's operations are usually reduced (Garbarski 2012: 66). However, many companies do not see these risks. Not only do they not create and adhere to any codes or ethical principles, but they consciously make decisions that have nothing to do with ethics or even simple honesty towards consumers or other stakeholders. The result of such proceedings is, inter alia, low social evaluation of companies' marketing activities in general.

**Nike Inc.**

Nike Inc. is an American multinational corporation engaged in the design, development, production, and worldwide marketing and sale of footwear, clothing, equipment, accessories, and services. In 2021, the brand alone was valued in excess of $30 billion, making it the most valuable brand among sports businesses (Brand Finance 2021).

The company has set its targets in three areas: People, Community, and Planet. As part of the Planet area, the company has set its, inter alia, goals such as:

- 70% absolute reduction in greenhouse gas (GHG) emissions in owned or operated facilities thanks to 100% renewable electricity and fleet electrification;
- 0.5 million tons of GHG emissions reduced by increasing the use of environmentally preferred materials to 50% of all key materials;
- 10% reduction in waste per unit in production, distribution, headquarters, and packaging thanks to better design and operational efficiency;
- 100% of landfilled waste in the company's extended supply chain, with at least 80% recycled back to NIKE products and other goods;
- 10X the amount of waste of finished products refurbished, recycled, or donated;

- 25% reduction in fresh water consumption per kg for dyeing and finishing textiles;
- 13 billion litres restored through a portfolio of watershed projects that support long-term resilience for water-stressed ecosystems and communities within their extended cotton supply chain.

Nike pays special attention to the process of designing and manufacturing its products, which reduce the amount of waste, use recycled materials and materials whose production process is minimally invasive from the point of view of environmental impact. The materials used include:

1. Nike Flyknit is a lightweight fabric with an average of 60% less waste than in traditional footwear upper manufacturing. Each shoe upper made from Flyknit contains six to seven plastic bottles.
2. Nike Flyleather that looks, feels, and smells like natural leather, but is made by binding at least 50% recycled leather fibres with synthetic fibres using a water-powered process. This process creates less waste and a lower impact on climate change compared to full-grain leather.
3. Recycled manufacturing waste, as of 2008, all Nike Air soles are composed of at least 50% recycled manufacturing waste. What's more, they reuse over 90% of the scrap materials used in Air soles to make new and innovative cushioning systems.
4. Recycled polyester, which is made from plastic bottles that are cleaned, shredded into flakes, turned into granules and then spun into high-quality yarn. In addition to reducing waste, recycled polyamide cuts carbon dioxide emissions by up to 30% compared to virgin plastic and diverts an average of 1 billion plastic bottles a year from landfills and waterways.
5. Sustainable cotton that is certified organic, recycled or Better Cotton sourced under the Better Cotton Initiative (BCI). All of the organic cotton used by Nike is grown without pesticides derived from fossil fuels or synthetic fertilisers, and we process over 1.5 million pounds of cotton annually.
6. Recycled nylon which is processed from a variety of materials such as carpet and used fish nets. The nylon is cleaned, sorted, and flaked, all before being chemically or mechanically recycled. The new recycled nylon yarn reduces carbon dioxide emissions by up to 50% compared to virgin nylon.

In a 2020 report, Nike declared that they use 100% renewable energy in the United States and Canada in their owned or operated sites. Globally, NIKE was powered by 48% renewable energy in 2020 (Nike 2020).

## The essence of value-based marketing. A place of social responsibility in value creation

The need to change the approach to the implementation of marketing in enterprises has been recognised for a long time. The role of marketing in creating shareholder value is primarily questioned. Highly insufficient is considered, inter alia, the use of a traditional approach to the implementation of marketing in services, where the main objection raised by both theoreticians and practitioners is insufficient customer orientation. This opinion is shared, among others, by B. Booms and M. Bitner (1981), C. Grönroos (1994), M. Rafiq and P. Ahmed (1995), F. Webster (1998), W. Gombeski (1998), L. O'Malley and M. Patterson (1998), G. Day and D. Montgomery (1999), and M. Akroush (2010). These authors emphasise that the specificity of services creates specific problems and challenges, requiring, inter alia, various marketing strategies, and the proposed, even extended marketing-mix allows for the implementation of individual transactions that do not build a relationship with the customer over a long period of time (transactional marketing). Such a procedure does not allow for the implementation of the added value, which would be of value for the customer and other stakeholders at the same time.

A paradigm shift is also expected due to changes in the political, legal, and socio-cultural environment of the company. Progress in information technology, changing the ways of communicating with consumers, and changing the expectations and requirements of consumers meant that enterprises should review the current methods of conduct. For some authors, relationship marketing is a solution adequate to the changes in the environment that will allow achieving the intended efficiency. They include, among others, F. Webster (1992), E. Gummesson (1994), R. Morgan and S. Hunt (1994), C. Grönroos (1994; 1996), and A. Payne and P. Frow (2005).

However, treating relationship marketing as a new approach to the implementation of the company's marketing functions has been criticised. For some specialists, relationship marketing is not a paradigm shift, but a supplement to the marketing-mix well-established in the world. Some researchers even prove that relationship marketing and transactional marketing paradigms are complementary paradigms rather than a paradigm shift, which still does not respond to the current expectations posed by the business sphere (Hakansson, Waluszewski 2005; Zineldin, Philipson 2007; Akroush 2010).

Technological progress and changes in the perception of the role of business in society mean that direct marketing is returning to the stage, leading to relationship orientation. Shaping the relationship, however, is not the same as shaping communication with the consumer. The current paradigm of marketing exchange is no longer sufficient. It is necessary to involve customers at every stage of product preparation, often including the production process (e.g. production of shoes for individual customer orders, in which customers not only choose the materials, but even the way they are made). Such an approach to the consumer means that results-oriented marketing will have to give way to marketing, which will have a process character and will be oriented towards creating, not distributing, value (cf. Sheth, Parvatiyar 1995: 414).

The first definitions of value-based marketing can be found in the publications of P. Kotler and co-authors (2002: 47–48), including P. Kotler and K. Keller (2006: 6). And the first publication devoted entirely to this subject is P. Doyle's book "Value-based Marketing. Marketing Strategies for Corporate Growth and Shareholder Value" released in 2000.

According to P. Kotler, in accordance with the concept of value-based marketing, the company should direct most of its resources to value-creating marketing investments. Kotler emphasises that such marketing activities as one-off sales promotions, small packaging changes, or pompous advertising can increase sales in a short period of time, but they add less value than a real improvement in quality, utility features, or convenience of the product would do. Meanwhile, the purpose of value-based marketing is to build long-term customer loyalty by constantly increasing the value of the enterprise, which can be obtained as a result of the company's marketing offer (Kotler et al. 2002: 47–48). The functionality of marketing in creating value is also highlighted by, inter alia, P. Doyle. For Doyle, creating shareholder value is all about building a sustainable competitive advantage, which is why customers should consistently prefer to buy a specific company's products. Marketing, in turn, provides tools for creating a competitive advantage (Doyle 2008: 20).

The need to return to shaping direct relations with the customer and creating real value for the customer is indicated, among others, by J. Sheth and A. Parvatiyar. According to these authors, the orientation towards building customer relations existed from the early years of industry development. The situation changed only when mass production led to a surplus of goods and the marketing activities of the companies became transaction oriented. However, changes in the market forced changes in the area of marketing and sales.

The orientation on transactions in marketing gives way to a return to relationship orientation, and further on to value creation. Enterprises are interested not only in repeated purchases, but also in long-term customer loyalty and commitment. This requires a paradigm shift in marketing theory. From the paradigm of exchange, focused on the distribution of value and the results of exchange, to relationship-oriented marketing and value creation for the company's stakeholders, where the process of creating value is at least as important, if not more important than the results of the exchange (cf. Sheth, Parvatiyar 1995: 414).

P. Doyle's book is treated as groundbreaking. Nobody has so clearly presented the impact of marketing activities on the real value generated for shareholders before. Earlier publications on marketing did not pay as much attention to revenue generation by the marketing area. On the other hand, publications devoted to creating goodwill paid little attention to marketing activities. Meanwhile, Doyle combined both of these areas and tried to show how marketing expenses can contribute to the increase in the value of the company and generate profits by it in the future.

P. Doyle defined value-based marketing as a management process that seeks to maximise profit for shareholders by developing and implementing a strategy of building trust relationships with high-value customers and creating a sustainable, sustainable competitive advantage. According to Doyle, marketing is not a cost-generating area, as is often perceived by companies, but a factor of value creation. The aim of marketing is to support activities aimed at maximising value for shareholders, and the basic resources on which the marketing of modern enterprises should be based are: brand image, loyalty of buyers, and relations with recipients (Doyle 2008: 74).

In order to ensure a balanced, sustainable, value-based development of the company, leading to a market advantage, it is necessary, however, to consider the requirements of not only the company's customers, but also other interest groups. Value-based marketing consists in considering the broadly understood, subjective environment of the company in the market service strategy and a responsible approach to all stakeholders by creating the desired value. The aim of this approach is to gain and maintain customer loyalty through extensive care for the needs, development, and environment of the customer (Howaniec, Waszkielewicz 2013).

The features that distinguish value-based marketing from marketing concepts such as mass marketing, segmentation-based marketing, and relationship marketing are presented in Table 3.3.

The resultant approach in marketing is no longer enough. Market share or increased customer satisfaction are not indicators whose achievement guarantees an increase in shareholder value. This makes it necessary to reformulate the marketing concept, among others in the creation and management of intangible assets, i.e. relationships with customers, channels, and brands, in order to maximise economic value. The new approach is called value-based marketing. However, such perception of the marketing function changes its place, placing marketing activities in a key role in the process of formulating the company's strategy (cf. Doyle 2008: 21).

Value creation assumes entering social activities into the company's strategy in such a way that they co-create the conditions of the environment (e.g. by solving social problems) and, as a consequence, contribute to the growth of the company's value. A significant problem in the area of value creating is the definition and selection of the support area that will have the potential to create value for both the society and the enterprise. The main financial goal in the concept of value creation is the economic value (EVA) of the enterprise.

Although value-based marketing is based on Shareholder Value Analysis (SVA), it doesn't just mean numbers or complex calculations. Value-based marketing is: (1) a set of beliefs about marketing goals – the primary task of marketing is to develop strategies that maximise shareholder returns; (2) a set of rules for selecting marketing strategies and making marketing decisions consistent with these beliefs – these rules are based on estimating future cash flows related to the strategy for calculating the added value for the shareholder; (3) a set of processes that ensure that marketing develops, selects and implements a strategy that aligns with these beliefs and principles – these processes

*Table 3.3* Characteristics of the concept of value-based marketing as one of the concepts of marketing (Howaniec, Waszkielewicz 2013: 230–231)

| *Marketing strategy* | *Mass marketing* | *Segmentation-based marketing* | *Relationship marketing* | *Value-based marketing* |
|---|---|---|---|---|
| Objectives | Large range of influence<br>High brand awareness<br>Large market share | Customers acquisition<br>Customer satisfaction<br>Building loyalty<br>Market share | Acquiring and maintaining customer loyalty<br>Participation (share) in customers<br>Customer development | Creating value for the customer<br>Acquiring and maintaining customer loyalty<br>Customer development<br>Social responsibility |
| The nature of marketing activities | Universal<br>Impersonal<br>Passive | Tactical<br>Connected<br>Dynamic | Strategic<br>Based on cooperation<br>1:1 | Responsible<br>Targeted at all stakeholders |
| Communication | One-sided (to the customer) | Double-sided<br>Transactional | Individual | Based on interaction |
| Media | Mass advertising<br>Mass communication channels | Selective promotion<br>Selected channels, effective from the point of view of selected segments<br>Call centres | Personal<br>Providing real-time responses<br>Internet (e-mail)<br>Fax<br>Telephone<br>Face-to-face meetings | Social<br>Enabling interaction between all interested parties<br>Internet websites<br>Social networks<br>Content networks<br>Virtual social worlds |
| Indicators | Based on mass demographics<br>Market research<br>Product profitability | Based on the demographics of the segments<br>Market research<br>Profitability of conducted campaigns<br>Customer retention rate | Based on individual behavioural research<br>Knowing "customer value" | Based on in-depth behavioural research<br>Research on the company's reputation and brand image |

relate to the management of financial, marketing, and organisational factors capable of creating or contributing to the value of the enterprise. The drivers of financial value are those key metrics that have the greatest impact on shareholder value. Marketing factors are customer-oriented plans necessary to improve financial performance. Organisational factors, in turn, are the basic skills, systems, and leadership styles needed to create and implement an orientation on creating shareholder value in a company (Doyle 2008: 36).

Due to the change in the approach to marketing, P. Doyle proposes to redefine not only the concept of marketing, but also marketing goals, which should be the maximisation of profits for owners, measured by the stream of long-term dividends and capital growth. The concrete contribution of marketing, in turn, should consist in formulating a strategy for selecting the right customers, building a trust relationship, and creating an advantage based on differentiation (Doyle 2008: 74).

The concept of value marketing really changes the current approach to both customers and other stakeholders, introducing changes to both the content of marketing activities and the recipients to whom they are addressed. Marketing activities of companies should increasingly consider the value that they can provide, in all areas of creating the company's offer, from shaping the features and usability of products, setting prices, through creating value-based communication between the company and the market, to value-based distribution of products. This change, however, is not dictated by fashion, but by a long-term search for a new marketing paradigm that would better meet the requirements of modern enterprises, largely determined by the expectations of the external environment.

Focusing on selling is not enough. Building relationships with customers without creating real value for them also involves some mistakes. Marketing will no longer rely on influencing the customer to buy what the company has to offer, but will move towards interactive communication focused primarily on listening and creating what the customer expects. The development of modern forms of communication is shifting the activities of enterprises towards mass customisation, and this approach will not only apply to aspects related to the product, but to all areas of customer contact with the enterprise, including prices, distribution, and communication. Value-based marketing is complemented by considering the interests of other stakeholders, including the natural environment, in the process of shaping and creating value. Value-based marketing is not only about taking customer expectations into account, but balancing them with the expectations of other stakeholders, as well as the expectations of business owners.

## Marketing and value creation

The goal that defines the business is to maximise the value for the owner in the long term through the sale of goods or services (Sternberg 1998: 59). For many years, the basis of the business of a commercial enterprise was the owner's profits, which was placed in the first place as the obvious and indisputable goal of economic activities (Sternberg 1998: 59). As the changes that took place in the company's environment, further financial goals, such as social, environmental, and ethical goals, were introduced. The way of looking at the company has also changed. Once an economic entity that was primarily supposed to provide financial benefits to its owners, now it is required to meet the requirements of broadly defined stakeholders. All this means that today's companies are under pressure from two sides: on the one hand, they are owners who expect an improvement in financial results in the long term, and on the other hand, they are stakeholders who expect socially responsible behaviour from the company.

Although social responsibility has become one of the important issues on the agenda of today's companies, it still does not occupy the main place in their strategies. One of the key problems is the lack of understanding of the impact of the application of CSR in the management and marketing activities of companies on their financial performance, value, and competitiveness. This includes causes that companies do not consider creating value for stakeholders as a long-term investment in the value of the company, which is also value for shareholders. Social involvement and managerial ethics, which are the basis for value creation, cannot be located peripherally. Such an approach to business execution influences the company's decisions at every stage of planning and operation, and should occupy a central place, that is, take precedence over the operational, functional, technical, and conceptual (strategic) levels of management in the enterprise (Hosmer 1994: 200). This is because creating value for stakeholders has a direct impact on the company's competitiveness.

There are many studies proposing the business rationale for corporate social involvement (Vilanova et al. 2009), trying to analyse the relationship between CSR and financial results (cf. Chand, Fraser 2006) or providing case studies of CSR practices. Previous studies have not shown a clear relationship between CSR and financial performance of companies (Chand, Fraser 2006)[2] or a relationship between CSR and the competitiveness of enterprises (Mackey et al. 2007). However, the conceptual extension introduced by the stakeholder theory caused CSR to be treated as a vehicle of broadly understood value. It is assumed that the social involvement of companies allows for an increase in value for share- and stakeholders in the long run, although the actions taken by companies may reduce the current value of their cash flows (Mackey et al. 2007: 833).

L. Hosmer tried to justify the positive relationship between efficiency and ethics. He argued that the reliable, honest, and fair conduct of the company towards all stakeholder groups is an absolutely necessary condition for a company to achieve lasting success, assuming that the company operates under conditions of free competition. According to Hosmer, this thesis is confirmed by the following relationships (Hosmer 1994: 193–200; cf. Lewicka-Strzałecka 1999: 159):

1 Enterprises depend on a variety of stakeholder groups that have the potential to influence their long-term competitiveness.
2 Enterprises depend on stakeholders not only for cooperation, but also for improvisation, creativity, and innovation, which are essential for their competitiveness.
3 It is difficult to motivate decisions and actions that are both creative and innovative on the part of all stakeholders within the extended organisation.[3]
4 Trust is a fundamental element that leads to commitment and managers should build trust in every contact with stakeholders by treating them properly, fairly, and honestly.

Success depends largely on the relationships that the company has with key stakeholders and its reputation. The key importance of stakeholders in creating the market advantage of enterprises (apart from R. Freeman) is indicated, among others, by T. Donaldson and L. Preston, who, when analyzing the validity of the stakeholder theory, indicate as one of the conclusions that the theory of creating shareholder value perspective is morally unsustainable (Donaldson, Preston 1995: 87–88).[4]

According to B. Rok, responsible business is (2004: 18):

- achieving sustainable profit while wisely shaping relations with all stakeholders,
- a management tool that allows to use the process of building a dialogue with stakeholders in order to improve the company's development strategy,
- philosophy of running a business based on building lasting, transparent relationships with all interested parties including employees, customers, suppliers, shareholders, competitors, and the local community,
- building a strategy of competitive advantage in the market, based on ensuring lasting value for both shareholders and other stakeholders,
- providing services and products in a way that does not degrade the natural and social environment,
- conducting business in such a way as to consider ethical values, law, respect for employees, society, and the natural environment,
- honest fulfilment of obligations,
- running a business in accordance with social expectations, which are ethical, legal, financial, and civic,
- building and implementing a strategy of social involvement, exceeding legal obligations, for the benefit of all citizens, in accordance with socially accepted ethical standards,

- managing the enterprise in such a way that the effects of economic activity are consistent with expectations and social values,
- contributing to sustainable development by working with employees, local and global communities to improve the quality of life for all citizens,
- sense of responsibility for the consumer, investor, society, and natural environment, for the success of the economy,
- voluntarily considering social, ethical, and environmental aspects in business activities and in contacts with stakeholders,
- applying transparent business practices based on respect for employees, the community, and the environment.

The creation of value for shareholders, i.e. the creation of economic value in the long term, must be related to the creation of value for the company's stakeholders. The element that connects these two planes is CSR.

L. Burke and J. Logsdon believe that there are as many as five dimensions of a company's strategy that may determine that CSR allows for the creation of value for various interest groups. These are: (1) centrality (central location), understood as the proximity of the mission and goals of the company, (2) specificity, i.e. the ability to generate benefits for the company, (3) proactivity, i.e. planning ahead (anticipating) social trends, (4) voluntarism, i.e. activity that involves voluntary action, and (5) visibility, i.e. actions taken are observed by stakeholders (Burke, Logsdon 1996).

In order for CSR to create value for shareholders, it is necessary to change the business approach to CSR and shift the activities undertaken in this area from the position of "expenditure" to the "inputs" item. The change that must take place is primarily a change in the perception of CSR as an element of the company's strategy. CSR should be treated as a long-term investment. The necessary condition, however, is to act in accordance with the concept of creating common value, i.e. undertaking CSR activities in a strategic manner, allowing the enterprise to increase its economic value in the long term. Stakeholder value creation should not be seen as a cost centre, but as a profit centre. Carrying out appropriate actions should deliver value not only to stakeholders, but also to the enterprise itself, i.e. its owners. P. Doyle cautions managers against misunderstanding the company's financial goals. In the concept of value creation, it is primarily shareholder value maximisation that is important, not short-term profit maximisation. Maximising profitability can lower a company's long-term competitiveness (in terms of lowering costs and freeing up resources to achieve a quick payback) while neglecting new market opportunities. Such strategies unfortunately destroy rather than create economic value (Doyle 2008: 3).

Strategic investments in socially responsible activities, even if they reduce the company's cash flow, are profitable in the long term. These investments also provide benefits other than the increase in the company's revenues. Generating economic value through CSR is particularly easy when the demand for socially responsible investments is greater than their supply. Unfortunately, if the conditions of supply and demand for socially responsible activities are not favourable, and their selection will not be based on creating shared value with stakeholders, engaging in CSR may actually reduce the company's market value. Therefore, it is necessary to shape the demand for this type of activity (cf. Mackey et al. 2007: 833) for example through appropriate marketing activities. Another solution is to work with the company's stakeholders. It is easier to contribute to positive change when we co-create this value with other stakeholders. Involvement in achieving a common goal of local communities or non-governmental organisations allows for finding more optimal solutions, which is particularly important when assuming a large-scale impact. M. Kramer and M. Pfitzer even point to the need to create an ecosystem supporting the creation of common value. In their opinion, companies belong to ecosystems whose social conditions, cultural norms, or government policy may affect the absorption of markets and the efficiency of enterprises. Effective collaboration between actors can therefore provide a value higher than acting alone. In order to achieve such benefits, according to Kramer and Pfitzer, five conditions must be met: (1) ensure a common program, (2) create a common measurement system, (3) plan mutually supportive activities, (4) ensure constant communication, and (5) implement targeted, basic support from one or more independent organisations (cf. Kramer, Pfitzer 2017).

Creating value for stakeholders should be a value for the enterprise itself, in line with the concept of CSV, i.e. creating shared value. Effective CSV is about creating new business opportunities, new markets, in a way that improves profitability and strengthens the company's competitive position, that is, following the formula of "doing well by doing good" (cf. Porter, Kramer 2006).

## Notes

1 Basic consumer rights in the United States were formulated in 1962 in the US Congress by President J.F. Kennedy.

2 Interesting research on the economic benefits of applying CSR principles in Polish enterprises was carried out by a team consisting of: P. Kulawczuk, M. Bąk, P. Bednarz, T. Kulawczuk and A. Szcześniak. Four research procedures were used as part of the study: (1) a statistical analysis of the differences in the distribution of variables determining the benefits of CSR in two groups of enterprises was performed: the group of enterprises that applied the CSR principles, which was confirmed by the "Fair Play Enterprise" certificate (hereinafter referred to as the CSR group) and a group of enterprises that were not certified as meeting the CSR principles under the "Fair Play Enterprise", selected from the Central Statistical Office database based on the identity of the industry and similar number of employees (hereinafter referred to as the CSO group); (2) the results of the mean variables determining the economic benefits of CSR were analysed for both studied populations (CSR and CSO) and in pairs (150 pairs); (3) the results of the CSR group divided into industries (64) were compared with the average

industry results (industries of the Central Statistical Office), with the analysis focused on presenting rankings of industries that provide the greatest benefits from the use of CSR for enterprises, employees and society; (4) the qualitative benefits of applying CSR principles for enterprises were determined on the basis of 24 interviews conducted in small and medium-sized enterprises with the owners and directors of these enterprises. According to the results obtained, CSR provides tangible benefits for enterprises, employees and society as a whole, and these benefits have their quantitative and qualitative dimensions (Kulawczuk et al. 2007: 55–112).

3 "Extended organization", "extended enterprise", a concept that emerges along with the topic of co-creating value with customers and other company stakeholders. Co-creation of value requires the ability to engage the "extended enterprise" by managing the processes of creating value for customers and suppliers (Payne et al. 2008, p. 93; Bobbink et al. 2016).

4 The relationship between ethical conduct and the company's success in the long term was researched in Poland by, among others, A. Lewicka-Strzałecka (survey of respondents' opinions). According to the results, as many as 38% of respondents believe that ethical behaviour definitely ensures the economic success of the company, and 45% of respondents agreed with such a position by answering "rather yes". Only 10% believed that ethical conduct was rather unrelated to the economic success of the company, and 2% that such a relationship absolutely does not exist. In the case of this question, only 5% answered that they had no opinion on this subject (Lewicka-Strzałecka 1999: 169).

# 4 Shaping value-based marketing

## A new look at product quality

One of the areas that society is interested in is the quality and safety of the products and services offered. Customers demand that quality be considered when planning and manufacturing products, and very often they are guided by quality when purchasing. Technological development and global competition significantly contributed to the improvement of quality. The approach to quality has changed and is still changing. Quality assurance nowadays is not only the responsibility of a small group of people who monitor performance and remove defective products, but it is a whole of activities that consider the expectations of society throughout the product life cycle, i.e. from the stage of product planning to its removal from the market. The inclusion of all quality assurance initiatives is now mandatory and quality, or rather the pursuit of continual improvement, must be organisation wide.

What is quality? The term quality has many meanings, in everyday language it is most often associated with product excellence. It is also often defined as meeting the requirements or standards. However, such an assessment may relate to different characteristics of the product. It should also be remembered that the perception of the product and its subjective assessment are influenced by the individual preferences of the buyer. It is therefore not easy to define quality in an unambiguous and categorical manner.

The literature is dominated by the definitions popularised in the 1950s with the development of the TQM (Total Quality Management) system. For example, W. Deming defines quality as meeting current and future customer requirements. J. Juran defines quality as the usability of a product. In turn, P. Crosby treats quality as compliance with the requirements, which, in his opinion, can be measured by the costs of non-compliance (Oakland 1992: 281–288). A. Feigenbaum defines the concept of quality in another way, for him quality is the overall characteristic of a product or service through which the consumer's expectations are met (Beckford 1998: 86).

The above-mentioned definitions of quality, despite some differences, also have a common part and it is meeting the customer's expectations. The quality is supposed to provide satisfaction to the customer (Parasuraman

DOI: 10.4324/9781003317364-5

et al. 1988: 16). Here, however, the question arises. Is the customer the only reviewer of the delivered quality? Are the customer's requirements the only requirements that the company should meet?

One of the tools that allow enterprises to improve the quality of their products is TQM, i.e. an idea, philosophy, or concept of management, which assumes that the proper (optimal) combination of acquired skills allows to obtain a result that will meet the needs of buyers. Quality, however, is no longer treated as merely adjusting product features to customer requirements. More and more often, the need to consider broader aspects, including environmental and social, is underlined.

The necessity to change the approach to quality assurance was mentioned many times. Preventing errors or adjusting the quality to the so-called minimum standard did not seem to be sufficient many years ago. It was assumed that the attitude of enterprises to the problem of quality should be changed and activities organised in such a way as not only to exclude wrong actions, but also to provide value to customers and society. It is the society's expectations of safety, functionality, and other product characteristics that create the standards that determine the desired product quality. And while quality management can be treated as a way of managing a business organisation, for many people the improvement of quality is a factor that may determine the success of an enterprise (Gilbert 1992: 22). This is how quality is perceived by, among others, K. Obłój or E. Skrzypek (Obłój 1997: 34–40; Skrzypek 2000: 18). Criticism of traditional quality models can be found, among others, in the work of E. Anderson, C. Fornell, and D. Lehmann (Anderson et al. 1994) and D. Iacobucci, K. Grayson and A. Ostrom (Iacobucci et al. 1994). These authors accused the traditional approach to quality for not considering clearly the customer's price or costs in assessing the quality of products. In their opinion, traditional quality models require a simple modification to consider financial factors, only then the evaluation of the offer by the customer would be a comparison of what they got for what they paid.

One of the researchers who drew attention to the necessity of a broad view of quality as a factor that may determine the competitiveness of an enterprise was J. Gilbert. He noticed and emphasised such an approach in the work of quality management pioneers, including in the works of K. Ishikawa (Gilbert 1992: 23). A. Feigenbaum also looked at quality more broadly. This author, considered a quality management guru, believed that quality has two parameters: it should provide the customer (1) with the best product in terms of use and (2) the best acceptable price (Beckford 2001: 87). Feigenbaum drew attention to the need to consider the quality of the product from both the technical and economic points of view. In his opinion, the lack of such verification may mean that the high level of quality features set by the manufacturer will not be accepted by the public. A very high level from a technical point of view does not have to mean an equally high economic evaluation of the product. The value for the customer is the combination of the benefits that the consumer will receive as a result of purchasing the product and the price that must be paid for these benefits. Feigenbaum saw the need to adapt to social expectations not only in terms of technical characteristics of the product, but also other parameters important from the point of view of potential customers' goals.

Combining quality with marketing aspects meant that apart from technical quality (objective, real), which is also considered in economic terms, there is also a perceived (marketing) quality. Perceived quality is the customer's overall impression of a product's quality and may differ from actual quality, i.e. how the manufacturer perceives it. These differences are additionally exacerbated by the discrepancy between the basic criteria of quality assessment performed by the consumer and the producer. The client is interested, inter alia, in usability and aesthetics of the product, comfort of use, or uniqueness of the product, while the most important dimensions of quality for a manufacturer are financial results, applications, technology, and the ability to compete with the product (Figure 4.1).

The importance of the quality of the product perceived by customers is also emphasised by, inter alia, D. Aaker. According to Aaker, it is one of the five elements that create brand value (the others are: customer loyalty to the brand, brand awareness, brand associations, and other values such as patents, trademarks, links in the distribution system, etc.), which is also value for the enterprise (Aaker 1991: 16).

This approach to quality is consistent with value-oriented definitions. These definitions consider product quality in terms of price and cost and analyse the relationship between these variables. In this sense, a high-quality product is one that ensures performance at an acceptable price or compliance at an acceptable cost. The key aspect in this approach is the analysis of the

| Quality from the consumer's point of view | | Quality from the producer's point of view |
|---|---|---|
| **The need for utility**<br>Functionality<br>Economic<br>Reliability | ↔ | **The need of profit**<br>Expense<br>Price<br>Sale |
| **The need for comfort and aesthetic experiences**<br>Esthetics<br>Ergonomics | ↔ | **The need for technological**<br>Modernity of technology<br>Possibility of improvement |
| **The need for prestige**<br>Uniqueness | ↔ | **The need for competitiveness**<br>Market size/Market share |

*Figure 4.1* Product quality perception: customer perspective vs. producer perspective (Hamrol 2005: 26)

benefits that the customer obtains by compiling information on the price, expected quality, and the cost of obtaining the product (Garvin 1984: 28).

However, changes that have occurred on the market require a further evolution of the approach to quality. This need is indicated, among others, by P. Ahmed and S. Machold. These authors advocate the rigorous incorporation of ethics and morality in the quality management process and consider virtue to be part of the quality paradigm. In their opinion, such an approach to quality will lead to the next stage of the evolution of the theory of quality and will increase the role, that this factor will play in the practice of managerial and social responsibility, in the future (Ahmed, Machold 2004: 527). R. Waddock and C. Bodwell take a similar position, with the difference that they emphasise the necessity to consider CSR in the quality management process, i.e. they do not refer to moral values, but to the broadly understood responsibility of the company. These authors emphasise that the requirements of the CSR concept go far beyond the quality of the product or service, focusing, inter alia, on areas such as labour standards, environmental sustainability, supplier relations, and supply chain management. Considering the increasing frequency of considering CSR during purchases, in their opinion, it is necessary to consider all areas of social responsibility also in the quality management process. The modern consumer is increasingly demanding social responsibility of companies and assessing how their operating practices (policies, processes, and procedures) affect all stakeholders, including the environment (Waddock, Bodwell 2004: 25).

The broad treatment of quality as a responsibility not only to customers, but also to other stakeholders, is also visible in the early definitions formulated in the standards for quality systems. According to ISO 8402 of 1994, TQM is defined as "(4) a method of managing an organization focused on quality, based on the participation of all members of the organization, aimed at achieving long-term success through customer satisfaction and benefits for all members of the organization and for society" (ISO 1994). The standard, which acted as a guideline (terminology standard) in the field of implementing quality systems into business practice, clearly indicated that the benefits for "members of the organization and society", i.e. the company's stakeholders, were considered. The perception of changes taking place in the economy can also be seen in other ISO documents. The International Organization for Standardization (ISO) has identified, inter alia, a crisis of confidence in relation to corporate and public management and the urgency of a responsible approach to sustainable development as a challenge that will have a significant impact on international standardisation in the near future (ISO 2003: 2).

The broadly understood responsibility is also considered, inter alia, in the prestigious Award of Excellence in the field of quality (EFQM Excellence Award), established by the European Foundation for Quality Management (EFQM). Already in the introduction to the assumptions of the model of excellence adopted, which is the basis for the assessment of companies applying for this award, the EFQM explains that the model is based on European values, first expressed in the European Convention on Human Rights in 1953 and in the European Social Charter, revised in 1996. They also indicate that the Convention was ratified by 47-member states of the Council of Europe and its provisions were incorporated into national legislative systems.

The EFQM excellence model also refers to the 10 principles of the UN Global Compact, assuming that excellent organisations respect and operate in accordance with them, regardless of whether they are legally obliged to do so or not (EFQM 2013: 6) (Figure 4.2).

The aspects assessed on the basis of the presented model are in the area of potential – leadership, employees, strategy, partnership, and resources as well as processes, products, and services, and in the area of results – results concerning employees, customers, society and ultimately financial results. At the same time, in the area of results, the emphasis is on achieving and maintaining very good results that meet or exceed the needs and expectations of individual groups.

This approach to quality is adequate to modern requirements. The quality provided by enterprises cannot be limited to the quality required by the customer, but should consider a broader aspect, i.e. the environmental and social aspect (e.g. in the area of culture and customs). The customer may at any given time justify requesting a product with certain specifications without considering its impact on the environment and society as a whole, for example for reasons of cost. However, the company's task is to consider all aspects of the product's impact on the environment and to offer products that, while meeting customer requirements, will also meet the expectations of other groups.

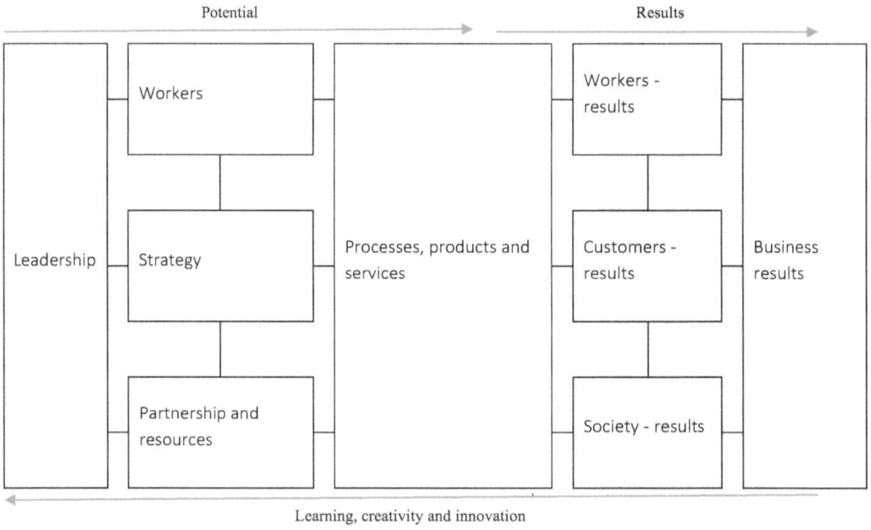


*Figure 4.2* EFQM Excellence Award Model (EFQM 2013: 13)

Considering quality in terms of value, one should therefore refer to certain moral obligations of the enterprise and its owners, even though this aspect is particularly difficult for enterprises. Many companies are still unable to define their commitment to maintaining high quality in moral terms. While a large proportion of the activities undertaken may be worthy of respect precisely from a moral point of view, the enormous potential for generating this involvement remains untapped due to the failure to apply moral discourse in the normal, day-to-day activities of enterprises. Companies see quality improvement as a path to certification that can help them cope with competitors. Meanwhile, a broader and less defensive attitude would be more beneficial (Pratley 1998: 121).

As P. Drucker emphasises, the right quality ensures regular customers and is the strongest weapon in the fight against competitors and the only way to the constant development of the company and achieving profit (Drucker 1995: 34). Despite the studies that do not confirm the relationship between quality management and the financial performance of companies (cf. Przybyłowski et al. 1998: 43), it is widely believed that poor quality can be a source of market loss. This regularity seems to be confirmed by the famous statement of P. Crosby: "quality is free, poor quality costs money".

High quality of products, services, and finally processes is a value for the company itself. The benefits that may result from the improvement of quality include, inter alia, lower costs (as a direct effect of reducing waste), greater efficiency, and ultimately the possibility of lowering prices. In order to achieve such effects, however, it is not enough to implement a quality assurance system in the company's practice, which, as the name suggests, is a confirmation of the repeatability of the process, and not a guarantee of high-quality product or service. The only weapon in the competitive struggle is the high and responsible quality of products and services compared to market standards.

Qualitative competition is therefore a prerequisite for survival in the current market, and a broader view of quality can provide benefits to customers, society, and, consequently, additional value to the company. Enterprises should therefore feel forced to constantly improve quality and look for more effective ways to provide consumers with products that meet their requirements, while considering the expectations of other stakeholders. A fairly original approach to quality is represented by R. Shaw, who makes the possibility of achieving success based on quality conditional on combining it with marketing. Shaw proposes to change the approach to quality and the measures used. In his opinion, the company's goal is, first of all, to study the perception of customers in terms of quality and value provided to them by the company and to fully and continuously satisfy their needs in this area (Shaw 2001: 41, 43–55).

The already mentioned environmental aspect is an essential element in the process of creating the quality of the products delivered today. Both consumers and opinion-forming circles formulate demands in the area of environmental performance of products. From the point of view of enterprises, however, there is doubt whether investing in green technologies is profitable. In practice, environmentally friendly products are basically similar to their conventional versions, with the difference, however, that they are less harmful to the environment, but often more expensive. Ecological aspects relate to all product characteristics and are assessed throughout the product life cycle, including the procedure after its end of use.

Consumers' preferences in terms of purchasing products from the so-called "green" companies cause that enterprises are more and more often interested in, inter alia, use of environmentally friendly technologies. Increased interest in purchasing "green products" and the ability to differentiate themselves from competitors in this way encourages companies to invest in environmentally friendly technologies. There is even the concept of ecological quality, i.e. quality based on ecological values, which has come to be perceived as a factor in the competitiveness of enterprises. According to A. Chodyński, quality in this approach is a competence consisting in creating added value by distinguishing a product, process, or the entire organisation in the eyes of the client and/or other stakeholders (Chodyński 2011: 183).

An important element of the process of creating and offering environmentally friendly products is also the possibility of specific labelling of these products, indicating their eco-labelling. Investments in environmentally friendly technologies give companies the right to "eco-labels", that is, ecological symbols.

Eco-labels are a potentially important variable as consumers are more likely to choose products with at least a neutral environmental impact. Research also shows that many consumers are willing to pay more for products that symbolise environmental values (EPA 1998; Teisl et al. 2002). Consumers prefer environmentally friendly production, natural raw materials, and boycott products that may be a threat to the future of society (Pratley 1998: 122). However, the degree to which these values are considered is not the same. The differences can be seen not only within the segments identified in the market, but also between countries. It also causes a diversified interest in the so-called environmental performance of products, which is still related to the relation of revenues that the company can obtain from the sale of these products with the costs of their production.

## Co-creation of value with customers as an element of value-based marketing

The company's primary goal is to create value for the customer in a better way than the competitors do (Brilman 2002: 54). Meanwhile, the key to creating value is co-creating offers that mobilise customers (Normann, Ramirez 1993: 69). Customers are one of the company's main assets that can generate value growth, thus creating value for shareholders. Achieving such an effect is possible only when the customers' problems, the values they expect, and, above all, when the customer becomes a co-creator of these values are well identified (Dobiegała-Korona 2008: 29).

Twenty-first-century customers have more options than just satisfaction with their purchase. The rapid development in the computer world has transformed modern society from a production culture focused on the production of goods and services to a culture that focuses on the exchange of information. This led to the emergence of a network society (Castells 2000). Changes in the market in conjunction with unlimited access to information have changed the customer from isolated, unaware, and passive to related to the company, informed and active. The modern client wants to influence every part of the business system (Prahalad, Ramaswamy 2004a: 4). The reasons for such changes include the departure of business from formal, defined, and well-established practices and roles over the years. Deregulation, globalisation, technological convergence, and the rapid evolution of the Internet have obliterated the roles we have become accustomed to as participants in the market exchange process. Suppliers are no longer passive suppliers of materials and parts, but active collaborators who contribute to the value of the enterprise. There was also a tightening of cooperation between enterprises and entities participating in the distribution process. However, these changes did not consider the changes in customers to the same extent. Meanwhile, the traditional way of delivering value to clients also ceased to be optimal for them (Prahalad, Ramaswamy 2000: 79–80).

The changes taking place on the market have changed the perception of value by customers. They are no longer interested in the purchase itself, and the physical characteristics of products and services are not of sufficient value to them. C. Prahalad and V. Ramaswamy called a "traditional" product an artefact around which the experiences of consumers who do not want to limit their experiences to patterns created by producers are shaped (Prahalad, Ramaswamy 2000: 83).

The authors of the concept of co-creating value together with clients are considered to be Prahalad and Ramaswamy, who in 2004 published a book entitled *The Future of Competition: Co-creating Unique Value with Customers* (Prahalad, Ramaswamy 2004). These authors argue that companies can no longer operate on the principles previously generally accepted. Until now, product design, development of production processes, creation of marketing messages, and control of sales channels have been carried out with little or no participation of the consumer. Meanwhile, armed with new tools and dissatisfied with the available choices, consumers want to interact with companies and participate in creating value for themselves, thus co-creating value for the enterprise (Prahalad, Ramaswamy 2004a: 5).

The idea of co-creating value appears in numerous publications. F. Kleemann, G. Voss, and K. Rieder identify the so-called a new type of consumer, i.e. the working consumer, showing his involvement in the crowdsourcing process.[1] For these authors, crowdsourcing is a solution that allows people who do not have any relationship with the company to work for it or its clients. By responding to crowdsourcing calls, consumers thereby contribute to the company's efforts to innovate either product or process. The authors also add that the emergence of a working consumer is independent of specific technologies, and his skills and willingness to engage in work are increasingly used for commercial purposes (Kleemann et al. 2008: 23).

For K. Rieder and G. Voss, these changes are nothing more than a consequence of the previously started process of transferring some business activities to customers. To the previous stages, these authors included: (1) the opening of warehouses (end of the 19th century), which enabled the customers to self-service and allowed the enterprise to save on personnel; (2) the introduction of self-service stores in retail (the first Piggly Wiggly Store in Memphis (Tennessee) opened in 1916), in this case written product information replaced the sales advisory service, companies also saved on the customer service process (e.g. packing of goods); (3) extension of self-service to the service sector (the 1970s): gastronomy (McDonald's), gas stations, etc. (the example is also given of IKEA, which moved product assembly to customers' homes); and (4) introduction of vending machines, including ATMs (1980s), which operated by customers perform some of the activities previously performed by employees (Rieder, Voss 2010: 2).

Each of these stages increased the involvement of consumers in processes previously perceived as activities assigned to business, reducing the activities performed by employees. A similar situation is taking place today. The consumer simply seeks to gain greater control over the production processes of products and services (Rieder, Voss 2010: 3). Therefore, the involvement of customers in the co-creation of value is not a sovereign decision of the organisation, but a response to reported customer expectations.

The concept of co-creating value with the customer partially refers to the concepts of prosumer and presumption. The concept of a prosumer was used for the first time by A. Toffler, who created it from the combination of the words producer and consumer (Toffler 1980: 27, 406–439). A prosumer is a consumer involved in the co-creation and promotion of goods or services and their simultaneous consumption. In the process of presumption, it is not only the production of the product that is valuable, but the activities related to it, which are the consumer's experience.

In the concept of presumption, the customer's participation in the consumption of the product is clearly emphasised, i.e. it is assumed that the actions taken by the customer allow for the creation of value, but the result of his involvement is the production of products that ultimately consumes and which become his consumption experience (Lusch, Vargo 2006: 284; Xie et al. 2008: 109). Meanwhile, the concept of value creation does not assume the need to consume manufactured products (Kleemann et al. 2008: 23).

The client began to be perceived as a source of co-creation of the company's value (Prahalad, Ramaswamy 2000) and also involved in the process of creating innovations. There were proposals for open source i.e. open innovations (OI) models and user innovation (UI) models that assumed the co-creation of new solutions by customers, using communities focused around a clearly defined, specific problem, which is developing new solutions, products, services, or concepts (Von Hippel 2001: 86).[2] Over time, these models have come to be referred to as user-driven innovation (UDI) and are treated as a consequence of the evolution of models and systems for understanding innovation (Howaniec, Okrzesik 2015: 13).

The possibilities of engaging customers in the processes of creating innovative solutions were also indicated, among others, by C. Prahalad and M. Krishnan (Prahalad, Krishnan 2010: 166) or C. Grönroos (Grönroos 2011). According to Grönroos, in the present conditions of competition, the client wants to control both the creation and determination of value (Grönroos 2011: 294). Meanwhile, the utility value of the process of co-creating value by the client is the function of his experience and logic (Grönroos, Voima 2013: 133).

The future of competition therefore lies in a completely new approach to value creation. The process of co-creating value with the client based on the principle of interaction will be effective. Consumers want to interact and co-create value, not only with one company, but with a community of professionals, service providers, and other consumers (Prahalad, Ramaswamy 2000: 83). Thus, providing the consumer with the opportunity to co-create value can contribute to the company's success. The consumer's potential is a valuable source of competences that may allow the company to grow.

Taking into account the customer's voice in the process of creating innovations and new solutions in the enterprise has its justification: (1) customers are the main generator of enterprise value, and at the same time a resource that is difficult to access, therefore enterprises must manage customers in such a way that their value is transferred to the enterprise value; (2) consumers as buyers are the best source indicating future trends in business development, and thus the directions of necessary investments ensuring an increase in the value of enterprises; (3) consumers are the best verifier of the adopted business models, the value offered and the effectiveness of companies' activities, through the acts of acquiring value at specific prices and ways of engaging in the activities of companies (loyalty, recommendations and co-creation processes) (Dobiegała-Korona 2014: 26).

The interactive and interdependent nature of value co-creation processes is a challenge for traditional management practices. It requires proper preparation of the organisation, including changes in management systems and traditional organisational structures. The traditional system of roles and functions assigned to the enterprise and other participants of the current exchange process must also be changed. The customer ceases to be an "entity" that buys a product designed and delivered by the enterprise and becomes a value co-creator. Marketing turns into a "structure" of relationships, meetings, and dialogue. The share of knowledge in creating a competitive advantage of enterprises is also increasing, which should focus on operational resources as a key unit of exchange (cf. Payne et al. 2008: 93).

The concept of a prosumer and the concept of co-creating value with the company's customers have changed the image of the traditionally understood process of planning, preparing, and delivering a product or service. In both cases, the customer takes an active part in the entire process. Through his commitment, he co-creates value that is also of value for the company. However, it is necessary to extend the concept of co-creation to other stakeholder groups, including suppliers, participants of distribution channels, or opinion-forming circles. Clients do not always have specialist knowledge in the area of creating a specific value, unlike some stakeholders who are also interested in the development of the company. Using the knowledge of suppliers, intermediaries and independent experts can bring an enterprise much higher value than co-creating products only with consumers. This means that value "co-creation" should be replaced by the term "co-innovation". A new global business ecosystem where individuals, organisations, governments, and economies are networked and interdependent needs a new model of innovation. A model that will be based on a platform on which internal, external, collaborative, co-created ideas will be able to create solutions based on shared value, considering the interests of all stakeholders (Lee et al. 2012: 818).

## A changing of nature of promotion: from traditional to the responsible

The area of marketing that is subject to a radical transformation in relation to the known, well-established solutions is also the process of communication of companies with the so-called market. The change in the nature of the communication process, the way of impact, and the entities to which the message is addressed puts into question the current way of defining promotion. From the point of view of marketing, the value of changes in the area of corporate communication concerns the following issues:

1. there is a change in the area of promotion channels used, from the channels typical for one-way communication, the interest of both broadcasters and recipients shifts to channels allowing direct interaction,
2. the content of the communication changes, i.e. the message must be meaningful to the recipient,
3. the ethics and responsibility of formulated messages increases.

The saying that a good product is not enough to be successful in the market is still valid. In order to sell it, you need a proper promotion. Today, this means, more than ever, effectively communicating information to the customer about the features and value of a product in a manner acceptable to the customer and maintaining customer satisfaction throughout the value creation process.

The reason for the biggest changes in the area of promotion is technological progress in the field of technologies related to information, communication, and the way in which data is collected in order to create new technologies and solutions for business. People all over the world are connected to each other via the Internet, which serves them as a tool for sharing information on an ongoing basis for personal, social, scientific, or business purposes. Telecommunications, medical, educational, entertainment, and social technologies flourished thanks to the network economy (Lee et al. 2012: 819). Currently, about 4 billion people worldwide use the Internet. Information and Communication Technologies (ICT) has become a catalyst for the digital world, thus changing the existing business models. Currently, all types of organisations, from global giants to entities from the group of small and medium-sized enterprises, use a network in which they establish and conduct cooperation, co-create values, implement distribution, and even consumption.

The progress in the field of ICT has increased the role of consumers in creating enterprise value, and thus in the process of communication between the enterprise and the market. Marketing communication is increasingly seen as two-way, and the process itself as interactive. Currently, customers can dialogue with suppliers at every stage of product design and delivery. Thanks to the wide access to information, incl. about companies, products, technologies, prices, or consumer reactions from around the world, consumers are no longer passive recipients of marketing messages created by enterprises. They are committed customers who, in a network environment, create value together with enterprises through custom, co-produced offers. Co-creating value with the client is desirable from the point of view of the company and is treated as an interactive process of shared learning (Ballantyne 2004: 121). Changing the nature of communication from one-way to interactive can help companies emphasise the point of view of consumers and improve the process of identifying their needs and desires.

Online consumer services are taking on a new meaning in most industries. Communities (consumer networks) have emerged, the involvement of which shapes the demands placed on the products and services offered, thus reversing the traditional top-down structure of marketing communication. For companies used to limiting the flow of information to consumers, this change is radical. Information restrictions still exist, but they are rapidly eroding, changing the conditions of competition. It has also become more difficult to communicate the values provided by brands. Traditional advertisements presenting the product in a positive light assumed the lack of verification of the information provided. With today's access to knowledge, the client has the opportunity to confirm the truthfulness of the message. Treatment of the client so far, therefore, it has ceased to be effective, and even companies with an established position are forced to constantly take care of their image, especially in terms of leadership and innovation. The introduction of new mobile communication devices, such as smartphones, tablets, made the competitive advantage based on new products, without constant innovation, fragile. This forces a change in the approach to the client. The communication technology revolution changed the flow of ideas and information, decentralising it from producers who had the capital to create and broadcast content to consumers. New communication technologies provide consumers with new and diverse forms of information, while being interactive, two-way means of communication. Providing interaction in such perceived marketing communication of companies is a very important element that determines its effectiveness. However, the interaction between the parties is only possible if the transmitted content is of good value. The message must be meaningful to the recipient, otherwise it will not get their attention. Contemporary marketing communication – as J. Wiktor writes – can basically only take place through a specific dialogue in which, on the one hand, the enterprise participates with its information and promotion activities, and on the other hand, the consumer – with the structure of his needs and preferences, and its task is to create and integrating values (Wiktor 2016: 50, 52–53).

Co-creating value changes the approach to the company's marketing activities that require a solid revision. The traditional roles of producer and consumer have faded away, and the control and predictability that have been used to rely on existing marketing lose their importance in this process. The ideal would be to create a balanced, collaborative, and harmonious relationship between producers and consumers, where controlling the co-creation process with consumers would ensure a predictable and satisfactory result for the company. Unfortunately, the reality is slightly different from this ideal. Co-creation of value is a cooperation of increasingly interconnected, chaotic environments in which control is rapidly shifting towards consumers (Fisher, Smith 2011: 325).

The need to create real value for the customers has increased the interest in using social networking sites, content sites, or – somewhat less frequently – virtual social worlds for marketing practice (Kaplan, Haenlein 2010: 59). There are new terms such as social media marketing or content marketing (cf. Howaniec 2014a: 172).

Marketing in social media is activities consisting in gaining traffic on a website and attracting attention through social media (Trattner, Kappe 2013: 88). More and more publications confirm the high efficiency of social media as a content carrier in modern marketing. Already in 2010, the results of M. Stelzner's research indicated a positive impact of social media on the effectiveness of companies' marketing activities. According to the report, 85% of respondents indicated that their activities in social media generated better exposure of the company on the market, 63% indicated increased customer traffic, and for 56%, marketing in social media resulted in new business partnerships (Stelzner 2010: 5). Also, in the 2018 report, the surveyed marketers confirmed the positive impact of social media on the company's results. As many as 87% of respondents indicated that their activities in social media resulted in greater exposure of the company, and 78% said that the benefit was the increased customer traffic. For 53%, activity in social media allowed for an increase in sales (Stelzner 2010: 11).

Content marketing is a general term that covers all marketing formats that rely on the creation or sharing of content to engage existing and potential consumers. Content marketing is, inter alia, on publishing and disseminating via the Internet, attractive and useful content, such as articles, e-videos, podcasts, graphic forms, etc., aimed at a strictly defined group of recipients (Handley, Chapman 2012; cf. Gębarowski 2007: 96–119). Live streaming is a popular way to ensure interaction with your audience in real time.

The emergence of new tools allowing for effective contact with the client inspired W. Visser to propose a new concept of CSR, i.e. the concept of CSR 2.0. Visser emphasises the convergence between Web 1.0. and traditional CSR and Web 2.0[3] and the concept of CSR 2.0 described by him. While one can argue with him as to the perception of CSR (which he described as philanthropy activities, subordinated to PR requirements), it is difficult to disagree with the author as to indicate a change in the scope of promotion measures used by enterprises and the methods of its implementation. The emergence of social media, user-generated content, and the open source movement[4] has introduced radical changes in the field of promotion, including in the area of CSR communication. The Internet has changed from a one-way communication driven by advertisers' demands to a collaborative communication. Tools provided by Google and Facebook allow for real-time interactions. According to Visser, similar changes are necessary in CSR communication, which should be more interactive and consider the voices of various stakeholders (Visser 2010). The similarity between Web 2.0 and CSR 2.0 is presented in Table 4.1.

The change in the nature of CSR activities towards creating common value has also changed the way of shaping the company's relations with other stakeholders. Ad hoc, dedicated business reactions undertaken in response to identified problems must be replaced by comprehensive, strategically justified

*Table 4.1* The similarity between Web 2.0 and CSR 2.0 according to W. Visser (2010: 317)

| *Web 2.0* | *CSR 2.0* |
|---|---|
| It is defined by the slogans: "collective intelligence", "collaborative networks" and "user participation". | It is defined by the slogans: "global communities", "innovative partnerships", "stakeholder engagement". |
| Tools include social media, content syndication,[5] and beta testing.[6] | Mechanisms include stakeholder panels, real-time transparent reporting and new wave social entrepreneurship. |
| According to the maxim: Is the state of being technical progress? A new philosophy or way of looking at the world has emerged. | There is a visible shift of power from centralised to decentralised, a shift of scale from a few large to many small, and a shift of applications from singular and exclusive to many and shared. |

solutions. The approach to CSR based on care for reputation and PR has ceased to be credible. Greenwashing is treated as a CSR trap, and as a justification I am saying that social responsibility is more than just communication. Social reporting should be reliable. Meanwhile, many companies treat social reporting as an additional element of marketing in such a negative way that they focus on highlighting activities that are not really of value to society or other stakeholders. Interest in the so-called "greenwashing" is particularly high among companies with a low level of social commitment, which tend to pay particular attention to social reporting and to present CSR practices in such a way that misleads the recipients of the report (Bazillier, Vauday 2009: 30–31). The use of "green argument" is, however, much less effective than it used to be. Consumers in particular have become more demanding and sceptical about the content on social engagement presented by companies. They notice that many companies emphasise, for example, their commitment to environmental protection, and the social reports lack evidence that confirms it or the actions taken are more "image-building" than they solve any problems. Such an approach results in lowering confidence in the information contained in reports on CSR practices, which are more and more often treated as an element of the company's PR, or even referred to as business rhetoric. This is solely due to a wrong approach to social reporting which should be simply accountable and honest. Even in the area of PR, greater attention should be paid to social and political effects.

The reliability of the formulated messages is an important aspect of today's marketing communication. From the interest in techniques of influencing the customer (cf. Howaniec 2000; 2001), the company's effort was shifted to content creation. Stakeholders generally do not react negatively to emphasising companies' commitment to CSR, but react negatively to any marketing strategies that appear to be manipulated or misleading (Forehand, Grier 2003: 355). Ethics and social responsibility are treated as the key to communication between business and the market. Marketing is less manipulative and more targeted at the target audience. However, in order to be able to talk about reliable or "moral" communication, it must be characterised by such features as, among others (Pratley 1998: 187):

1 openness – all participants of the exchange and negotiation process should have the right to express their opinion (this means, among others, respect for the moral autonomy of employees and open relations with the company's environment),
2 mutual respect – all participants have equal rights, including the right to be solicited for their own interests, which should be accepted by each of the parties (formulating statements based on mutual benefit),
3 logical consistency – using reasoned arguments.

This means that in addition to the economic aspect, which is very important in shaping the company's marketing communication, it is also, or maybe most of all, its substantive content that counts. However, the change in the approach to the communication process means that the costs of communication between the company and the market in the current conditions cannot be treated as company expenses, as it has been the case so far, but as an investment in brand development. Such an investment increases both current sales and future sales (Doyle 2008: 304). It is a mistake to judge marketing and communication expenses in terms of sales or immediate profits. Rather, these expenses should be assessed in terms of their expected impact on the net present value of the future cash flows. A significant part of the expenditure on communication with the market is an investment in building intangible assets, i.e. brands, relations with customers, and other stakeholders of the company. Developing a communication strategy also builds the company's knowledge and allows to understand the markets, which increases the efficiency of basic business processes. Strong brands, marketing expertise, and strong relationships enable the company to introduce new products more efficiently, maintain customer loyalty, and run an efficient supply chain. In turn, these processes increase the company's potential to increase the value of the enterprise itself, which is tantamount to increasing the value for shareholders (Doyle 2008: 304). The communication model based on P. Doyle's value is presented in Figure 4.3.

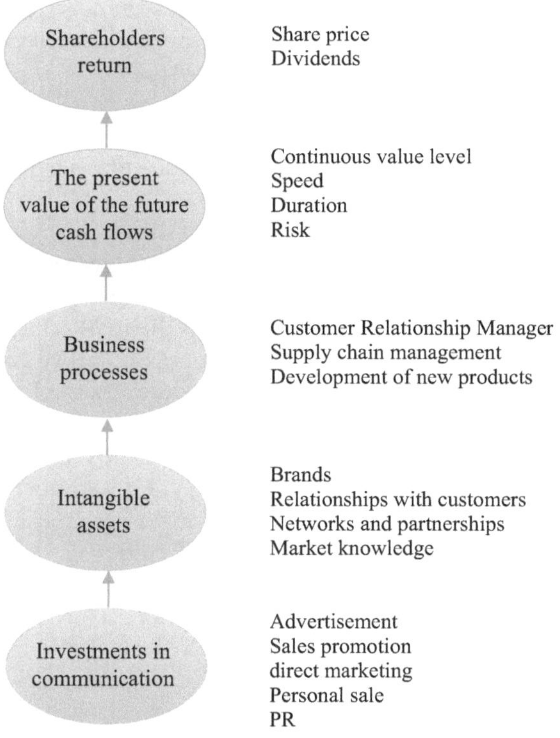


*Figure 4.3* Model of communication based on P. Doyle's values (Doyle 2008: 305)

The co-production of value with the client, which means his involvement in the entire value creation chain, the need to shape positive relations with all stakeholders and the requirements for content caused that marketing is not only moving towards "real-time" marketing, but the market has become a place of active customer involvement. The consequence of changes in the area of promotion is the increased importance of marketing communication and dialogue in the co-creation process identified in this way. Communication with the marketplace must focus on all relevant channels and consider all kinds of "meetings" (contacts) that will support cognition, emotion, and action-based learning. From the perspective of benefits, one can also consider broader communication of corporate social commitment. Thanks to CSR, consumers can implement important goals and values in their daily activities by identifying with the company involved in social problems that are important to them.

## Price responsibility

The approach to marketing activities from the point of view of creating shared value assumes that both the product and other elements of marketing will be able to generate, or at least consider, additional value for the customer, thus contributing to an increase in shareholder value. While it is relatively easy to imagine delivering real value for customers or other stakeholders in the area of the company's product or communication, some difficulties may arise from the idea of creating value in the pricing process. Meanwhile, the need for change is also recognised in this area. The rationale is based on two issues: (1) the importance of price in creating enterprise value and (2) resulting from external conditions the increase in the importance of price in creating the value for customers.

Although the importance of prices from the point of view of the company's financial indicators is high – prices affect, among others, on shareholder value by influencing the margin and sales volume – the subject of pricing is not as popular in the literature as it is related to the other elements of the marketing composition. The impact of even a modest price increase on profitability is much higher than that of other operating management levers. For example, a 5% increase in the average selling price increases profit before interest and taxes (EBIT) by an average of 22%, while adequate changes in turnover and cost reductions lead to an increase of 12% and 10%, respectively (Hinterhuber 2004: 766).

Despite the perceived increased price competition and difficulties in setting prices, some managers are convinced that the only regulator in this area is the market. Businesses focus on costs and volumes, not price. They do not even collect the relevant information that would allow them to fix their prices more efficiently. Methods consisting in adding a standard margin to the estimated cost of a product or service are still widely used (Howaniec

2009: 175). Pricing based on costs or in relation to competitors in most cases leads to profitability below the target.

The development of the social approach to marketing activities contributed to a different view of the pricing policy of enterprises. The term value-based pricing has emerged, which means a type of pricing policy in which, when making pricing decisions, the benefits that customers perceive in relation to the purchase of a product or service in relation to their price are considered (Ingenbleek 2014: 33). Value to the customer is thus defined as the difference between the net benefit received and the price paid. These benefits include not only economic benefits, but also functional and psychological benefits.

Proponents of value-based pricing policies include, among others, A. Hinterhuber. The author points out that there are two misconceptions in the market in terms of pricing that contribute to pricing based on the cost or price of competing products: (1) it is assumed that premium prices and high market share do not coexist; and (2) it is assumed that customers know product prices and are price sensitive. As Hinterhuber proves, these assumptions are incorrect in both cases. First, the assumption that only low prices and the use of a penetration strategy can achieve a dominant position in terms of market share is not supported by any evidence. The products whose prices have been established on the basis of a skimming strategy (high-price strategy) often have a high market share. Second, consumers show little interest in the prices of the goods they buy, while managers generally tend to believe that price is the most important issue for customers. High market share and high prices can be achieved when they truly reflect high customer value. It is only necessary to have a solid understanding and quantification of the product's value for the customer, and a tool that is helpful in this area is customer value analysis (CVA) (cf. Hinterhuber 2004: 766–767, 777).

Customers are often unaware of the prices paid, and for them the price is one of the least important criteria for choosing a product or service. When making a purchase decision, they are guided by the perceived value of the products. If they can get more value from another supplier, they will probably choose that. The advantage of customer value (CV) analysis is that it helps a company identify specific attributes of its products or services that increase the perceived customer value (PCV). Thus, CVA measurement is an effective way to track the company's competitiveness in relation to the characteristics of the product or service that customers value the most. These data allow the company to react quickly and appropriately, which in turn allows to protect or improve the company's position on the market.

Knowing the perceived value to the customer can suggest when and where prices can be increased without risking losing sales and is also a good clue for pricing new products. The relentless focus of enterprises on price competitiveness is unjustified. Moreover, rather than creating and transferring value to customers, enterprises risk undue attention to the current characteristics of competitors' products, regardless of whether they meet customer requirements and truly offer them real value.

A price calculation based on the perceived value by the customer allows the company to perform better in the sector. Firms using value appraisal as their core pricing principle consider themselves ahead of the competition when it comes to managing their prices. They rate their own pricing outcomes as better than those using a cost or competitive approach. Moreover, not only their self-esteem turns out to be better. Value-driven pricing seems really worthwhile when it comes to closing trades. Firms using conventional pricing methods often win by undercutting competitors' prices, but risking margin erosion and price wars. Participants driven by a value perspective succeed by drawing customers' attention to product parameters and winning through strong business relationships and knowledge of customer needs (cf. Kurz, Többens 2012: 10). A positive relationship between the value-based price and the company's results was also found by S. Liozu and A. Hinterhuber (2013: 605–606).

The need to reformulate the current way of setting prices also results from changes in the market. Today's dynamic markets are more price sensitive, necessitating a discussion of current pricing methods. Broader consumer control of range, price, and cost in different geographic areas restricts businesses' freedom to set and change prices. Prices offered in one market affect prices that may be offered in others.

The information revolution and the Internet have also destroyed the simplicity of uniform prices, restoring individual negotiated prices and bargaining. Widely available price comparison websites allow to check sellers' prices across the market, intelligent sales agents find the best deals for customers, and online auction sites allow buyers and sellers to negotiate prices. We can also come across solutions that completely reverse the existing purchase process, where the customer places an order by specifying the conditions to which potential suppliers of products or services meet.

Price decisions are becoming more and more critical due to the increasing complexity of the markets. Meanwhile, pricing based on value for the customer requires the company to apply additional organisational solutions. The most important of them is the change in the company's pricing policy, which forces, among others, support from top management. Among other issues, the literature highlights the need to implement appropriate pricing processes, the availability of customer value data, and the adjustment of the sales force to value-based pricing (cf. Kienzler 2018: 86).

## Creating value in the area of distribution

The information revolution has a large impact not only on the promotion strategy, but also on the distribution strategy. As has been shown in the previous chapter, the company's website is increasingly becoming the first source of information about the company's products and offers. However, this means that the existence of intermediaries between the producer and the consumer ceases to be justified. The main distinguishing feature of the new approach to shaping distribution is the integration of distribution channels and the return to direct sales. Suppliers having direct contact with the customer in the process of communicating the offered values, determining the desired product characteristics (mass personalisation of the offer) and prices, cease to need intermediaries. The only effort to deliver the product in a timely manner to the place requested by the customer is to ship the product to the address provided by the customer. Such a view of distribution necessitates changes in its basis. The functions traditionally assigned to intermediaries in the process of delivering the product to the market will be taken over by producers, or the nature of the support provided by distribution will change. The task of intermediaries will not only be the traditional transfer of the product from the place of its production to the place of consumption, but also a wide customer service, including, inter alia, product and price arrangements (e.g. online stores).

The reason for changes in the area of distribution is changes in the area of communication and information technologies. New opportunities not only allow for increasing the integration of activities carried out by the company, but also cause, inter alia, disappearance of the differences between the company's communication with the market and distribution (cf. Lipowski 2016: 101–104). There is an integration of marketing and logistics in the structure of enterprise management (cf. Kauf 2005: 13–15). A commonly used solution is the omnichannel strategy ("omnis" is Latin for "every/all") i.e. strategy where is an integration of all physical channels (offline) and digital channels (online) to offer a unified customer experience.[7]

Research on the integration of distribution channels was carried out, among others, by X. Koufteros, M. Vonderembse, and J. Jayaram (Koufteros et al. 2005) and M. Swink, R. Narasimhan, and C. Wang (Swink et al. 2007). The role of information technologies (IT) in the integration of the production supply chain was also investigated by S. Devaraj, L. Krajewski, and J. Wei (2007) and M. Swink and A. Nair (2007). The shortening of distribution channels is also indicated by P. Doyle, for whom the evolution that is currently taking place on the market is primarily the transformation of the traditional business model into a model based on coordination and concentration (Doyle 2008: 12).

In the traditional model, there were intermediaries, who were the link between the producer and the final recipient of the product. However, the changes that occurred on the market, and in particular in the IT area, resulted in closer contact and increased integration with the buyer, which in turn resulted in shortening the channels and excluding intermediaries (Figure 4.4). This model, called by P. Doyle direct, is a model, in which the sale is made directly to the customer and to the customer's direct order. Instead of traditional vertical integration of the distribution channel, i.e. control and coordination through ownership, we have virtual integration, i.e. control and coordination through information.

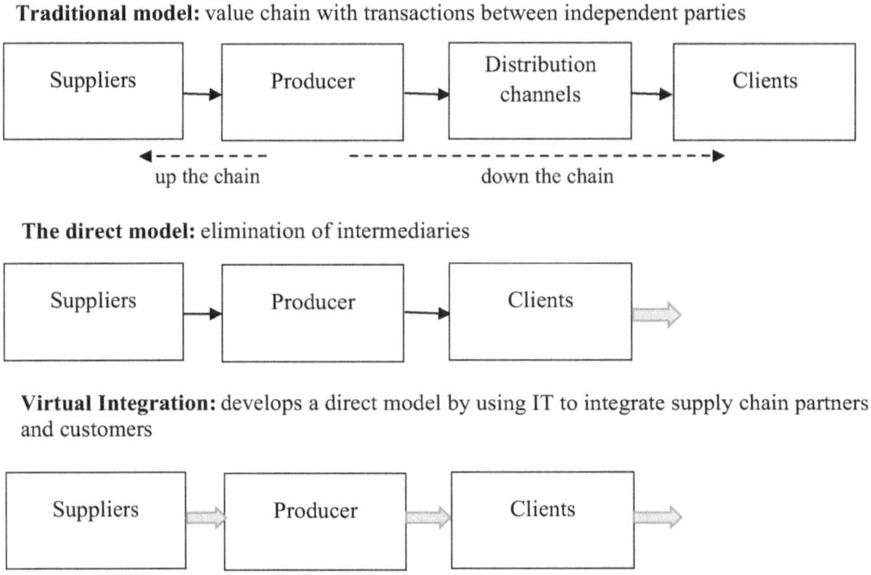


*Figure 4.4* Evolution of the new business model according to P. Doyle (2008: 13)

Eliminating intermediaries from distribution channels provides additional benefits to both the business and the consumers. Integration in the area of distribution allows, among others to (cf. Doyle 2008: 12):

1. improvement of customer relationship control – functions performed so far by an intermediary are performed by the producer who, through direct contact with the customer, will be able to influence the quality of maintained relationships,
2. reduction of distribution costs – the execution of orders for individual customer orders allows for the elimination of stocks and reduces the risk resulting from forecasting the size of consumption demand,
3. increasing value for the customer – adjusting the offer and communication to the exact requirements of the customer increases the value delivered to the customer, contributing to the growth of his loyalty,
4. shortening the time of purchase – purchases made with the use of modern distribution channels allow you to make them without leaving a home,
5. lowering purchase costs – shortening the distribution channel by eliminating intermediaries will significantly reduce transaction costs and the product itself (elimination of intermediaries' margins).

As we can see, shortening the distribution channels may be associated with an increase in value for the consumer and the enterprise. Customer participation in the product delivery process, on the one hand, will increase his involvement in the consumption process, and on the other hand, it will provide him with additional benefits, which are a real value, primarily of a material nature. Changing the approach to distribution will also change the value realised by the company, which will not only establish direct contact with the customer, but by individualising the approach to the customer, it will eliminate the entities that have been distributing products so far.

## Brand as value for stakeholders

According to the classic definition, a brand is a name, concept, graphic symbol, drawing, colour, melody, or a combination of these elements, created to mark a product or service and to distinguish it favourably from the competition's offer. Such an approach to the brand is presented, among others, by P. Kotler and G. Armstrong (cf. Kotler, Armstrong 1989: 248) or T. Kramer and J. Altkorn (cf. Altkorn and Kramer 1998: 140–141). The brand is defined in a similar way by D. Aaker, which defines it as a name and/or symbol (such as a logo, trademark, packaging) designed to identify a good or service of an individual or group of vendors and to distinguish them from competing products (Aaker 1991: 7). L. De Chernatony and M. McDonald, on the other hand, define a brand as a product or service, person or place, clearly distinguishable from others and presented in such a way that the buyer or user can easily perceive significant, unique added values, preferably satisfying his needs (De Chernatony, McDonald 1998: 25).

J. Kall defines the brand much more broadly, according to which it is such a combination of a physical product, brand name, packaging, advertising, and accompanying activities in the field of distribution and price, which, by distinguishing the offer of a specific marketer from competitive offers, provides the consumer with distinctive functional benefits and/or symbolic, thanks to which it creates a loyal group of buyers, thus enabling its owner to achieve a leading position on the market (cf. Kall 2001: 12).

Considering the definitions in the literature, it can be assumed that a brand is the sum of tangible and intangible elements, such as name, sign, symbol, packaging, price, promotion, and distribution activities as well as myths, values, and emotions associated with it, which provide consumers with functional and symbolic benefits, positively distinguish it from competing brands, thus enabling its owner to gain an advantage on the market (cf. Howaniec 2008: 485).

Branding, however, is not only about adding value to the product. When analyzing brand definitions, it can be noticed that there has been a certain shift in the area of brand functions. Originally, the brand was defined as an element whose main and often the only task was to identify the products marked with it, thus distinguishing them from the products of the competition. Currently, the brand, in addition to identifying and distinguishing the company's offer, performs a number of other functions, equally important from the point of view of the marketing process, including those related to the broadly understood business environment. By creating an emotional bond with customers, a brand identifies not only the company's offer, but also the company, becoming a synonym for the policy it adopts.

The interest in the brand as an element of communication with all the company's stakeholders results mainly from the trust that customers place in the company's brand. This trust creates a brand-customer relationship that encourages preference, brand loyalty, and a willingness to incorporate new products and services that the company may offer in the future (cf. Doyle 2008: 227). The influence of the brand cannot, however, be considered only in terms of the brand owner – customer. A brand is a tool that has a more or less direct impact on all stakeholder groups (Figure 4.5). Thus, branding is of value not only to customers, who are the company's key stakeholder, but also to other groups, namely (cf. Howaniec 2013: 12):

1 The brand provides benefits to customers – a strong brand provides consumers with values such as: high quality, responsibility, it is an element of psychological satisfaction of consumers; identifies actions taken by the company, influencing the possessed values, beliefs, and attitudes of consumers.
2 A brand influences the culture of its owner – brand management within the organisation becomes culture management, consisting in creating the right organisational climate and nurturing values important for the organisation. A good, responsible brand is also an important element of the HR policy, which affects both current and future employees of the company.
3 A strong brand contributes to strengthening the positive opinions of consumers regarding the high quality of the offered products, their reliability, the attractiveness of the price-quality relationship (i.e. the perceived value of products and services) and to creating the belief that the company cares for both consumers and the well-being of the entire society.
4 Strong brands contribute to the improvement of the standard of living by offering products that use the latest technologies, including environmental protection technologies, appropriate selection of product or service attributes, and social commitment to solving problems important from the point of view of society.
5 Strong brands care for relations with cooperators, including by maintaining long-term, development-based relationships with suppliers and entities in the area of distribution.
6 Enterprises with strong brands are more interested in creating a positive image of the company on the market, therefore they engage in sponsorship and charity activities more often than others, thus influencing local communities and/or society in general.
7 Interest on the part of the society and the media in the activities of entities with strong brands makes them particularly responsible in terms of contacts and obligations towards public administration and the media.

Therefore, a strong brand is not a resource that provides benefits only to customers and the enterprise itself (a brand, by increasing its value, significantly increases the value of the enterprise, contributing to an increase in value for shareholders). Brand management has clearly shifted from customer-oriented management towards a more balanced approach of considering the interests of all groups around the company with which it interacts in any way (cf. De Chernatony 2003: 12).

By representing and promoting a lifestyle, brands influence the internal life of consumers, i.e. their values, beliefs, and attitudes. Increasing commitment to CSR is at least partly stimulated by the growing belief that consumers reward companies that are good citizens through greater and more lasting patronage (cf. Lichtenstein et al. 2004; Luo, Bhattacharya 2006). Consumers do tend to choose products of companies that engage in CSR activities, especially in areas that consumers find appropriate and relevant (cf. Sen, Bhattacharya 2001; Klein, Dawar 2004; Sen et al. 2006].

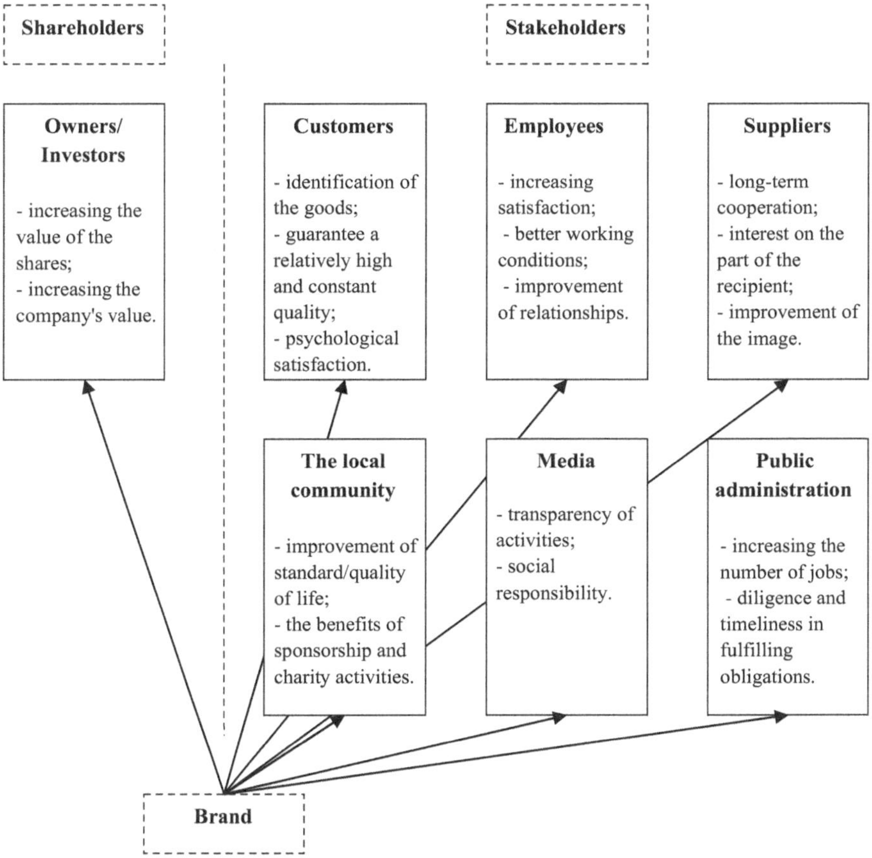


*Figure 4.5* Brand influence on the company's stakeholders (Howaniec 2013: 59)

Brand, trust, and reputation are also the main reasons why companies are interested in CSR. To the question: What factors prompted you, as CEO, to act on the issues of sustainable development, as many as 72% responded that it is a brand. The next ones are the increase in revenues and reduction of costs (44%), personal motivation (42%), and customer demand (39%) (Figure 4.6).

The brand's communication value goes well beyond the customers' area. CSR contained in brand capital - brand social equity[9] repositions the brand not only in the minds of consumers, but also other stakeholders. A brand identity based on CSR is (at least at the present time) not only fundamental and relatively durable, but also more distinctive than identities based on innovation or other values. Unlike other positioning strategies, CSR-based positioning humanises a company or brand by encouraging consumers not only to like, respect, or admire the company, but actually identify with it (cf. Bhattacharya, Sen 2003). The brand's social capital also positively influences the brand's value (Howaniec 2010). However, corporate social engagement is more effective when it is linked to the core competencies of a brand. S. Du, C. Bhattacharya, and S. Sen argue that the same CSR activities can trigger different consumer reactions depending on the extent to which they are perceived as separate activities from the brand base. Strategic linking of CSR with the brand brings more benefits than the mere involvement in CSR, even when such commitment is known and liked. CSR reveals the core values or character of a brand and is more clearly related to the desired deeper, longer-term relationships with consumers than other positioning strategies (cf. Du et al. 2007: 237).

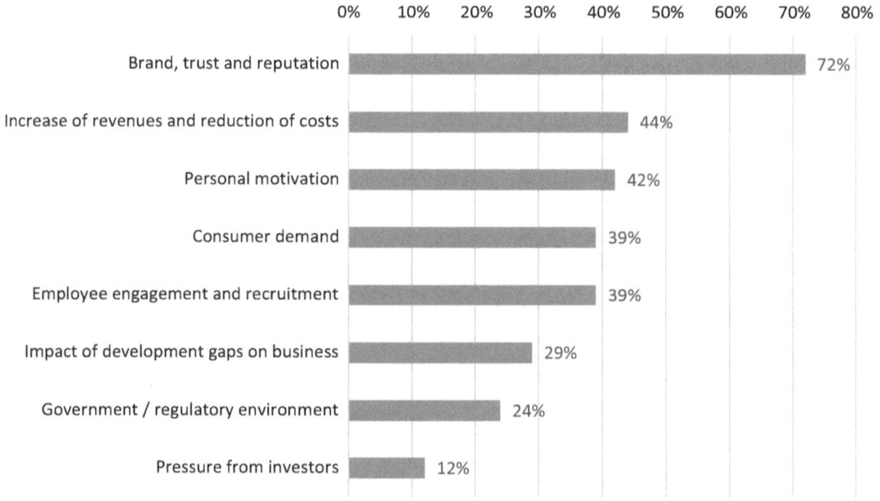


*Figure 4.6* Motives for acting in the area of sustainable development[8] (UN Global Compact 2010: 20)

## Employer's brand as an element of value-based marketing

Although people who are workers enjoy the same natural rights as everyone else, they do not have any additional rights as workers. In particular, they do not have any special moral rights to a specific wage or job, to collective bargaining, to job security, organisation, or privacy. According to E. Sternberg, the only rights we have at the time are those granted to us under applicable law or in the employment contract. Meanwhile, moral or natural laws result from human nature and their justification is based on human nature. This means that these rights belong to human beings as moral entities (Sternberg 1998: 149).

A brand traditionally related to the company's products or services, more and more often is also related to a company (corporate branding), even though it was emphasised a few years ago that in the case of enterprises we are talking about corporate image or corporate reputation. The brand is even related to other functional areas of the enterprise (cf. Keller, Lehmann 2006). For example, in the area of human resources management, such a concept as employer branding has appeared. Enterprises wanting to ensure access to properly prepared employees more and more often take actions aimed at shaping their brand as a good employer.

Employer branding has the same theoretical foundations as consumer branding or corporate branding. The employer communicates his goals, values, and strategy to current and potential employees, using available communication channels, including social media, in a way that will allow it to be better distinguished from the offers of the competition (Howaniec 2018a: 167).

In the era of public acceptance of the CSR concept, more and more enterprises are not limited only to care for safe working conditions, which for some means only compliance with the provisions shaping the health and safety at work in the enterprise, but consciously shapes the employer's brand, caring for the development and satisfaction of employees. The justification for this approach to the employee is also the situation on the labour market. Employers are trying harder and harder, on the one hand, not to lose a good employee, and, on the other, to encourage potential interested parties to join the company.

The concept of an employer brand suggests that the company distinguishes itself from its competitors in the area of those characteristics of the company that identifies it as an employer. The brand, or how often it can be found in the literature – the image of the employer, emphasises the unique aspects of the employment offer or the company's environment (Backhaus, Tikoo 2004: 502–503). T. Ambler and S. Barrow define the employer's brand in terms of benefits, calling it a package of functional, economic, and psychological benefits identified with the company provided by employment in a particular company (the employer's brand image can be defined analogously) (Ambler,

Barrow 1996: 187). S. Lloyd from employer branding defines it as the sum of the company's efforts to convey to current and future employees that it is a desired workplace (Lloyd 2002: 64). The addressees of the activities undertaken are therefore not only potential employees, but also people already employed. From this point of view, it is important that the communication of the adopted strategy, i.e. the company's value system, policy, and behaviour, is directed both outside and inside the company (Howaniec 2018: 135).

The high importance of employees as recipients of marketing activities of enterprises is indicated, inter alia, by W. George and C. Grönroos (1989; George 1990) who argue that the organisation's personnel is any company's first market. L. Berry and A. Parasuraman think similarly. These authors emphasise that the product of work must attract, develop, and motivate employees who are also consumers. In this case, employees buy a product from the employer, which is work (Berry, Parasuraman 1991: 169).

When creating an employer's brand, one should influence two groups: (1) currently employed and (2) potential employees. According to K. Backhaus and S. Tikko, these activities should run in two ways. The main factor influencing the already employed is the image of the company and its organisational culture. The employer consciously forms his identity in the area of the so-called place of work and shapes ties with employees, thus influencing the loyalty of employees towards the company. With regard to potential employees, meanwhile, they are much more important the so-called associations related to the employer's brand and the image of the employer's brand. They ultimately shape the perceived attractiveness of the employer (Backhaus, Tikoo 2004: 505).

Therefore, the recommended two-track actions exclude the legitimacy of using the same tools for current and potential employees. After defining a specific "employee value proposition" (EVP), which should communicate what the organisation has to offer to employees, it directs this message outside in order to attract desired employees and inside (internal marketing – IM) – in order to consolidate the image of the organisation in existing employees (Backhaus, Tikoo 2004: 502–503). The proposed activities in the area of employer branding are presented in Table 4.2.

K. Backhaus and S. Tikko distinguish the three-stage process of employer branding. First, the company must develop a "value proposition" to be embedded in the brand that will be the main message to current and future employees. Using information about the culture of the organisation, management style, characteristics of current employees, the current picture of employment, etc., the company should develop a concept of value that will be consistent with other messages of the form, and that it wants to offer to current and future employees. After the value proposition has been developed, the company should begin the process of selling it. In addition to current and future employees, the addressee of the prepared value proposition should be recruitment agencies, employment agencies, etc. The main goal of the activities undertaken is to attract the so-called target market. The third stage is the

*Table 4.2* Activities in the area of employer branding (Howaniec 2018a: 170)

| | *Employer branding targeted at potential employees* | *Employer branding targeted at current employees* |
|---|---|---|
| Activities in the area of employer branding | Internship programs<br>Activities of the company ambassador<br>Activity in social media<br>Promotion of offers in search engines, SEO, SEM positioning, AdWords and AdSense advertisements<br>Recruitment Videos<br>Participation in job fairs<br>Active presence of the company at universities<br>Organising open days | Employee opinion surveys<br>Communication with employees: newsletter, brochures, Intranet, information boards<br>Good communication on the line: manager – employee<br>Meetings with the management<br>No discrimination in hiring, promotion and layoffs<br>Enabling professional development/career path<br>Appropriate motivating system (material and non-material motivators)<br>Additional amenities program, e.g. medical care, facilities for young mothers, etc. |

internal marketing of the employer's brand, the aim of which is the development and involvement of the company's employees in the established set of values and organisational goals (Backhaus, Tikoo 2004: 502–503).

Employers are increasingly using non-standard methods of attracting and retaining employees, and they are also expanding the list of amenities addressed to people already employed. Pro-social companies are more inclined to better motivate employees, avoid lawsuits and penalties, and care for a positive public opinion. The starting point for employer branding is the conviction that in order to have satisfied customers, the company must also have satisfied employees

## Notes

1 Crowdsourcing is a process in which an organisation (company, public institution, non-profit organisation) outsources tasks traditionally performed by employees to an unidentified, usually very wide group of people in the form of an open call.
2 Open innovation (OI) and user innovation (UI) are two separate concepts, introduced by H. Chesbrough (father of open innovation) and E. von Hippel (father of user innovation). Open innovation is a company-oriented paradigm that primarily deals with the use of external knowledge to improve internal innovation and thus the company's economic performance. User innovations mainly concern people who use innovations to meet their own (often unique) needs, without considering the company's success (Piller, West 2014, p. 29).
3 Web 2.0 – definition of websites in which the content generated by the users of these websites plays a fundamental role.
4 Open source – open access, or open software, the license of which allows for legal and free copying of content.
5 Content syndication (web syndication) is a solution that allows you to collect and share information on the Internet.

6 Beta testing – operational testing of computer software by potential and/or existing users (customers), usually on a voluntary basis, to determine if a component or system meets their needs. Testing is done on an external site that is not related to programmers.
7 Omnichannel strategies unite user experiences across multiple touchpoints, including brick-and-mortar, web, and mobile apps.
8 UN Global Compact survey based on 766 responses. The respondents were choosing the three most important factors.
9 The social value of a brand is a set of features attributed to a brand by stakeholders in connection with its ethical, social and environmental activity.

# 5 Value creating in practice – social responsibility as an element of value of enterprises, research results

## The awareness and perception of the social responsibility of business

The first step to identify the role of CSR in creating value for enterprises is to determine what is the awareness of CSR and to what extent both groups, i.e. enterprises and customers, take it into account in their actions.

As shown by the research conducted so far on the Polish market by the Responsible Business Forum, Polish consumers perceive themselves as responsible (68%), i.e. they think that they make deliberate purchases, which means they only purchase the necessary products. Only 7% of respondents who described themselves as responsible consumers admitted that they buy products of companies that act ethically. The respondents highly appreciate the activities of companies in the field of environmental protection, ensuring adequate remuneration and working conditions for employees, or activities such as ensuring appropriate conditions for animal husbandry and not testing products on animals.

Each of these elements was approved by almost 90% of respondents. When confronted with examples of unethical behaviour, such as destroying the ecosystem, expressing racist views by an entrepreneur, violating children's rights, or leading to the death of an employee, they do not indicate that such activities affect their market choices. Destruction of the ecosystem and expression of racist views by the owner for 50% of respondents is not a reason to give up the services of a certain company. In the event of violating the rights of children and leading to the death of an employee, 40% of respondents would remain faithful to their choices (RBF 2018: 9).

As the results of the survey show, the awareness and considering of CSR in the conditions of the Polish economy are not high and have remained at this level for several years.

In order to determine the awareness and perception of CSR by the respondents, these studies tried to determine the following issues: (1) what is the level of knowledge of CSR in Poland, (2) how CSR is understood, (3) how the implementation of CSR is perceived in the practice of companies operating

DOI: 10.4324/9781003317364-6

in Poland, and (4) what role, in the opinion of the respondents, is played by CSR in the functioning and competitiveness of enterprises.

## Social responsibility of business in the perspective of customers

The obtained results confirm that Polish consumers have little knowledge about CSR. Only 32% of respondents declared that they had encountered the notion of CSR before. The rest (68%) have never had contact with this term before, or at least they do not remember it.

For the respondents, social responsibility is primarily the voluntary inclusion of social and environmental aspects in the strategies and activities of a company (43%) or maintaining good relations with the environment (42%). Some responses indicate that the respondents associate CSR with activities for environmental protection. They answer, inter alia, that CSR is a preventive approach to the natural environment (25%), undertaking initiatives aimed at promoting the attitudes of ecological responsibility (37%) and the use and dissemination of environmentally friendly technologies (35%). For some of the respondents, CSR also means supporting social campaigns (36%), adherence to the principles of sustainable development (23%), and the application of ethics in business (27%) (Figure 5.1).

As in the cited RBF research, the respondents have a positive opinion of Polish enterprises. As many as 61% of respondents believe that they undertake

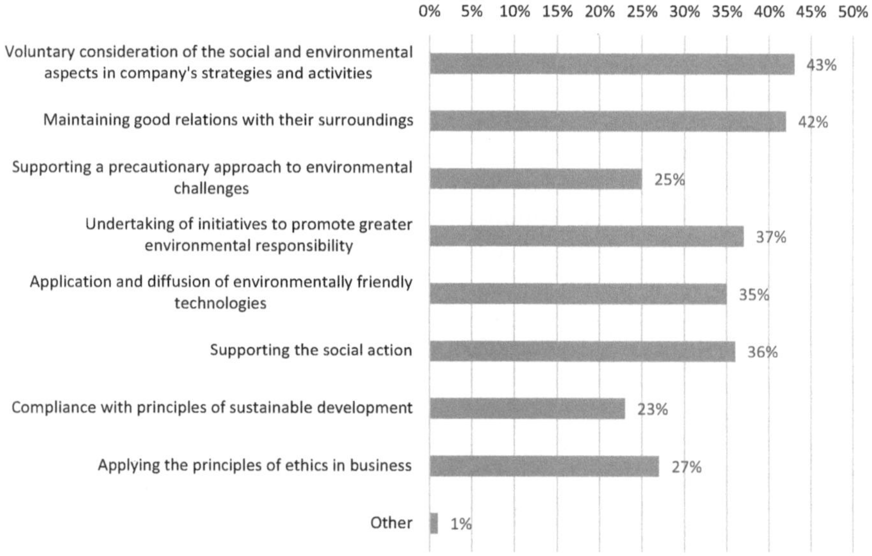


*Figure 5.1* Perception of CSR – customers' perspective (*N* = 502. The results do not add up to 100 because respondents could choose more than one answer. Own study)

CSR activities. However, when assessing the degree of implementation of CSR in enterprises operating in Poland, they are not so optimistic. Only 2% of respondents believe that enterprises operating on the Polish market have definitely implemented CSR principles, 22% believe that the degree of implementation of CSR is rather high. The vast majority are of a different opinion. As many as 64% of respondents are convinced that the degree of CSR implementation is rather low, and 12% believe that the implementation of CSR principles is at a very low level (cf. Howaniec 2015).

The justification seems to be found in the responses to subsequent questions in which the respondents should have specified whether individual CSR principles are implemented in enterprises. The vast majority of respondents (66%) believe that enterprises support and respect human rights adopted by the international community, but only 35% believe that they eliminate all violations of these rights by organisations. As many as 65% believe that companies are not engaged to that extent. The vast majority (60%) believe that enterprises respect the freedom of association. Unfortunately, the respondents poorly assess the current solutions in the field of equal opportunities (discrimination) in the field of employment in enterprises, indicating that most enterprises do not comply with the rules applicable in this area (69% of responses; only 31% of respondents confirmed that enterprises do not allow discrimination in the field of employment). They are also not satisfied with today's approach of enterprises to environmental protection, indicating that enterprises do not present such an approach (57%; 43% of the respondents stated that enterprises have a preventive approach to the natural environment). On the other hand, they positively refer to the involvement of enterprises in initiatives aimed at promoting the attitudes of ecological responsibility (55%) and positively assess the issue of using and disseminating environmentally friendly technologies by enterprises (52% of respondents believe that such technologies are used and popularised by enterprises). The area of "corruption" was assessed the worst. As many as 76% of respondents believe that enterprises operating in Poland do not counteract corruption or its manifestations (cf. Howaniec 2015a) (Figure 5.2).

However, the respondents do not indicate enterprises as the group that is most interested in CSR. When asked to indicate the entities that are most interested in implementing CSR, the vast majority believe that it is a local community (32% answered that it is very important for the indicated group, 28% that it is important). The media was listed in second place (27% and 33%, respectively). And only in third place – in the opinion of the respondents – were enterprises (25% replied that it was very important for this group, and 30% that it was important). According to the respondents, the next groups are customers (according to 21% of respondents it is very important), employees (15%), public administration (13%), investors (12%), and suppliers (5%) (Figure 5.3).

The main difficulties which, according to the respondents, hinder the implementation of the principles of social responsibility in practice are

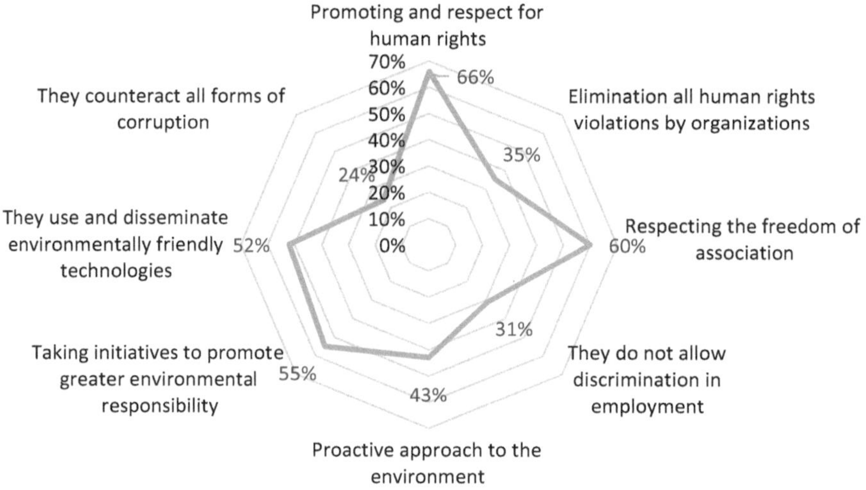


*Figure 5.2* Compliance with CSR principles in enterprises in Poland – customers' perspective ($N$ = 502. Own study)

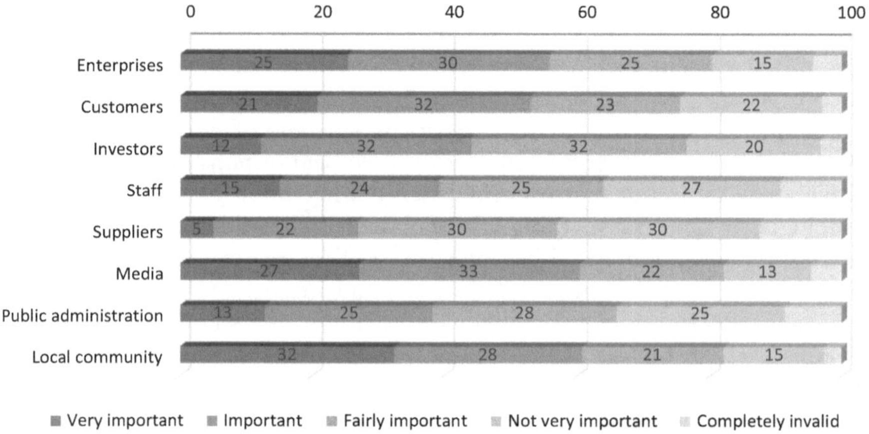


*Figure 5.3* Groups most interested in CSR implementation – customers' perspective (%) (N = 502. Own study)

(in order): (1) insufficient financial resources (60%), (2) lack of interest in corporate social responsibility (40%), (3) insufficient potential of companies (39%), lack of knowledge about CSR (39%), and (4) lack of interest in CSR by company supervisors (31%) and low efficiency of such activities – the costs incurred related to the implementation of CSR into the practice of companies do not, according to the respondents, affect their market effects (26%).

It is not a big surprise how customers perceive the importance of individual stakeholders to enterprises. The obtained answers clearly favour customers – as many as 68% of respondents believe that this group is very important for enterprises, almost one-fifth – that it is at least important (19%). However, investors came second. Half of the respondents believe that they are very important for enterprises (52%) and it is them that enterprises devote a significant part of their attention to. In the case of such stakeholder groups as employees, suppliers, and the media, the vast majority of respondents answered that these groups are important, but not the most important for the company (33%, 46%, and 33%, respectively). In the case of public administration and the local community, the responses indicated a lack of conviction as to the importance of these groups for the current functioning of the enterprise. The dominant indications are that these groups are fairly important (34% and 32%, respectively). A relatively large group of respondents indicated that they are not very important for enterprises (26% and 31%), or even completely irrelevant – such an answer appeared in a large group of respondents (12%) in the case of the local community. In the light of the answers received, several questions can be asked: Do companies operating in Poland really try to implement CSR principles and consider the needs of all stakeholders? Are, perhaps, the actions taken in the area of CSR focused solely on the quick effect of PR? The respondents' lack of knowledge about the importance of individual groups for the enterprise indicates that business practice differs from the theoretical assumptions defining the CSR theory. Consumers apparently have no experience with engaging enterprises in the development of the local community, they do not perceive such activities as employees. They also do not perceive cooperation with public administration or the media as something valuable (Figure 5.4).

However, the respondents believe that enterprises should apply CSR principles in their business activities. This opinion is unequivocally shared by a quarter of the respondents (25% of respondents answered "definitely yes"), and more than half chose the answer "rather yes", thus pointing to some doubts, but presenting a positive position on this issue. Less than 15% of respondents had a negative opinion, while nearly 13% replied "rather no", and less than 2% were unambiguously negative in this matter.

For CSR proponents, enterprises should implement CSR principles into business practice because: (1) they have an impact on the environment, contributing to the emergence of numerous problems (e.g. environmental pollution), in solving which they should also participate (40% of respondents), (2) have a personality legal, they are a kind of citizens who should take care of their environment (28%), (3) thanks to social responsibility, companies can improve their reputation, which affects their competitiveness and thus their competitive position (25%), (4) enterprises have a surplus of income that they can donate to social, local (23%), and ultimately (5) the benefits of using CSR are undeniable (7%).[1] These responses show overwhelmingly moderate support for CSR. The respondents, being at the same time consumers,

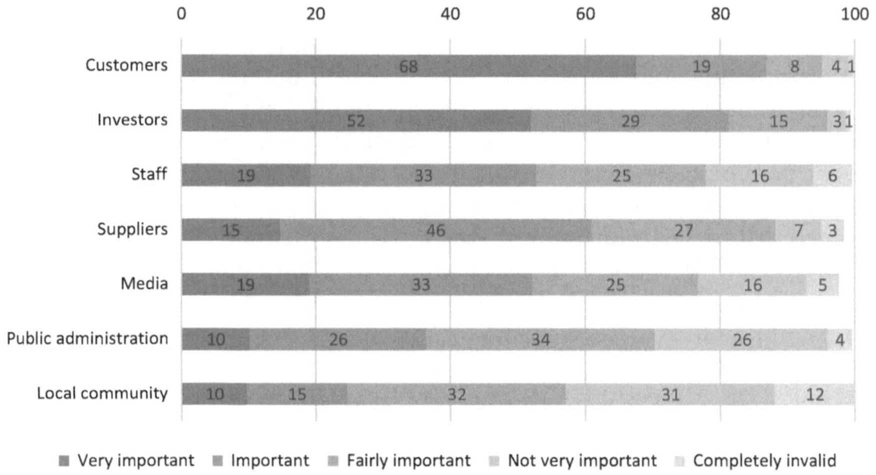


*Figure 5.4* The degree of importance of individual stakeholders for enterprises – customers' perspective (%) ($N = 502$. Own study)

employees, or members of the local community, do not see the need and justification for greater involvement of enterprises and their broad responsibility.

Despite such moderate expectations, the respondents believe that the application of CSR is in line with the interests of the company – 13% answered "definitely yes", 65% "rather yes", in total 78% of the respondents gave an affirmative answer. Only 4% of the respondents believe that it is absolutely inconsistent with the interests of the company, and 18% replied "rather inconsistent", which may indicate some doubts of the respondents in this respect.

In justifying the adopted position, the respondents indicate that: (1) the role of business is a service in the understanding of the obligation to meet the expectations of the company's environment and to balance the interests of groups that operate in it (43%), (2) business is not only about generating profits (35%) and finally that (3) a company is an organisation that serves the interests of a wide group of constituent entities, who should be seen as partners of the company (30%). Unfortunately, a significant proportion of respondents perceive CSR only as an effective PR tool (23%).[2]

When asked about the impact of applying CSR principles on the company's turnover, the respondents were also not enthusiastic about it. Only 10% of the respondents clearly indicate that in their opinion there is a positive correlation in this area. The vast majority of respondents chose the answers indicating the uncertainty as to such an impact, i.e. almost half believe that there is a relative positive impact of CSR on the value of the company's revenues (48%), but as many as one-third (34%) is of the opposite opinion, i.e. they claim that such an impact is unlikely to occur. Almost 8% of the respondents gave a negative answer.

According to the respondents, compliance with the CSR rules by the company has a positive impact on the company's image (the answers "definitely yes" were given by as many as 28% of the respondents, and the answers "rather yes" – 54% of the respondents). Only 3% of respondents believe that there is no relationship between these variables, and 15% believe that the impact is ambiguous.

The respondents also see the impact of CSR on customer loyalty to the brand. It is true that in this case only 13% of respondents are convinced of such a dependence, but as many as 59% believe that such practices have a rather positive impact on the repeatability of customer choices. One-fourth of respondents do not see such a relationship, but provided a conditional answer ("probably not"), and only 3% believe that such an impact does not take place.

## Perception of social responsibility among enterprises

The level of CSR awareness among respondents on behalf of enterprises is slightly higher than among customers. Only 37% of respondents indicated that they had encountered the term CSR earlier.

For the respondents – as in the case of customers – CSR is primarily the voluntary inclusion of social and environmental aspects in the strategies and activities of the company (67%) and maintaining good relations with everyone in the company's surroundings (59%). However, the respondents in this group rank further the use and dissemination of environmentally friendly technologies (38%) and a preventive approach to the natural environment, supporting social campaigns, and applying the principles of ethics in business (27% of responses each). Slightly fewer respondents believe that it is undertaking initiatives aimed at promoting the attitudes of ecological responsibility (22%) and adherence to the principles of sustainable development (17%) (Figure 5.5).

The respondents were also asked: Do they think their company undertakes CSR activities? However, the answer to such a question may surprise. According to the answers provided, as many as 65% of respondents perceive themselves as responsible because they gave an affirmative answer.

A contradiction of this position is the answers to the question about the degree of implementation of CSR principles in the companies they represent. Only 2% answered that it was definitely high, and a quarter of the respondents believed that it was high (25%). This means that despite the fact that the respondents perceive themselves very well, in fact they do not believe that the actions taken by the represented enterprises were sufficient. This way of looking at own enterprises confirms the point of view of customers for whom the degree of implementation of CSR in enterprises operating on the Polish market is rather low (Figure 5.6).

Respondents were also asked about the implementation of individual principles, which were announced at the World Economic Summit in Davos

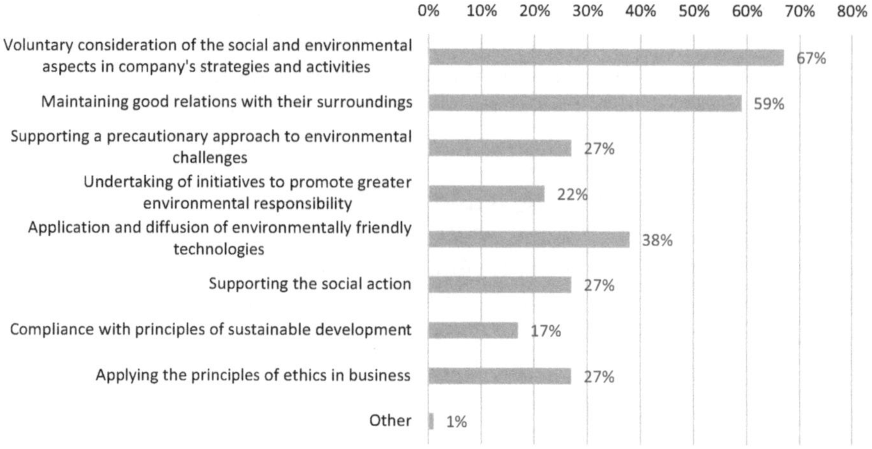


*Figure 5.5* Perception of CSR – enterprises' perspective ($N$ = 150. The results do not add up to 100 because respondents could choose more than one answer. Own study)

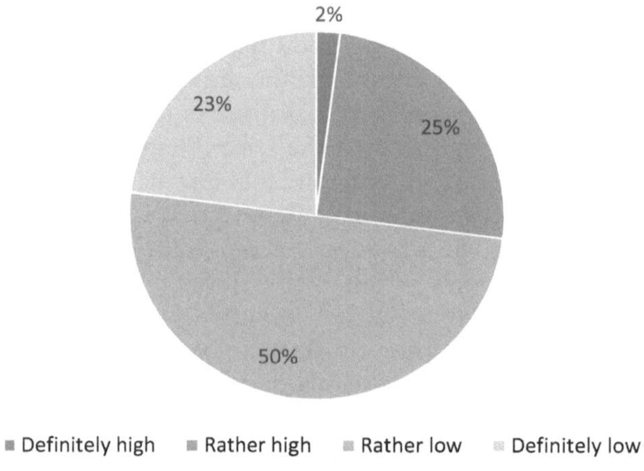


*Figure 5.6* Assessment of the implementation of CSR principles in enterprises operating in Poland – enterprises' perspective ($N$ = 150. Own study)

(supplemented in 2004), and which – according to the Global Compact program – enterprises should follow, regardless of whether they are required by the law of a given country, or not.

The obtained answers clearly confirm that entrepreneurs perceive themselves much better than their recipients of the activities in question. For example, as many as 96% of respondents believe that their companies support and respect human rights adopted by the international community. They also rate themselves very high in the area of care for the employee, i.e. as many as 89% believe that enterprises do not allow discrimination in the area of employment. A very large group also believe that enterprises eliminate all human rights violations by organisations (73%) and respect the freedom of association (81%). This would even indicate the priority of human rights in the management of enterprises operating on the Polish market and their market behaviour, including contacts with other stakeholders, for example suppliers. At this point, it would be justified to ask about monitoring, for example, working conditions in enterprises performing orders for Polish enterprises. Do Polish enterprises really show such a far-reaching concern for respecting human dignity? The area related to the natural environment is also positively assessed. As many as 86% of the surveyed enterprises have a preventive approach to the natural environment, 67% use and disseminate environmentally friendly technologies, and 54% undertake initiatives to promote the attitudes of ecological responsibility. A relatively large proportion of respondents also indicated that they counteract all forms of corruption (77%) (Figure 5.7).

According to the results, CSR in the everyday practice of enterprises is quite important. The respondents not only indicate that activities were undertaken in this area (it is assumed that the indications regarding the company's ecological responsibility resulted from the actual activities undertaken by companies), but also confirm that the companies themselves are interested in CSR. When asked to indicate entities that are most interested in implementing social responsibility in economic practice, they indicate public administration in the first place (27% answered that it is very important for

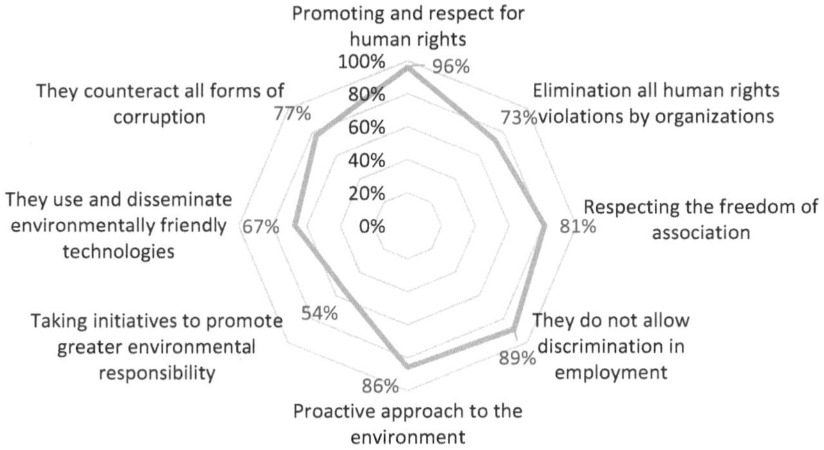


*Figure 5.7* Compliance with CSR principles in enterprises in Poland – enterprises' perspective ($N$ = 150. Own study)

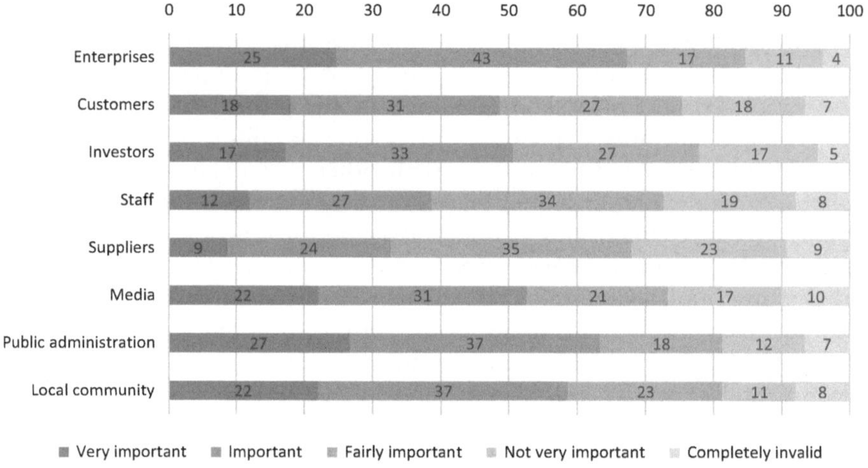


*Figure 5.8* Groups most interested in CSR implementation – enterprises' perspective (%) ($N$ = 150. Own study)

the indicated group, and 37% that it is important), but in their opinion, in second place is business (with the number of responses, analogously: 25% and 43%). Respondents answering on behalf of enterprises also see high interest in CSR among local communities (22% replied that it was very important for this group, 37% that it was important) and among the media (22% and 31%, respectively). The next in order (according to the highest priority assignment) are, according to the respondents: investors (17%), employees (12%), and suppliers (9%) (Figure 5.8).

The main obstacles, perceived by the respondents as difficulties in implementing the principles of social responsibility in practice, are insufficient financial resources. This opinion is shared by slightly more than half of the respondents (51%). For the respondents, it is also the low potential of small companies – as many as 43% share this opinion and the low effectiveness of CSR activities (34%). Therefore, as the answers show, the surveyed enterprises do not combine CSR with the possibility of increasing the economic value of the enterprise, which is certainly one of the most serious reasons for not taking social responsibility into account in the strategies and activities of enterprises. As many as one-third of respondents are convinced that the costs incurred in connection with the social involvement of enterprises do not affect their market effects. In the opinion of the respondents, the interest in social responsibility is also low. This opinion is shared by as many as one-third of respondents (33%). A similar number of respondents also believe that the level of knowledge on CSR is low (29%). Some respondents attribute the blame to supervisory authorities, indicating that they are not interested in CSR (20%) (Figure 5.9).

Confirmation of the presented position is the indication of the priority of customers as the most important group of recipients of enterprises' activities, in combination with a relatively low assessment of the importance of other stakeholders. According to the answers, the most important group for the respondents are customers – as many as 88% of respondents indicated that they are very important, and 11% that they are important. In contrast to the answers obtained in the group of the so-called customers who indicated investors in the second place, entrepreneurs indicated employees as a group that is particularly important in the opinion of enterprises. As many as 54% believe that this group is very important for the company, and 37% believe that it is important. Suppliers were indicated next, with the number of responses: 38% as the most important and 40% as an important group for business. Investors were classified by respondents in fourth place. Nearly one-third consider this group to be very important (27%) and almost the same number consider it important (29%). The respondents attribute low importance to the local community. About one-fifth of respondents believe that this group is very important for companies (23%). The lowest ratings were given to the importance of public administration (12% believe that it is a very important group) and the media (11%) (Figure 5.10).

Despite ignoring the importance of, among others groups such as the local community, which indirectly confirms both the low knowledge of CSR assumptions and the lack of practice in this area, the respondents believe that enterprises should be socially involved. As many as 18% of the respondents answered "definitely yes", clearly confirming the need to implement CSR in business practice, and as many as 70% of respondents answered "rather yes",

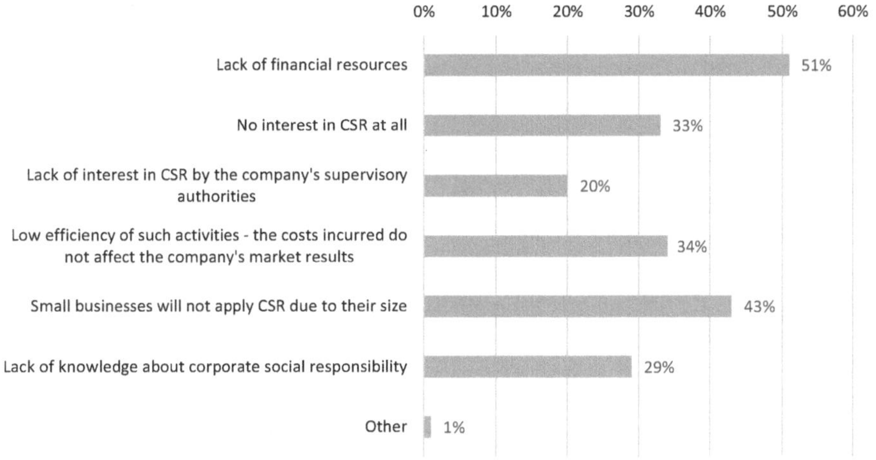


*Figure 5.9* Barriers to the implementation of CSR in practice – enterprises' perspective ($N = 150$. The results do not add up to 100 because respondents could choose more than one answer. Own study)

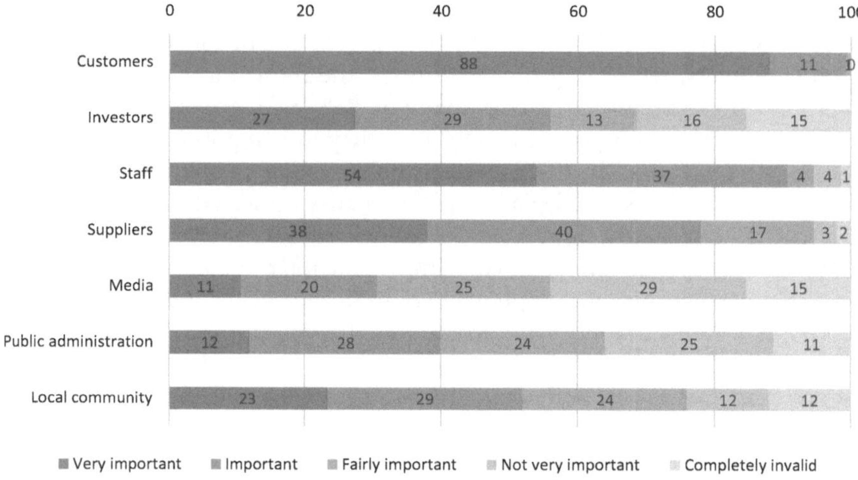


*Figure 5.10* The degree of importance of individual stakeholders for enterprises – enterprises' perspective (%) (*N* = 150. Own study)

which means that in case of partial doubts they believe that considering CSR in the company's activities is necessary. A total of 12% of respondents have a different opinion, but only 1% of respondents strongly believe that enterprises should not apply the CSR concept in practice.

As a justification for their involvement, entrepreneurs mention primarily the impact of business on the environment (40% of respondents). The respondents agree with the statement that enterprises contributing to the emergence of numerous problems (e.g. environmental pollution) should also participate in solving them. Almost one-third of the respondents (30%) see the potential of CSR as a tool to improve the reputation and thus the competitiveness of enterprises. A similar number believe that enterprises have legal personality, so they are a kind of citizens who should simply take care of their surroundings (29%). A very small number of respondents agreed with the statement that companies have surplus income that they can donate to social purposes or to the local community (11%). Such an answer is somewhat contradictory in perceiving oneself as a good citizen. This means that, on the one hand, the respondents confirm their willingness to be a good "neighbor", but they do not associate it with sharing income surplus. This, of course, may also mean that they do not have the surplus and therefore do not have the opportunity to share it with society. The smallest number of respondents indicated the benefits of implementing CSR in practice – only 3% of respondents (Figure 5.11).

The respondents also believe that the application of CSR is in line with the interests of the company (19% answered "definitely yes", 68% "rather

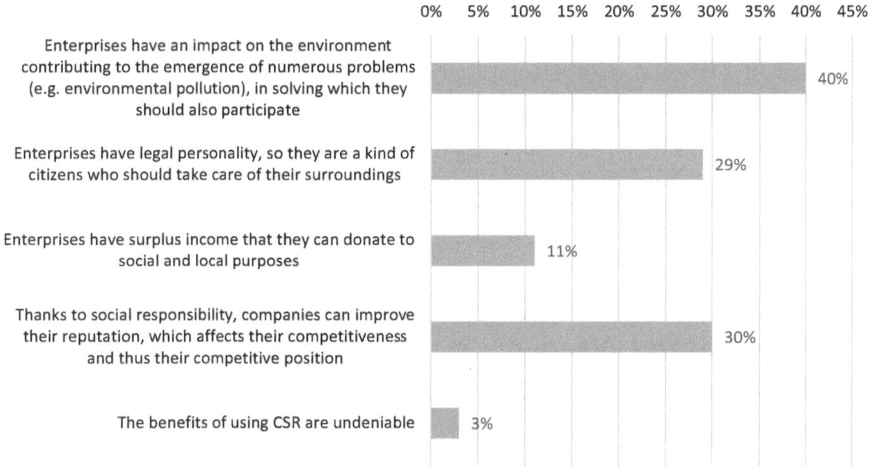


*Figure 5.11* Justification of considering CSR in practice – enterprises' perspective ($N$ = 150. The results do not add up to 100 because respondents could choose more than one answer. Own study)

yes"), in total 87% of the respondents gave an affirmative answer. Only 1% of the respondents believe that this is absolutely inappropriate from the point of view of the company's goals, and 12% replied "rather inconsistent", which may indicate some doubts of the respondents in this respect.

In justifying the adopted position, the respondents – as opposed to the dominant responses in the group of customers – indicated in the first place that an enterprise is an organisation that serves the interests of a wide group of entities that constitute it, who should be perceived as partners of the company (41%). A quarter of respondents also believe that the role of business is not only about generating profits. Slightly fewer people agree with the statement that the role of business is a service in the sense of the obligation to meet the expectations of the enterprise's environment (19%). And the least number of respondents, because only 12% believe that CSR is an effective PR tool.[3]

The respondents are very positive about the relationship between the social commitment of the enterprise and the size of its turnover. Although only 8% of respondents believe that such an impact definitely occurs, more than half indicate such an impact conditionally, giving the answer "rather yes" (52%). In the group representing business, fewer people believe (also in relation to customers) that there is no positive dependency between CSR and the value of the company's revenues (40% in total), and only 3% are unequivocally convinced that there is no such relation.

According to the vast majority of the respondents, the social commitment of enterprises has a positive effect on the image of the enterprise (the answer "definitely yes" was given by 9% of the respondents, and the answer "rather yes" was given by as many as 65% of the respondents). Only 1% of respondents believe that it has no impact on the image of the company, and 15% do not have an unambiguous opinion, but believe that such an impact does not exist.

The respondents also see the impact of CSR on customer loyalty to the brand. Admittedly, in this case 14% of respondents are convinced of a definite dependence, but as many as 60% believe that such an influence exists (the respondents answered "rather yes"). Nobody answered that there was no such dependence, and only 26% gave a conditional answer "probably not".

## Activities in the area of business social responsibility as an element of value creation

Determining the values of corporate social involvement is not easy, both from the perspective of customers and companies. When it comes to consumers, the level of knowledge of the assumptions of the CSR concept, and even of the term itself, is primarily low. Therefore, it is difficult to use the available research tools and at the same time to ask about the awareness of CSR and the perception of the impact of activities that fit into the concept of social responsibility on value. In the case of enterprises, the situation is very similar. The respondents also did not confirm the high knowledge of CSR assumptions. Social aspects are not included in the company's accounting documents, which results in the lack of specific data both in the area of expenses and the impact of possible actions on the company's financial results. A limitation was the questionnaire used, which was still the easiest-to-use tool, considering the goals adopted in this study. In order to overcome the inconvenience resulting from the tool used, the respondents were asked a few questions, which largely led to interesting answers. The aim in this area was to determine: (1) whether the respondents perceive CSR in the market activities of enterprises, (2) whether they see value in CSR activities undertaken by companies, and (3) whether they consider the company's social commitment when purchasing. Meanwhile, in the group of enterprises, attempts were made to determine: (1) whether the respondents perceive CSR in the activities of their enterprises, (2) whether they perceive value creation in the activities undertaken in the area of CSR, and (3) whether, in their opinion, the actions taken to influence the market decisions of consumers.

## Social responsibility and value creation – customer's perspective

Despite the relatively positive assessment of enterprises operating in Poland in terms of the application of CSR principles in general, the respondents do not perceive CSR activities as customers and do not consider the social involvement of companies in purchasing decisions. Namely, to the question: have you met CSR activities in the market activities of companies? Most often they answered in the negative (choosing the answer "no"). As many as 89% of respondents did not notice such practices when providing services, and 69% did not experience any activity of enterprises in the area of CSR during purchases. Moreover, these activities are also not noticed in advertisements for products – 63% of respondents, and 80% did not notice advertisements promoting CSR initiatives undertaken by enterprises (cf. Howaniec 2016a). These results are obviously highly unsatisfactory, considering that many companies, including multinationals, not only consider CSR aspects in their activities in the current functioning on the Polish market, but also try to emphasise their activity in promotional activities.

The research also confirms the very low knowledge of the respondents about CSR initiatives undertaken and promoted by enterprises. The respondents, when asked about campaigns promoting responsible behaviour of enterprises, confirm their knowledge of them, however, to a moderate extent.

The largest number of respondents confirmed contact with the campaign conducted by Żywiec Zdrój entitled "Plant a million trees with us" (76%). This campaign is related to the program run under the name "On the side of nature" (in the first years "My Strong Tree"), implemented since 2008, with the next edition taking place every year. The term "Plant a million trees with us" is an advertising slogan used both in advertising messages in traditional media and social media. The program is a long-term activity, by definition it was a response to the need to revitalise the tree stand destroyed by the bark beetle in Żywiec Beskid, and the initiator of the campaign states that by 2018, together with the ARKA Ecological Foundation and the State Forests, 1,000 hectares of land planted with 8 million trees were afforested under this program (Żywiec Zdrój: 9).

The following initiatives are also highly aware of the respondents: "Milk start" (67%), "Tesco for schools" (64%), or "We are proud to support moms" (56%).

According to RBF, "Milk Start" is the first socially useful product on the Polish market (semolina with milk sold in a sachet, which costs about USD 0.15), developed under the Partnership for Health program. Partnership, producer – Lubella company, coordinator – Danone company, distributor – chain of Biedronka stores, and a scientific unit – Institute of Mother and Child, was established in 2004 to prevent malnutrition. The profit generated under the project is allocated to nutritional education, and additional activities undertaken under the program include, inter alia, a competition aimed at students for a drawing on the importance of the first breakfast in the student's diet, a survey on a group of 1000 children on the eating habits of schoolchildren and a series of articles on the functioning of a child at school, with particular emphasis on the impact of the first breakfast on its development (RBF 2011: 37).

The "Tesco for schools" program is one of the programs that has been implemented by Tesco Poland since 2003. The aim of the program is the environmental education of primary and secondary school students by participating in annual competitions aimed at showing children that green solutions are a simple way for environmental protection, and ecology can be profitable. A form of encouragement in this case is numerous awards, also for schools (RBF 2011: 84–85).

"We are proud to support moms", in turn, is the motto of the Procter & Gamble program implemented as part of the global campaign "Thank you, Mom". As part of the program, the company not only conducts philanthropic and charity activities, such as the renovation of a part of the Surgery and Urology Clinic of the Polish Mother's Memorial Hospital in Lodz, or the creation of free social and hotel rooms in Polish hospitals intended for mothers, but also a media campaign, which the goal is, among others fight against prejudices (RBF 2016: 112).

Less known among the respondents are the campaigns carried out by entities on the brewing market: "Enjoy Heineken – be responsible" – a social campaign conducted by Żywiec Group[4] (30%) and "For what it's worth!" – Kompania Piwowarska[5] (17%). The social campaign "Coffee with Fair Trade certificate" by PKN Orlen (17%) is also characterised by very low awareness. However, these campaigns are not promoted as much as the examples that received a greater number of indications, so their knowledge may be conditioned by the degree of reaching the average citizen in Poland with the message.

It should be emphasised, however, that the respondents confirmed the knowledge of individual campaigns from a prepared list of ready-made answers (assisted awareness). Even though there was such a possibility, none of the respondents provided an example other than those listed in the research tool. This, unfortunately, also confirms the low public awareness of the social involvement of enterprises, often involved in the social life of Poles for many years, and making CSR one of the elements in the competitive struggle.

A positive example deliberately omitted from a research tool is, inter alia, social activity of Nivea Beiersdorf. It is a company whose main values, communicated both in promotional messages and undertaken actions, include care, simplicity, courage, and trust, and undertakes a number of activities on the Polish market. They include, among others "Blue Sails", "Safely with NIVEA and WOPR", "100 playgrounds for 100 years of NIVEA", "NIVEA football schools" or "NIVEA yard" (Howaniec 2017a: 103–104). Despite the relative popularity of the above-mentioned actions, unfortunately, no one indicated any of them in the survey.

Polish consumers, however, notice the involvement of companies in sponsorship activities. As many as 57% claim that companies undertake sponsorship activities (6% of respondents answered "definitely yes", 51% "rather yes"), 33% were of the opposite opinion (28% answered "probably no", 5% "definitely not"). Exactly 10% of respondents do not have an opinion on this subject.

The involvement of companies in charity activities is assessed slightly less. In this case, only 4% of respondents strongly believe that enterprises engage in charity activities, and 38% confirm such commitment, but conditionally, giving the answer "rather yes". A total of 43% are of the opposite opinion, where 37% believe that enterprises rather do not undertake charity activities, and 6% firmly deny such activity of companies operating on the Polish market. In this case, as many as 15% of the respondents replied that they had no opinion on this subject.

Despite a positive response to the involvement of companies in sponsorship or charity activities, not all of the respondents provide examples of the discussed activities. In the case of sponsorship activities, at least one example is given by approx. 43% of respondents, and many of them are the activity of multinational companies, such as Coca-Cola, McDonald, about which the respondents have rather heard about in advertising messages. In the case of charity activities, only 18% of the respondents gave the example of at least one entity and its activities. In this case, however, the interest in the activities of the Great Orchestra of Christmas Charity, the Polsat Foundation, the TVN Foundation, Danone, Avon and several other entities whose activity is directly related to the local community is visible.

The adopted attitudes towards CSR were verified by asking more detailed questions, such as: What specific actions do enterprises take in relation to their customers? When asked in this way, more than half of the respondents stated that it was the implementation of systems confirming the quality of the offered products and services (55%), and a comparable number indicated that it was reliable product labelling (53%). Slightly fewer people believe that such action is a reliable indication of the place of production of the product (45%) or having complaint procedures available to consumers (42%). Some believe that enterprises simply provide valuable products – 25%, apply the principles of fair sales and advertising – 20%, are simply fair – 11%, or apply pure rules of the market game – 9%. Unfortunately, nearly one-fourth of respondents believe that enterprises do not undertake any specific activities that are dedicated to customers or are of value to them (24%). The respondents also did not indicate any additional activities which, in their opinion, would be of value for customers.[6]

The respondents were also asked about actions taken for the benefit of employees. In this case, the answers are more positive. More than half of the respondents positively assessed the implementation and compliance with occupational health and safety standards (56%). Improving safety in the workplace was also rated well (49%). The respondents also indicated care for the development of employees. According to the respondents, enterprises provide employees with appropriate training (46%), and most of the respondents indicated that this is free training. The company's activity in the area of employee integration was also assessed positively. Almost half of the respondents indicated that enterprises organise employee meetings, such as picnics (44%). About a third of respondents claim that enterprises respect employee rights (36%) and that they engage in dialogue with employee representatives such as trade unions or works councils (31%). Much less, i.e. about a quarter of the respondents indicate that companies provide good working conditions (27%), treat women and men equally when deciding to laid off from work (26%) or apply a policy of gender equality in access to promotion and professional development (20%). Only a few indicated that enterprises provide special conditions for children of employees (16%) or mothers (7%). A fairly large group, however, believe that companies do not undertake any specific actions for the benefit of employees (19%), which means that they are not fully satisfied with the activities of companies in this area (Figure 5.12).

The respondents perceive the activity of enterprises in contact with the local community much worse. Less than half of the respondents notice activities in the area of sponsorship (41%) and involvement in the promotion of pro-ecological activities (40%). One-third of respondents believe that enterprises reduce the negative impact of their activities on the natural environment (32%) or conduct social or educational projects (30%). One-fourth also believe that companies support employee involvement in social activities (26%). Despite such low ratings, a quarter of respondents claim that companies consider the needs and opinions of the local community (25%). However, definitely fewer respondents believe that companies engage in dialogue with the local community (18%). The involvement of business in

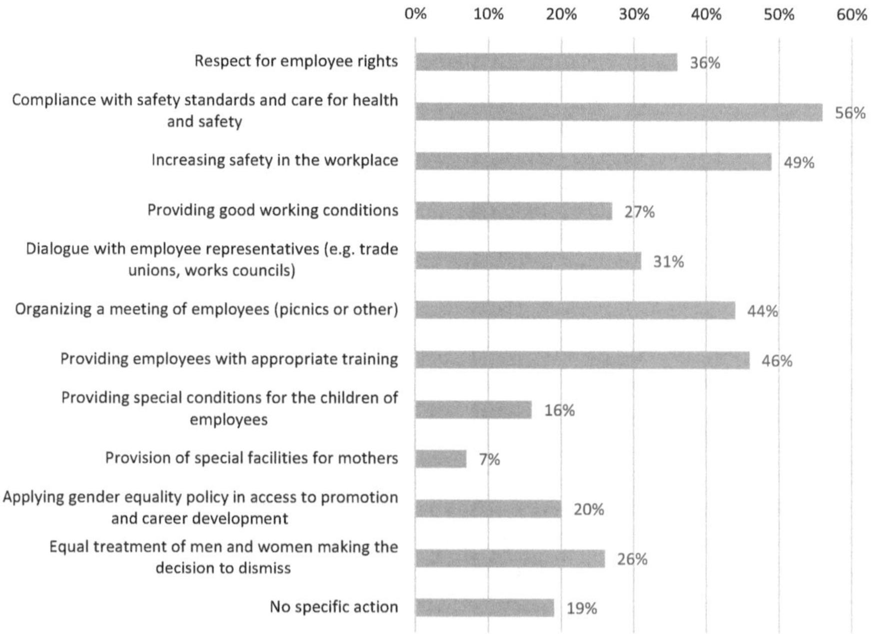


*Figure 5.12* CSR activities aimed at employees – customers' perspective ($N$ = 502. The results do not add up to 100 because respondents could choose more than one answer. Own study)

charity is also rated low (17%). A larger number than in the previous questions also believe that economic entities do not undertake any specific actions for the benefit of local communities (25%), which indicates that, according to the respondents, the social commitment of companies in this area is insufficient.[7]

When asked about environmental issues in the activities of enterprises, they also do not rate them very highly. The respondents see primarily activities aimed at the protection of natural resources, i.e. introducing programs for saving energy, natural resources, paper, etc. (53%). They also believe that enterprises implement regulations and recommendations to reduce the negative impact of their activities on the natural environment (45%). A relatively large group of respondents is convinced that the industry offers environmentally friendly products or services (46%). About one-third of respondents believe that enterprises operating in Poland promote pro-ecological behaviour among their employees, subcontractors, suppliers, or customers (28%). This most likely proves their contact with such activities in practice. Indeed, many companies operating on the Polish market promote pro-ecological attitudes, new certificates appear (e.g. the Green Office certificate), companies boast about implementing new programs. Building an eco-image of the company is also popular. However, confronting the number of people who see it is not beneficial. Almost a quarter believe that companies invest in environmental protection (24%), but only one-fifth believe that they monitor their environmental impact on an ongoing basis.[8]

As the answers to date present, Polish consumers – unfortunately – do not pay attention to the social commitment of companies. They have the same position in relation to the undertaken market activities. Only 5% of respondents say that they pay attention to CSR when buying products or services. An answer partially confirming such a procedure was given by 30% of the respondents (the respondents replied "rather yes"). Unfortunately, much more people, more than two-thirds of the respondents, answered that they did not pay attention to the social commitment of companies when shopping (as many as 49% answered "rather no", and 16% "definitely not").

## Social involvement and value creation – enterprises' perspective

Enterprises operating on the Polish market, even if they have not come across the term CSR, take actions, in particular in the field of environmental protection or directed at employees, which allow them to assess their activities positively. However, these activities are largely the result of the necessity to adapt to legal provisions or common law, developed in Polish conditions. From the management point of view, however, it is important to provide more detailed information on the social commitment of enterprises and to determine to what extent these activities are undertaken in a strategic manner, i.e. in order to obtain specific financial results. The respondents were asked a number of questions, including activities targeted at individual company stakeholders.

Positive responses prevailed when asked about specific actions taken for the benefit of customers. The respondents in the first place emphasised that they are "fair" (89%). Honesty is, as it shows, a special value for respondents, which they perceive as important in running a business. A lot of respondents also believe that they apply pure rules of the market game (80%), reliably label products (77%), and apply the principles of fair sales and advertising (71%). These responses confirm a kind of reliability in individual decision-making areas. A significant number also say that they reliably inform customers about the place of origin of the product (62%), have implemented quality assurance systems, which has a positive impact on the quality of the products and services offered (63%), and that they have complaint procedures open to consumers (80%). As many as three-quarters of respondents are convinced that they simply provide valuable products (75%). Such an answer may very well prove economic activity conducted in Poland. The respondents who are decision-makers in the surveyed companies have knowledge about the quality of the products themselves and reliability in the market service process. Of course, one should remember, however, that despite the anonymity of the survey, this is an individual assessment of enterprises, so these responses may present enterprises in a better light (Figure 5.13).

The respondents were also asked about actions taken for the benefit of investors. In this case, the results are not so enthusiastic. It is true that 68%

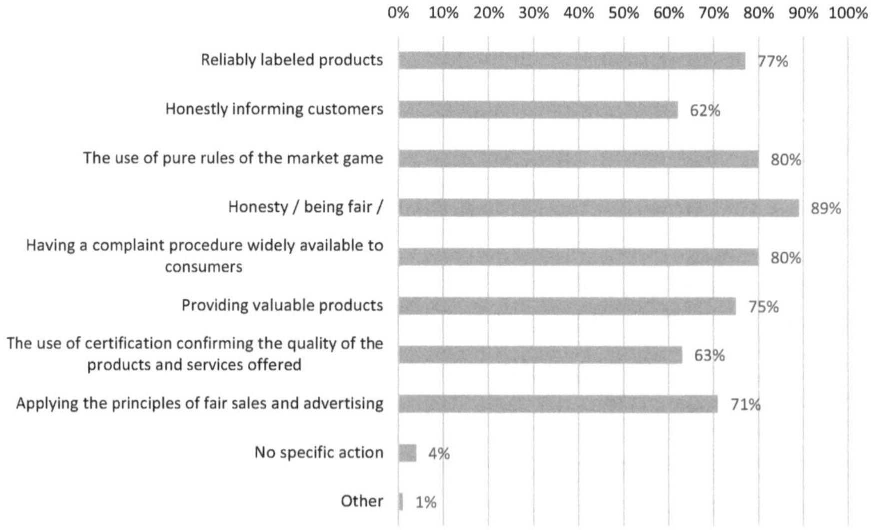


*Figure 5.13* CSR activities aimed at customers – enterprises' perspective ($N = 150$. The results do not add up to 100 because respondents could choose more than one answer. Own study)

answered that they maintain good business contacts with investors, but relatively few respondents indicate the forms that could be used to maintain these contacts. For example, only one-third of respondents claim that they systematically inform them about the development and activities undertaken in the company (33%). Confirmation of such a relation would actually prove cooperation and maintaining contacts with investors, while many companies do not maintain such contact or seek such contact. Only 11% replied that the company was trying to improve its business relationship with investors. The respondents mark, inter alia, that they maintain non-business contacts with investors (28%) and send greeting cards (30%). A lot, because almost one-third of the respondents indicated that they did not undertake any specific actions targeted at this group (32%) (Figure 5.14).

The next group that the respondents were asked about were employees. In this case, it must be admitted that enterprises do a lot for the safety of personnel, unfortunately in areas where they could demonstrate initiative themselves, the actions taken by them do not confirm the special treatment of these stakeholders.

Compliance with occupational health and safety standards is indicated by 91% of respondents. A similar number indicates that employee rights are respected (89%) and that good working conditions are ensured (85%). A relatively large group of respondents also indicates that they improve safety in the workplace (62%). Here, however, it should be noted that the vast majority of these activities are only adapting to legal provisions. Enterprises are obliged to ensure appropriate working conditions, adequate safety in the workplace,

*Figure 5.14* Activities aimed at investors – enterprises' perspective (*N* = 150. The results do not add up to 100 because respondents could choose more than one answer. Own study)

and compliance with health and safety standards (Journal of Laws No. 1997 no. 129, item 844). Therefore, these are not only voluntary actions, directed at the health and comfort of employees.

More than half of the respondents believe that the represented enterprises apply a policy of gender equality in access to promotion and professional development (51%) and treat women and men equally when deciding to dismiss (54%). In this case, it is also required by law. The Labor Code obliges employers to apply the principle of equality in employment in all its aspects, with particular emphasis on equality between women and men in employment (Journal of Laws No. 1974 No. 24, item 141: Art. 11). Moreover, the promotion of equality policy in the workplace and a strong emphasis on its application, for example in the implementation of projects partially financed from external sources, changes the habits in this respect into more favourable for employees. In the face of these conditions, the obtained results may, unfortunately, surprise negatively. It is assumed, however, that some enterprises are sole proprietorships, so they could not indicate this answer.

Much fewer respondents, approximately one-fourth, answered that they conduct a dialogue with employee representatives, such as trade unions or works councils (26%). Relations with these authorities are established by appropriate acts that define the employer's obligations in this respect. The obtained results could therefore be assessed as insufficient to confirm the proper conduct of enterprises in the area in question.[9] However, in this case, as in the previous question, not all respondents had the opportunity to mark this answer, because not all of them are obliged to create or permit the functioning of the said bodies within enterprises. Meanwhile, the additional support that is directed to employees is varied. Respondents indicate that employees are provided with appropriate training (62%), they also organise employee meetings, such as picnics (48%), but when asked about additional activities, they occasionally indicate them. Only 15% of the respondents indicated that they provide special conditions for the children of employees, and 12% that they have additional facilities for mothers.[10]

Despite the presented results, the respondents assessed themselves positively. Only 2% of respondents believe that enterprises do not take any particular actions for the benefit of employees (Figure 5.15).

Suppliers are also an important stakeholder for the company's success. In this case, the respondents were also asked about specific activities that could be of value for this group. However, the responses do not indicate any special interest in suppliers among the respondents, although it is difficult to call it unambiguously confirming the lack of attention for this group.

The respondents mainly indicate the timely payment of payments and compliance with the terms of contracts (85%). The joint resolution of supply or supplier development problems should also be seen as favourable (58%). More than half of the respondents also monitor the development of suppliers (55%). A positive aspect is also the constant contact with the supplier, which is related to, inter alia, with the ongoing provision of information about the

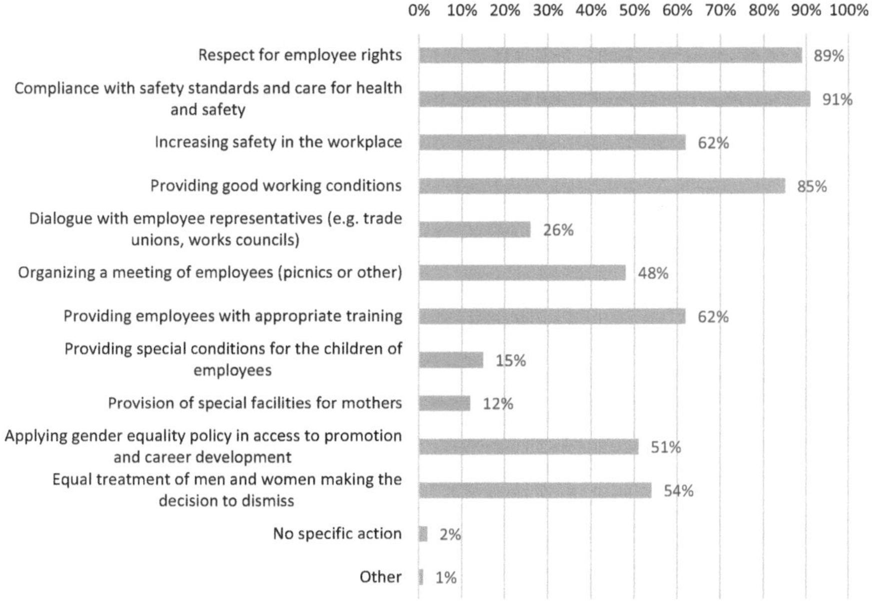


*Figure 5.15* CSR activities aimed at employees – enterprises' perspective ($N$ = 150. The results do not add up to 100 because respondents could choose more than one answer. Own study)

development and activities undertaken in the company (44%). Such action is beneficial for both parties, both for the supplier and the recipient, i.e. in this case the company. Discussing plans together allows for greater integration of activities, which may translate into better market results of companies (e.g. obtaining information about the supplier's industry, including product changes, innovations, adjusting production plans, etc.). In terms of other possible forms of maintaining relationships with suppliers, the respondents indicate: maintaining non-business contacts with suppliers (29%), sending greeting cards (25%), or giving suppliers small gifts (11%). There is little activity of the respondents in planning joint activities in the field of social responsibility with the supplier. Only 10% of respondents indicated that they educate suppliers in the area of CSR, and 14% verified them in terms of CSR. As many as 9% of the respondents answered that they did not take any specific actions, but this number may be dictated by the nature of the business (e.g. consulting services, interested in purchasing mainly office supplies) (Figure 5.16).

The group of "enterprises" was also asked about shaping relations with the media. As could be expected, the vast majority of respondents replied that they did not undertake any special activities related to this group (61%). It is surprising, however, that nearly one-fifth of the respondents systematically

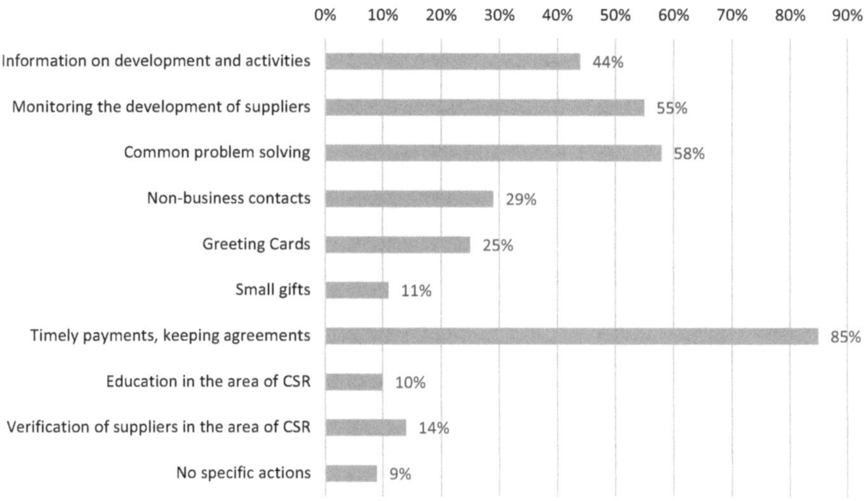


*Figure 5.16* Activities aimed at suppliers – enterprises' perspective (*N* = 150. The results do not add up to 100 because respondents could choose more than one answer. Own study)

inform the media about the development and activities undertaken in the company (23%) as well as crisis situations that take place in the company (21%). The smallest number – only 16% of respondents – provides information on activities in the field of CSR (Figure 5.17).

The responses to the question regarding specific measures directed at public administration, also in the understanding of public finance sector units, were slightly better. In this case, as many as 69% of respondents emphasised that they settle their obligations towards the state in a timely manner. However, this is almost mandatory in Poland, and there are penalties for failure to fulfill obligations. A relatively large group, however, indicated that they cooperate with the employment office (45%) or employ school graduates for internships (39%). The deliberate creation of jobs for the disabled (14%) should also be viewed positively. Nearly one-third of the respondents replied that the company did not take any specific actions targeted at this group (Figure 5.18).

The respondents were also asked about shaping relations with the local community, treating this group as one of the most important from the point of view of the company's social commitment and the creation of common value by the enterprise. In this case, the respondents emphasise, first of all, considering the needs and opinions of the local community (45%) – this answer had the most indications. Unfortunately, on the same point, only 18% of respondents indicated that their enterprises conduct a dialogue with the local community (18%). This means that while enterprises are willing to engage in society and support the local community, they do not do it strategically. Unfortunately, they exclude cooperation, thus depriving themselves

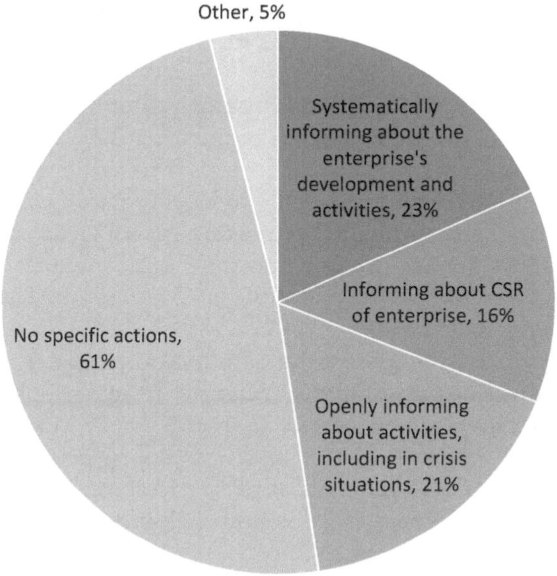


*Figure 5.17* Shaping relations with the media – enterprises' perspective ($N = 150$. The results do not add up to 100 because respondents could choose more than one answer. Own study)

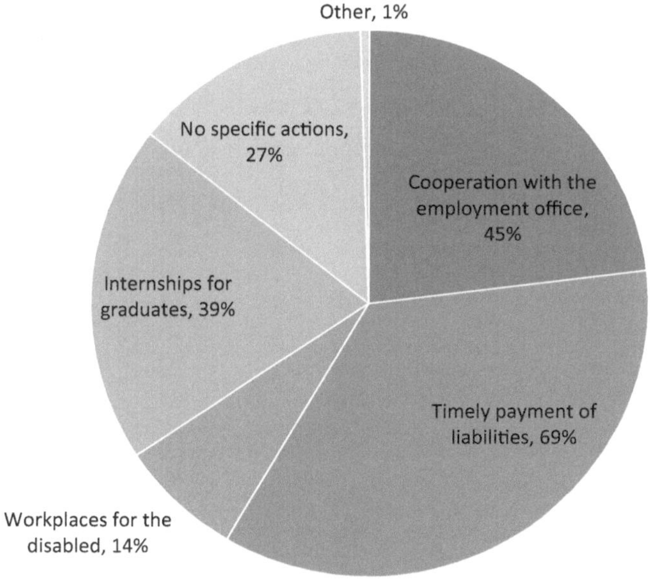


*Figure 5.18* Shaping relations with public administration – enterprises' perspective ($N = 150$. The results do not add up to 100 because respondents could choose more than one answer. Own study)

of the chance to establish a common goal for the enterprise and the local community, which could result in better outcomes for the enterprise, and even finding a support domain that could be the basis for creating value for the enterprise.

The aspect that companies pay attention to is environmental protection. Almost half of the respondents indicate the limitation of the negative impact of the company's operations on the natural environment (43%). Pro-ecological activity is visible in many responses of enterprises. Due to legal requirements and the pressure of public opinion, environmental protection is a subject that is considered in the practice of enterprises. Almost one-third of respondents indicate that the activity carried out for the benefit of the local community is promoting pro-ecological behaviour (32%).

A relatively large group also indicates sponsoring activities aimed at the immediate environment of the enterprise (39%). Slightly fewer people answered that these entities are involved in charity activities for the local community (24%). However, such a distribution of answers is not surprising. Sponsoring has gained its popularity, also in terms of tax settlements. Many managers believe that it is a more effective tool for both helping the local community and building the company's image.

The respondents also indicated that they support employee involvement in social activities (18%) and conduct social or educational projects (15%). A very large group of respondents replied that they did not undertake any specific activities for the benefit of local communities (24%) (Figure 5.19).

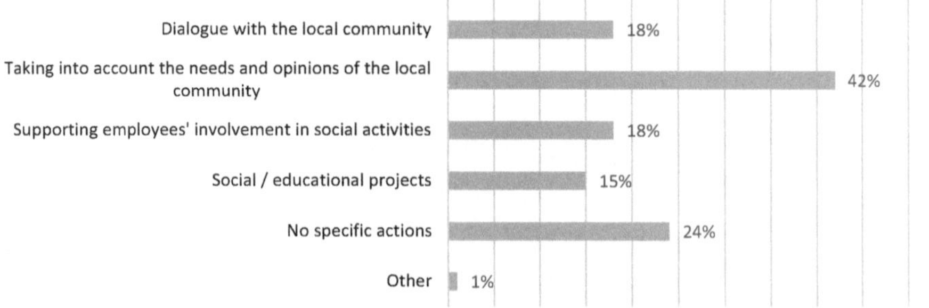


*Figure 5.19* Activities aimed at the local community – enterprises' perspective ($N$= 150. The results do not add up to 100 because respondents could choose more than one answer. Own study)

When asked about environmental issues, they mainly indicate the implementation of saving programs of energy, natural resources, paper, etc. (65%). It is a kind of fashion in Polish conditions, including informing in the content of the correspondence about implemented programs (e.g. the very popular idea of "Zero Waste").[11] This way of promoting environmental responsibility infects others who are eager to imitate ready-made solutions. Thus, they not only follow the general trend but also create some savings for the company and force additional solutions.

Entrepreneurs also believe that the products or services they offer are environmentally friendly (42%). This assessment is consistent with the assessment of consumers who had a similar opinion (46% of respondents in the group of consumers believe that the enterprises offered by companies operating in Poland are environmentally friendly).

Other activities undertaken by enterprises include: (1) promoting pro-ecological behaviour among their employees, subcontractors, suppliers, and customers (35%), (2) implementing regulations and recommendations to reduce the negative impact of the company's operations on the natural environment (31%) and ongoing monitoring of the company's impact on the environment (26%). Very few respondents indicated that they invest in environmental protection (13%) (Figure 5.20).

Respondents were also asked about the percentage of profits that are spent on environmental protection in the enterprise. The answers basically confirmed the position presented by the respondents in the previous question.

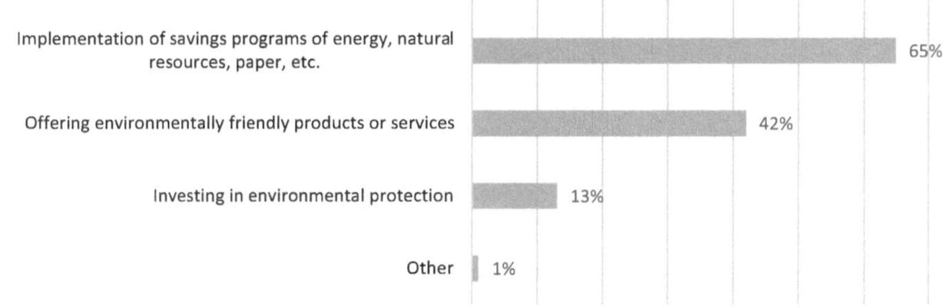


*Figure 5.20* Actions taken for the environment – enterprises' perspective ($N$ = 150. The results do not add up to 100 because respondents could choose more than one answer. Own study)

As many as 41% of enterprises do not incur any expenses on environmental protection, and 48% allocate for this purpose from 1% to 3% of annual profits. Only 11% of respondents replied that they invest in environmental protection spending 4 to 6% of annual profits for this purpose. None of the respondents indicated the answer that they spend more than 6% of annual profits on environmental protection.

The respondents were asked to provide more detailed answers and indicate the type of investments that are being implemented by the enterprise to protect the natural environment. The obtained responses indicate a multifaceted solution to problems related to the elimination of the negative impact of the enterprise on the environment, i.e. undertaking many of the various activities aimed at the protection of the natural environment. The largest number of respondents indicated waste management (60%). The topicality of the problem and attempts to solve it centrally in Poland force enterprises to take specific actions.

On the next places were investments in: (1) air and climate protection (33%), wastewater management and water protection (31%) as well as noise and vibration reduction (11%). These areas are most likely dictated by the form of companies' impact on the environment and the need to limit the negative impact on them. A small number of respondents indicated investing in the protection and restoration of the use value of soils, protection of groundwater and surface waters (4%), protection of landscape biodiversity (1%), and protection against ionising radiation (1%). It is surprising that about 5% of the respondents incur expenditures on research and development activities aimed at environmental protection (Figure 5.21).

In the area of air and climate protection, the surveyed companies invest primarily in the modernisation of boiler houses and heating plants (21%). The aim of these activities is to reduce the emission of pollutants generated by the enterprise. Some of the respondents installed cleaning and deodorising devices, i.e. dedusting, reducing, or neutralising gaseous pollutants (11%). A small number indicated the use of new combustion techniques and technologies (5%) and unconventional energy sources (3%).

In the area of sewage management and water protection, the main investments concern sanitary sewage systems (17%) and construction of sewage treatment plants or their elements (14%).

In the most frequently indicated area of waste management, the most frequent are investments related to the collection and selection of waste (48%) and waste recycling (42%). Some respondents also indicate the modification of technological processes, including the use of low or no-waste techniques or technologies (15%) and activities related to the use or disposal of waste (14%). Actions indicated by enterprises are basically compliant with the requirements imposed on them by the relevant legal regulations. The act indicates that an entrepreneur who undertakes activities causing or likely to generate waste should plan, design, and conduct them so as to: (1) prevent

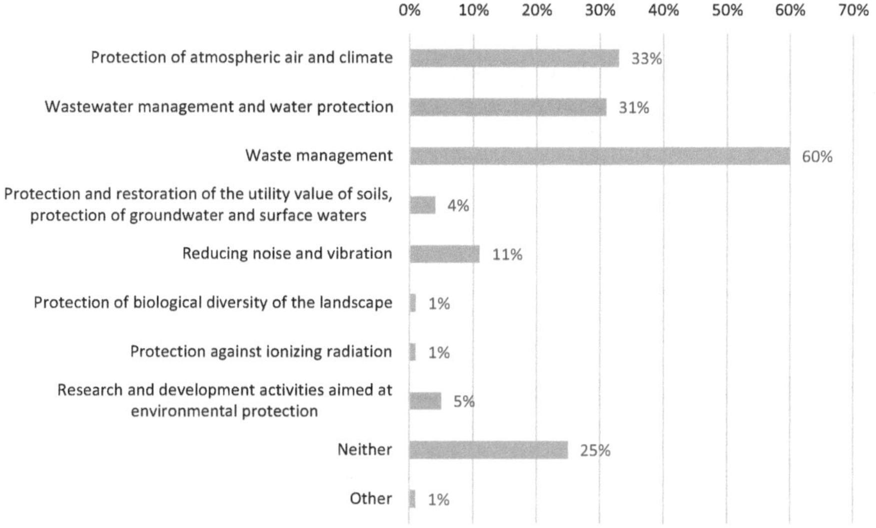


*Figure 5.21* Type of investments for environmental protection in the surveyed enterprises in the last five years ($N$ = 150. The results do not add up to 100 because respondents could choose more than one answer. Own study)

the generation of waste or reduce the amount of waste and its negative impact on the environment in the production of products, and after the end of their use, (2) provide recovery in accordance with the principles of environmental protection, if the generation of waste has not been prevented, and (3) ensure the disposal of waste that was not prevented or recovered in accordance with the principles of environmental protection (Journal of Laws of 2001, No. 62, item 628). The indicated investments are therefore not something additional that the enterprise performs for the environment, but the obligatory adaptation to the requirements of the law in force in Poland.

The respondents were also asked about documentation that would indicate conscious undertaking of CSR activities, including social reporting. The answers to this question are not, however, edifying. While nearly half of the respondents indicated that the company has a code of ethics (45%), only 6% of respondents indicate having a CSR policy in the company. Even fewer people indicated the preparation of CSR reports – 4%.

Such results mean that even if the enterprise has some framework defining its assumptions in the area of social involvement, it is not interested in paying more attention to these activities, and elements such as social reporting, which are also part of communication with stakeholders, are not prepared. Some of the respondents indicated that they had other documents related to CSR, but did not indicate their specificity, despite such a possibility.

An activity that is interesting from the point of view of corporate social involvement is also its activity – as it was originally included in A. Carroll's CSR pyramid – philanthropic. Therefore, the respondents were asked both about engaging in the form of sponsorship and charity, i.e. activities undertaken without expecting a return, for example in the form of advertising.

According to the answers obtained, most of the surveyed companies do not use sponsorship in their activities (63%). The remaining part confirms such commitment (37%), and 3% of the respondents indicate that it is sponsorship under barter agreements. When asked about the nature of the support, the respondents indicate primarily financial (21%), long-term sponsorship (20%), directed rather for institutions (17%). However, it also happens sponsorship in kind (17%) or service sponsorship (6%), one-off sponsorship (11%), for people (13%), or for specific projects (3%) (Figure 5.22).

The distribution of answers looks similar in the case of the question about the involvement of companies in charity activities. As many as 67% of the respondents answered that they did not conduct such activity. Among the enterprises that support various types of charity and social events, financial support (16%), one-off (15%), aimed rather at institutions (16%), prevails. Much fewer respondents indicated a donation in kind (11%) or a service donation (3%). Directing the support is also not of a long-term nature (7%) and less often it is directed to people (9%) than to projects (11%) (Figure 5.23).

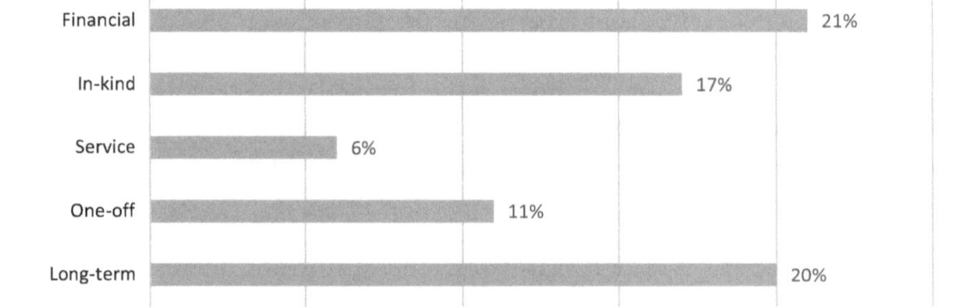


*Figure 5.22* Involvement of the surveyed companies in sponsorship (by type of sponsorship) ($N = 150$. The results do not add up to 100 because respondents could choose more than one answer. Own study)

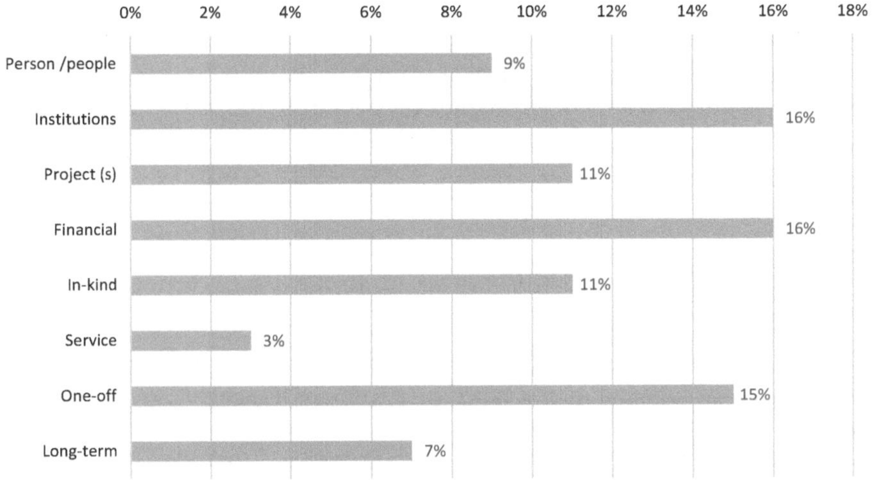


*Figure 5.23* Involvement of the surveyed companies in charity activities (by type of support) ($N = 150$. The results do not add up to 100 because respondents could choose more than one answer. Own study)

## Perception of the benefits arising from the implementation of social responsibility measures

The element justifying the implementation of CSR into the company's practice is the benefits that can be obtained as a result of this process. In line with the concept of creating shared value, shaping activities in the area of corporate responsibility may also be of a strategic nature and contribute to increasing the company's future cash flows. The benefits of corporate social involvement, however, do not only concern the enterprises themselves, the society is also a huge beneficiary of all profits.

As for the positive impact of CSR on the financial results of enterprises, almost no one has any doubts. Most researchers assume that social commitment contributes at least to the company's future cash flow. Various additional benefits that affect the company's financial results are also mentioned. Unfortunately, there is no research showing a direct relationship between the costs incurred in connection with social involvement and the benefits resulting from it. One of the reasons given as the justification is the difficulty in determining the direct impact of the applied CSR practices on the company's financial results due to the visibility of the effects only in the long term. The undoubted difficulty in estimating the aforementioned benefits is also the difficulty in assigning individual effects to specific activities in the CSR area (it is difficult to be sure whether the occurrence of specific benefits is due to the company's social commitment or the effects of the company's marketing activities). Moreover, enterprises very often do not analyse costs in terms of

CSR, so it is difficult for them to relate their CSR expenses to the actual benefits achieved by the enterprise.

Due to the many difficulties in determining the impact of CSR expenditure on the benefits that can be derived from it for enterprises and society, it was relied on qualitative data that could be obtained from answers to questions addressed to both groups of respondents.

In this part of the study, the respondents were asked to refer to the benefits that CSR can provide: (1) to the enterprise and (2) to society.

## Perception of the potential benefits of social involvement of business in the customers' perspective

In the group of customers, more than one-third of people believe that corporate social involvement has a positive effect on improving or strengthening the company's image (36%). A similar number is convinced of the positive impact of CSR on strengthening the company's brand (34%). While a large group notices the impact of CSR on acquiring new customers (27%), which may be justified in the case of previous responses, the area of company-employee relations was quickly noticed – as many as 27% believe that CSR influences the perception of the company as attractive employers. The respondents also believe that corporate social involvement increases the profits of enterprises (25%).[12]

Much fewer, i.e. about one-fifth of respondents, see a relationship between CSR and the increase in competitiveness and innovation of enterprises (21% each one), an increase in sales (21%), or the loyalty of existing customers (20%). A similar group of respondents is convinced of the positive impact of social involvement of enterprises on the interest of investors, improvement of the company's credibility, or an increase in sales profitability (19% of responses each one). For the respondents, CSR also has a more practical dimension, i.e. it allows for the deduction of social donations from the tax base (19%).

The respondents in the group of consumers also see the broader impact of CSR and associate it with other stakeholders. For 18% of respondents, CSR allows for the improvement of cooperation with international corporations. Almost similar number see a positive impact of CSR on shaping long-term, trust-based relationships with external stakeholders (17%). The same number of respondents believe that CSR has a positive impact on increasing employee satisfaction and commitment (17%), and even increasing the efficiency and quality of work (16%).

Relatively few respondents believe that following the principles of the CSR concept allows for efficient and conflict-free operation (15%), increased satisfaction of the company's management board (15%), or higher rates of return (15%). Despite the high assessment of the impact of CSR on the perception of the company as an attractive employer, only 14% believe that social responsibility of the company increases the possibilities of attracting and retaining employees. Also, 14% believe that CSR allows them to better adapt to the needs of customers.

For a very small group, CSR is associated with reducing operating costs (13%), increasing the effectiveness of business operations (12%), improving the level of the company's organisational culture (11%), or increasing resistance to the possibility and effects of crisis situations (9%). Only for 7% of respondents, CSR allows for risk reduction, and for 5% – reduction of the need for formal management (Figure 5.24).

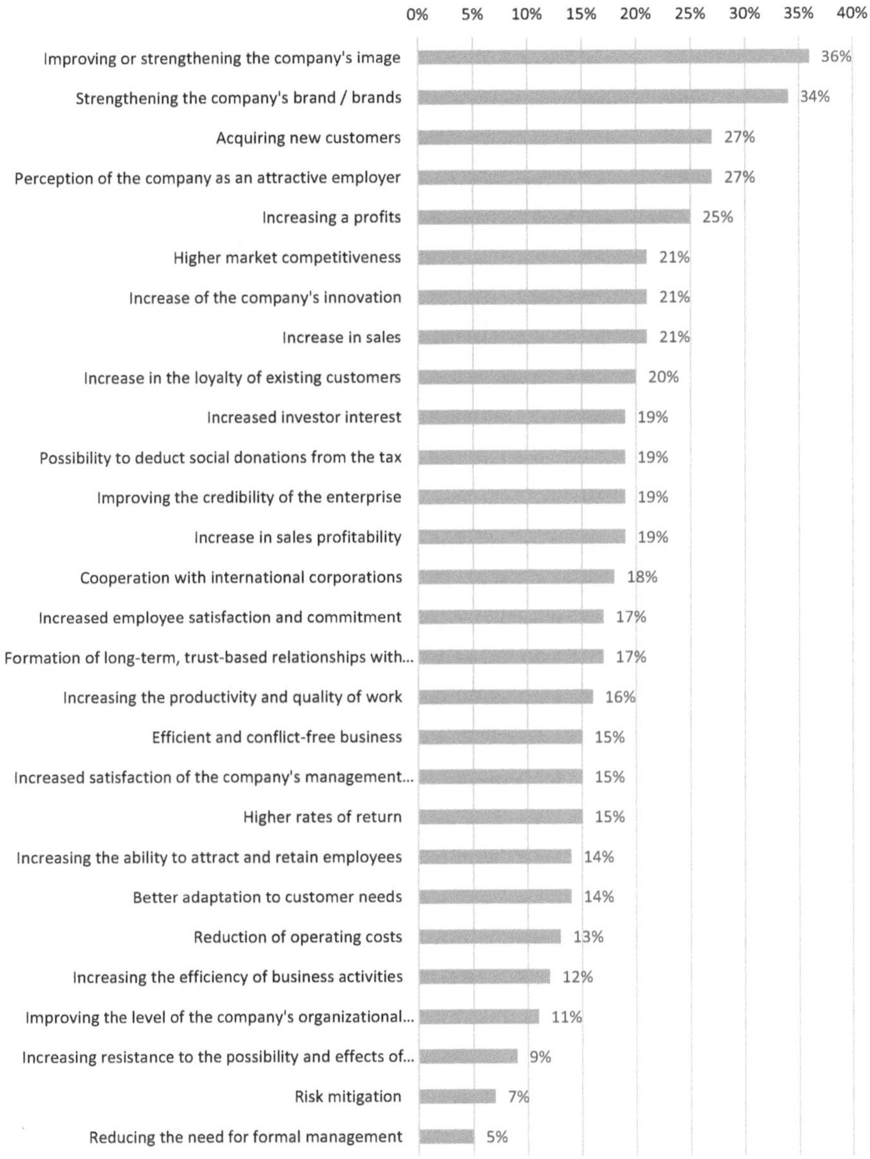


*Figure 5.24* Benefits that can be obtained by enterprises as a result of implementing CSR according to the highest assigned probability of occurrence – customer rating ($N$ = 502. Own study)

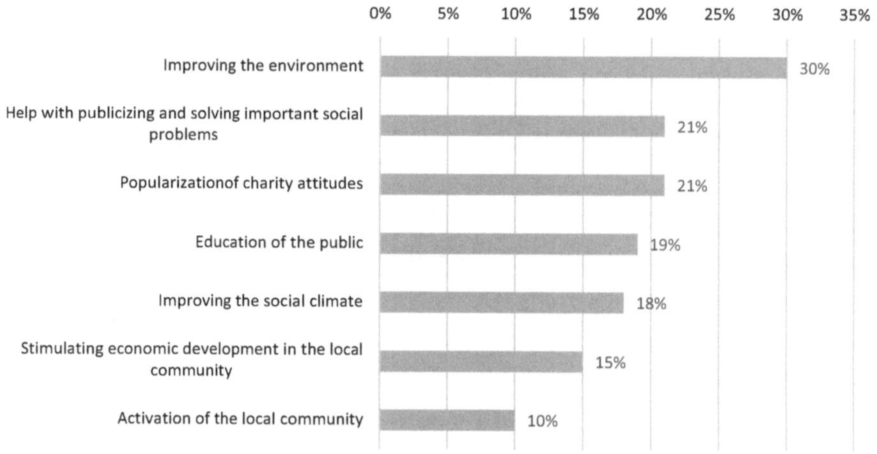


*Figure 5.25* Benefits for society that can be obtained by enterprises as a result of implementing CSR according to the highest assigned probability of occurrence – customer rating ($N = 502$. Own study)

From the point of view of benefits for society, as a result of implementing social responsibility in business practice, for the respondents it is primarily an improvement in the condition of the natural environment. Such opinion is shared by nearly one-third of respondents (30%). It is also significant for the respondents that CSR contributes to publicising and solving important social problems (21%). In this case, it is difficult to assess what part of this benefit is attributed to the surveyed enterprises, and what part they associate with simply publicising the concept of social involvement and engaging in solving other stakeholders' problems that are important from the point of view of society. Public opinion and opinion-forming circles are more and more active, and the support of business means that many problems are publicised and solved (e.g. child labour).

CSR is also perceived as a concept that serves to popularise philanthropic attitudes (21% of respondents think so) and educating the society (19%), which, according to the respondents, contributes to the improvement of the social climate (18%). For some respondents, these activities also allow for stimulating economic development in the local community (15%) and activation of the local community (10%) (Figure 5.25).

A detailed distribution of responses regarding the perceived probability of individual benefits for the enterprise and society from the perspective of consumers is presented in Tables 5.1 and 5.2.

*Table 5.1* Benefits that can be obtained by enterprises as a result of implementing CSR – the probability of occurrence in the opinion of customers (%) (N = 502. Own study)

| *Type of advantage* | *Very big* | *Big* | *Medium* | *Small* | *Very small* |
|---|---|---|---|---|---|
| Improving or strengthening the company's image | 36 | 51 | 11 | 2 | 0 |
| Efficient and conflict-free business | 15 | 34 | 42 | 7 | 1 |
| Acquiring new customers | 27 | 43 | 21 | 8 | 1 |
| Increase in the loyalty of existing customers | 20 | 40 | 29 | 9 | 2 |
| Increasing the efficiency of business activities | 12 | 40 | 32 | 15 | 1 |
| Higher market competitiveness | 21 | 36 | 24 | 15 | 3 |
| Increased investor interest | 19 | 39 | 29 | 9 | 4 |
| Possibility to deduct social donations from the tax | 19 | 38 | 26 | 14 | 3 |
| Perception of the company as an attractive employer | 27 | 35 | 23 | 14 | 1 |
| Increased employee satisfaction and commitment | 17 | 34 | 28 | 19 | 2 |
| Increased satisfaction of the company's management board | 15 | 32 | 35 | 14 | 3 |
| Improving the level of the company's organisational culture | 11 | 33 | 34 | 20 | 2 |
| Increase of the company's innovation | 21 | 38 | 25 | 13 | 3 |
| Increasing the productivity and quality of work | 16 | 29 | 30 | 20 | 6 |
| Increasing the ability to attract and retain employees | 14 | 37 | 29 | 16 | 3 |
| Reducing the need for formal management | 5 | 21 | 43 | 24 | 8 |
| Improving the credibility of the enterprise | 19 | 44 | 32 | 4 | 1 |
| Formation of long-term, trust-based relationships with external stakeholders | 17 | 33 | 40 | 8 | 2 |
| Increasing resistance to the possibility and effects of crisis situations | 9 | 31 | 30 | 24 | 5 |
| Risk mitigation | 7 | 27 | 38 | 22 | 6 |
| Better adaptation to customer needs | 14 | 39 | 29 | 16 | 2 |
| Increase in sales | 21 | 42 | 23 | 12 | 3 |
| Increase in sales profitability | 19 | 29 | 32 | 16 | 3 |
| Increasing a profit | 25 | 32 | 24 | 12 | 8 |
| Reduction of operating costs | 13 | 24 | 36 | 19 | 7 |
| Higher rates of return | 15 | 22 | 38 | 19 | 6 |
| Strengthening the company's brand/ brands | 34 | 37 | 19 | 6 | 4 |
| Cooperation with international corporations | 18 | 32 | 30 | 13 | 8 |
| Creating relatively greater added value | 14 | 29 | 40 | 13 | 5 |
| Others | 0 | 0 | 0 | 0 | 0 |

*Table 5.2* Benefits that may be obtained by the society as a result of implementing CSR – the probability of occurrence in the opinion of customers (%) (N = 502. Own study)

| *Type of advantage* | *Very big* | *Big* | *Medium* | *Small* | *Very small* |
|---|---|---|---|---|---|
| Help with publicising and solving important social problems | 21 | 48 | 24 | 6 | 1 |
| Activation of the local community | 10 | 38 | 34 | 16 | 2 |
| Stimulating economic development in the local community | 15 | 44 | 29 | 11 | 1 |
| Education of the public | 19 | 47 | 22 | 10 | 2 |
| Improving the environment | 30 | 35 | 25 | 8 | 1 |
| Popularisation of charity attitudes | 21 | 37 | 31 | 10 | 1 |
| Improving the social climate | 18 | 32 | 37 | 12 | 2 |
| Other | 0 | 1 | 1 | 0 | 0 |

## Perception of the potential benefits of social involvement of business in an enterprises' perspective

As in the group of customers, managers associate CSR primarily with improving or strengthening the company's image – so nearly one-third of respondents (31%) believe it and strengthening the company's brand or brands. However, only one-fifth of respondents (19%)[13] indicate the positive impact of CSR on the brands owned. In the next place, the respondents did not mention acquiring new customers, which was indicated by only 15% of the respondents, but benefits related to the staff. For enterprises, corporate social commitment improves their image among employees (17%), and therefore is perceived as an element of branding addressed to the company's current and future staff and contributes to the increase in employee satisfaction and commitment (17%). An important element for this group is the possibility of deducting social donations from the tax base (16%).

The respondents also see the impact of CSR on the improvement of the company's credibility, efficient and conflict-free conduct of business, increase in the loyalty of existing customers, improvement of the company's competitiveness on the market, increase in the company's innovation, as well as increasing the possibility of attracting and retaining employees. A very high probability of these benefits was indicated by 15% of respondents.

A small number of respondents believe that CSR can increase the company's profits (13%) or generally the effectiveness of business activity (11%). A similar group sees a relationship between CSR and an increase in the satisfaction of the company's management board and an improvement in the level of the company's organisational culture (13% of respondents each one). Under Polish conditions, it can be considered encouraging that for some respondents it is also a remedy for various types of crisis (11%), it may mean that the awareness of social responsibility increases and it ceases to be associated with charity, on the contrary, some managers perceive its importance in a strategic perspective.

For some respondents, CSR is simply an opportunity to cooperate with international corporations (11%). Responsibility in running a business and social commitment is very often a requirement of cooperation with foreign entities with a much longer tradition, in particular with multinational corporations. These entities, often under the pressure of international public opinion, take their contacts with stakeholders very seriously, taking care, inter alia, of to ensure that the entities they cooperate with are "flawless" in terms of image. Any mistakes in this regard may result in consumer boycotts and loss of some profits.

Few of the respondents also saw a relationship between CSR and the increase in investor interest (9%), increasing the efficiency and quality of work (9%), shaping long-term, trust-based relationships with external stakeholders (9%), or risk reduction (8%). For the respondents, social responsibility is not a guarantee of better adaptation to customer needs (8%), increased sales (8%), or improved profitability of sales (7%). It was also sporadically indicated that CSR allowed for the reduction of operating costs (7%), higher rates of return (6%), and the creation of relatively higher added value (4%). Enterprises operating in Poland, even if they have not encountered the term CSR, perform a number of activities that are part of the concept of CSR, and moreover, they are convinced of the legitimacy and effectiveness of such a procedure (e.g. action aimed at employees or the local community). The liability of entities operating in Poland, however, is most often liability at the level of compliance with the law. As confirmed by the responses in the area in question, the respondents clearly do not see the benefits of being socially involved with the company's financial results, even in the long term (Figure 5.26).

In the area of benefits for society, the first two places – as in the group of consumers – were taken by improving the condition of the natural environment and helping to publicise and solve significant social problems. The difference, however, is in the number of people convinced of such an impact of corporate social responsibility. In the case of consumers, it was 30% and 21% of the respondents, respectively, and in the case of respondents on behalf of business, it is 22% and 17%. In further places, the respondents among enterprises indicated education of the society (17%), popularisation of charity (17%), activation of the local community (13%), stimulation of economic development in the local environment (13%), and improvement of the social climate (11%) (Figure 5.27).

A detailed distribution of responses concerning the perceived probability of individual benefits for the enterprise and society from the perspective of respondents on behalf of enterprises is presented in Tables 5.3 and 5.4.

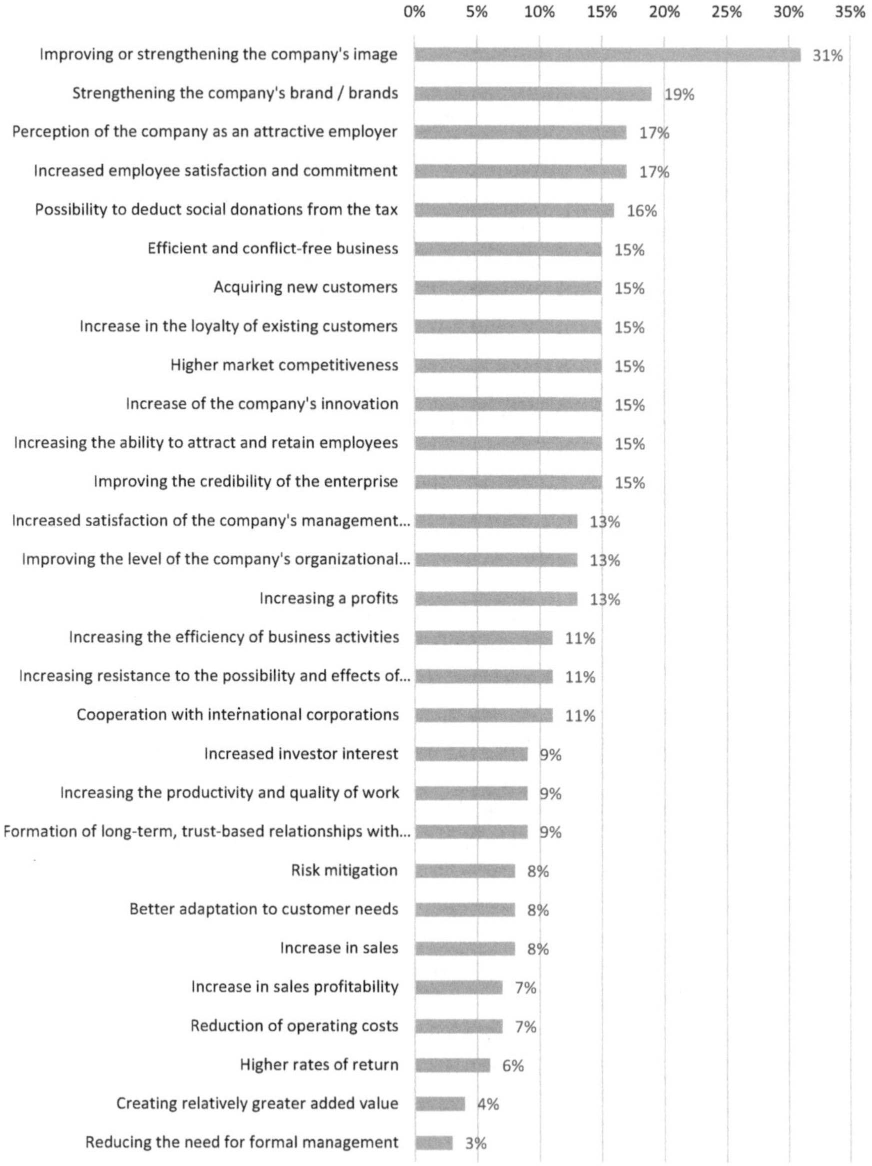


*Figure 5.26* Benefits that can be obtained by enterprises as a result of implementing CSR according to the highest assigned probability of occurrence – managers' rating (*N* = 150. Own study)

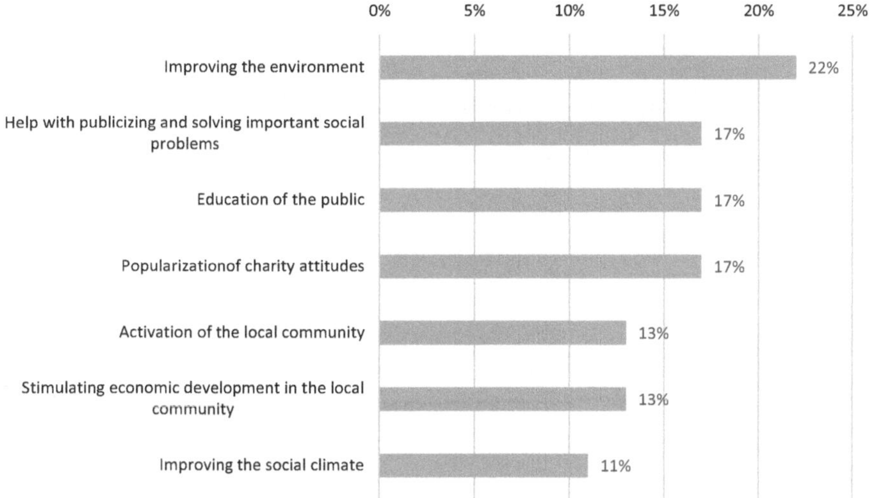


*Figure 5.27* Benefits for society that can be obtained by enterprises as a result of implementing CSR according to the highest assigned probability of occurrence – managers' rating ($N$ = 150. Own study)

*Table 5.3* Benefits that can be obtained by enterprises as a result of implementing CSR – the probability of occurrence in the opinion of managers (%) (N = 150. Own study)

| *Type of advantage* | *Very big* | *Big* | *Medium* | *Small* | *Very small* |
|---|---|---|---|---|---|
| Improving or strengthening the company's image | 31 | 48 | 14 | 6 | 1 |
| Efficient and conflict-free business | 15 | 42 | 29 | 9 | 4 |
| Acquiring new customers | 15 | 43 | 26 | 10 | 6 |
| Increase in the loyalty of existing customers | 15 | 41 | 25 | 11 | 9 |
| Increasing the efficiency of business activities | 11 | 42 | 28 | 10 | 9 |
| Higher market competitiveness | 15 | 39 | 27 | 11 | 7 |
| Increased investor interest | 9 | 41 | 28 | 13 | 9 |
| Possibility to deduct social donations from the tax | 16 | 29 | 29 | 16 | 11 |
| Perception of the company as an attractive employer | 17 | 37 | 31 | 8 | 8 |
| Increased employee satisfaction and commitment | 17 | 33 | 34 | 11 | 6 |
| Increased satisfaction of the company's management board | 13 | 41 | 27 | 10 | 9 |
| Improving the level of the company's organisational culture | 13 | 39 | 29 | 14 | 5 |
| Increase of the company's innovation | 15 | 47 | 23 | 8 | 7 |
| Increasing the productivity and quality of work | 9 | 39 | 28 | 15 | 9 |

(*Continued*)

*Table 5.3* Continued

| *Type of advantage* | *Very big* | *Big* | *Medium* | *Small* | *Very small* |
|---|---|---|---|---|---|
| Increasing the ability to attract and retain employees | 15 | 35 | 33 | 11 | 7 |
| Reducing the need for formal management | 3 | 27 | 33 | 26 | 11 |
| Improving the credibility of the enterprise | 15 | 41 | 26 | 9 | 10 |
| Formation of long-term, trust-based relationships with external stakeholders | 9 | 42 | 28 | 12 | 9 |
| Increasing resistance to the possibility and effects of crisis situations | 11 | 29 | 32 | 17 | 11 |
| Risk mitigation | 8 | 23 | 33 | 19 | 17 |
| Better adaptation to customer needs | 8 | 39 | 33 | 11 | 9 |
| Increase in sales | 8 | 38 | 28 | 15 | 11 |
| Increase in sales profitability | 7 | 37 | 29 | 16 | 11 |
| Increasing a profit | 13 | 33 | 29 | 18 | 8 |
| Reduction of operating costs | 7 | 29 | 33 | 19 | 12 |
| Higher rates of return | 6 | 35 | 29 | 19 | 12 |
| Strengthening the company's brand/brands | 19 | 45 | 21 | 7 | 7 |
| Cooperation with international corporations | 11 | 25 | 35 | 16 | 13 |
| Creating relatively greater added value | 4 | 27 | 38 | 17 | 14 |
| Others | 0 | 1 | 1 | 1 | 13 |

*Table 5.4* Benefits that may be obtained by the society as a result of implementing CSR – the probability of occurrence in the opinion of managers (%) (N = 150. Own study)

| *Type of advantage* | *Very big* | *Big* | *Medium* | *Small* | *Very small* |
|---|---|---|---|---|---|
| Help with publicising and solving important social problems | 17 | 44 | 27 | 7 | 5 |
| Activation of the local community | 13 | 31 | 39 | 11 | 7 |
| Stimulating economic development in the local community | 13 | 32 | 31 | 15 | 9 |
| Education of the public | 17 | 38 | 27 | 10 | 7 |
| Improving the environment | 22 | 40 | 29 | 5 | 4 |
| Popularisation of charity attitudes | 17 | 43 | 26 | 9 | 6 |
| Improving the social climate | 11 | 39 | 35 | 8 | 7 |
| Other | 0 | 1 | 3 | 0 | 13 |

## Conditions of shaping of the value-based marketing through social involvement – polish experiences

The adopted research hypotheses were verified in two groups: (1) consumers and (2) enterprises on behalf of which their owners or senior managers were responsible (Figure 5.28).

In relation to the group of consumers, it was assumed that they positively assess CSR activities and, seeing their value in them, consider the social commitment of enterprises when making purchases (Ha1). The Polish market is

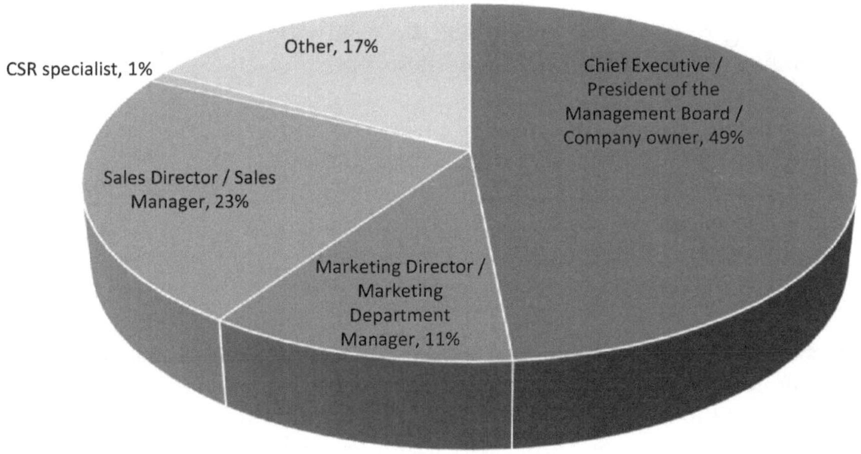


*Figure 5.28* Structure of the respondents answering on behalf of enterprises ($N$ = 150. Own study)

characterised by a different experience in the area of CSR than the more developed markets of Western Europe or the United States, which is understood as lower sensitivity of both consumers and managers to the broadly understood responsibility. From this point of view, it is important to explain whether Polish consumers really perceive the social commitment of enterprises and whether they take CSR into account when making purchases. The answer to this question is the key to further designing corporate marketing strategies and incorporating CSR into the company's management policy in general. Considering the results of previous research describing consumer behaviour on the Polish market and considering, or rather not considering, their social responsibility in purchasing decisions, which clearly confirm their ignorance of the assumptions of the CSR concept (RBF 2018: 9), it was decided that the verification of this hypothesis would consist in to consumers who are familiar with the concept of CSR. It was assumed, inter alia, that the mere awareness of the CSR concept is not tantamount to support for its application in practice, i.e. a positive assessment of the activities undertaken in this area. Consumers who know the assumptions of CSR may also have a negative or indifferent attitude towards activities in the area of CSR, which in practice means not taking this factor into account when making purchases. Moreover, the mere positive attitude towards CSR also does not mean that consumers treat the social commitment of enterprises as a value that is important to them and that they support through certain market choices. People with a positive attitude to CSR may or may not include CSR in practice. An element determining this approach to the verification of the hypothesis was the conviction that respondents who do not know the basic assumptions of the CSR concept are not able to refer to activities that fit into the area of CSR as a value that can be positively perceived and considered in market decisions consumers.

Considering the adopted reasoning, the following statistical hypotheses were formulated for the auxiliary hypothesis Ha1:

Hs1 Knowledge of the CSR concept influences the perception and assessment of activities in the area of social responsibility.
Hs2 Knowledge of the concept of CSR influences the perception and consideration of corporate social involvement during purchases.
Hs3 Consideration of CSR while purchasing results from a positive assessment of the concept and practice of CSR.

In the case of the first and the presented statistical hypotheses, a statistically significant relationship exists between the awareness of CSR declared by consumers and the conviction that CSR is consistent with the interests of the enterprise and that the concept is justified in practice. This means that consumers who come across the concept of CSR perceive this concept as justified and appropriate for use by enterprises. They also believe that CSR is consistent with the goals adopted by business entities or set for business. There is also a statistically significant correlation between the knowledge about CSR and the perception of the impact of applying the concept on consumer loyalty to the company's brands and on its financial results.

In each of these cases, there is a weak correlation between the variables, however, it proves that people who understand what CSR is more often notice the positive impact of CSR on selected performance indicators of enterprises. No statistically significant relationship was found between the awareness of the CSR concept among consumers and the perceived impact of CSR on the company's image (Table 5.5).

*Table 5.5* CSR awareness declared by consumers and perception of CSR – Pearson correlation coefficients (In the absence of a statistically significant relationship, the responses were omitted. Own study)

| *Variable A* | *Variable B* | *Pearson's CHI2* | *p-value* | *V Cramer's coefficient* |
|---|---|---|---|---|
| CSR awareness | Compliance of CSR with the interests of enterprises | 15.228 | 0.002 | 0.174 |
| | The legitimacy of applying CSR in business | 8.829 | 0.032 | 0.133 |
| | Assessment of the impact of CSR on the loyalty of consumers to the company's brand/brands | 21.134 | < 0.001 | 0.205 |
| | Assessment of the impact of CSR on the company's turnover | 24.071 | 0.001 | 0.219 |

- very weak correlation, - weak correlation, - moderate correlation

For the purposes of verifying the Hs1 hypothesis, attempts were also made to confirm whether there is a statistically significant relationship between the declared knowledge of the CSR concept and the perception of activities in the area of corporate social responsibility in practice. In this case, the hypothesis was largely confirmed, i.e. there is a correlation between the awareness of CSR declared by consumers and the perception of companies' involvement in sponsorship and charity activities and the perception of special treatment of customers and employees by enterprises. No statistically significant relationship was found between CSR awareness and the perception of activities addressed to local communities. However, this result may be conditioned by a very low involvement of enterprises operating on the Polish market in the development of the environment. Therefore, the respondents, not noticing the activity in question, did not include it in their responses. There is also no statistically significant correlation between CSR awareness and a positive assessment of the social commitment of enterprises operating on the Polish market or the assessment of the degree of implementation of CSR principles in these enterprises, which partially confirms the assumptions made in this study (Table 5.6).

There is also a statistically significant relationship between the CSR awareness declared by the respondents and the perception and consideration of social responsibility in the market practice of enterprises (Hs2). Significant relationships exist in all cases that were asked in the questionnaire, i.e. between awareness and perception of CSR during purchases, in product advertising, in advertising of CSR initiatives, and in-service delivery processes. The strength of the relationship between these variables is weak, apart from the correlation between the awareness of CSR and the perception of activities in this area in the advertisements of socially responsible initiatives.

*Table 5.6* CSR awareness declared by consumers and their perception of CSR activities – Pearson correlation coefficients (In the absence of a statistically significant relationship, the responses were omitted. Own study)

| *Variable A* | *Variable B* | *Pearson's CHI2* | *p-value* | *V Cramer's coefficient* | *Coefficient $\phi$* |
|---|---|---|---|---|---|
| CSR awareness | Assessment of companies' involvement in sponsorship | 17.267 | 0.001 | 0.185 | |
| | Assessment of companies' involvement in charity activities | 30.902 | < 0.001 | 0.248 | |
| | Taking specific actions for the benefit of customers | 11.304 | 0.001 | | 0.150 |
| | Taking specific actions for the benefit of employees | 4.384 | 0.036 | | 0.093 |

[legend box] - very weak correlation, [legend box] - weak correlation, [legend box] - moderate correlation

In this case, the correlation is moderate. These results prove that knowledge of corporate social responsibility senses consumers' attention to aspects related to CSR and more often than consumers unfamiliar with the concept of corporate social responsibility, they pay attention to the social commitment of enterprises (Table 5.7).

Based on the results of the research, it was also confirmed that there is a statistically significant relationship between the knowledge of CSR by the respondents and considering CSR activities during purchases. Therefore, CSR awareness is important in the market behaviour of consumers and the higher it is, the more often these aspects are considered in decisions about the selection of products or services.

In the research, attempts were also made to determine the implications for enterprises of considering CSR in market decisions (Hs3). As presented by the results of the performed statistical analysis, considering CSR during purchases is positively correlated with the belief that CSR is consistent with the interests of enterprises and the belief that enterprises should consider the principles of CSR in their practice. People declaring paying attention to CSR during purchases also tend to positively assess the impact of the company's social involvement on its image, financial results, and consumer loyalty to the company's brands/brands (Table 5.8). This means, inter alia, that people positively assessing CSR consider the activities of enterprises in this area when making purchases.

The research also confirmed the relationship between including CSR while purchasing and a positive assessment of the perceived activities of enterprises in the area of CSR and the degree of implementation of these activities

*Table 5.7* Consumers' awareness of CSR and the inclusion and perception of CSR in market activities of enterprises – Pearson correlation coefficients (In the absence of a statistically significant relationship, the responses were omitted. Own study)

| *Variable A* | *Variable B* | *Pearson's CHI2* | *p-value* | *V Cramer's coefficient* | *Coefficient ϕ* |
|---|---|---|---|---|---|
| CSR awareness | Noticing CSR while shopping | 38.312 | < 0.001 | | 0.276 |
| | Noticing CSR in product advertisements | 20.861 | < 0.001 | | 0.204 |
| | Noticing CSR in the advertising of CSR initiatives | 67.405 | < 0.001 | | 0.366 |
| | Noticing CSR in the process of providing services | 22.848 | < 0.001 | | 0.213 |
| | Consideration of CSR when purchasing | 15.184 | 0.002 | 0.174 | |

- very weak correlation, - weak correlation, - moderate correlation

*Table 5.8* Consideration of CSR when purchasing and the perception of CSR by consumers – Pearson correlation coefficients (In the absence of a statistically significant relationship, the responses were omitted. Own study)

| *Variable A* | *Variable B* | *Pearson's CHI2* | *p-value* | *V Cramer's coefficient* |
|---|---|---|---|---|
| Consideration of CSR when purchasing | Compliance of CSR with the interests of enterprises | 40.868 | <0.001 | 0.165 |
| | The legitimacy of applying CSR in business | 45.480 | < 0.001 | 0.174 |
| | Assessment of the impact of CSR on the company's image | 62.408 | <0.001 | 0.204 |
| | Assessment of the impact of CSR on the loyalty of consumers to the company's brand/brands | 46.349 | < 0.001 | 0.176 |
| | Assessment of the impact of CSR on the company's turnover | 77.973 | < 0.001 | 0.228 |

- very weak correlation, - weak correlation, - moderate correlation

in practice. There is a weak correlation between these variables, but it can be said that people who pay attention to CSR while shopping also positively assess the practice in this area. Consumers who are considering of CSR when purchasing, also positively evaluate the involvement of enterprises in the area of sponsorship, charity activities, activities undertaken for the benefit of the natural environment, and stakeholders such as customers, employees, and the natural environment. All the correlations found are weak, however, there is a positive relationship between these variables (Table 5.9).

A kind of confirmation of the positive attitude of consumers, who consider social responsibility when shopping, to the activity of enterprises in the area of CSR is their sensitivity to the aspects of social involvement of enterprises, which can be noticed in activities directed at consumers. The conducted analysis confirmed a weak, but statistically significant relationship between including CSR while purchasing and noticing CSR in this process. The respondents also see social responsibility in advertising products and in the process of providing services (Table 5.10).

In order to deepen the explanation and understanding of consumers' motives, another assumption was made that the perception of CSR as a value and taking it into account when making purchases by consumers is conditioned by their sociodemographic features (Ha2). For the auxiliary hypothesis adopted in this way, the following statistical hypotheses were formulated:

Hs4 There is a relationship between the knowledge of the CSR concept and the characteristics of consumers.

Hs5 There is a relationship between the perception of CSR and the characteristics of consumers.

*Table 5.9* Consideration of CSR when purchasing and assessing corporate social involvement in practice – Pearson correlation coefficients (In the absence of a statistically significant relationship, the responses were omitted. Own study)

| *Variable A* | *Variable B* | *Pearson's CHI2* | *p-value* | *V Cramer's coefficient* |
|---|---|---|---|---|
| Consideration of CSR when purchasing | Undertaking CSR activities by enterprises operating in Poland | 10.727 | 0.013 | 0.146 |
| | Assessment of the degree of implementation of CSR principles in enterprises operating in Poland | 35.748 | < 0.001 | 0.154 |
| | Assessment of companies' involvement in sponsorship | 40.750 | < 0.001 | 0.165 |
| | Assessment of companies' involvement in charity activities | 54.794 | < 0.001 | 0.200 |
| | Taking actions for the natural environment | 23.111 | < 0.001 | 0.215 |
| | Taking specific actions for the benefit of customers | 19.885 | 0.001 | 0.200 |
| | Taking specific actions for the benefit of employees | 10.979 | 0.012 | 0.148 |
| | Taking special actions for the benefit of the local community | 37.782 | < 0.001 | 0.275 |

- very weak correlation, - weak correlation, - moderate correlation

*Table 5.10* Consideration of CSR when purchasing and noticing CSR in the market activities of enterprises – Pearson correlation coefficients (In the absence of a statistically significant relationship, the responses were omitted. Own study)

| *Variable A* | *Variable B* | *Pearson's CHI2* | *p-value* | *V Cramer's coefficient* |
|---|---|---|---|---|
| Consideration of CSR when purchasing | Noticing CSR while shopping | 21.735 | 0.001 | 0.208 |
| | Noticing CSR in the advertising of CSR initiatives | 10.172 | 0.017 | 0.142 |
| | Noticing CSR in the process of providing services | 18.416 | 0.001 | 0.192 |

- very weak correlation, - weak correlation, - moderate correlation

Hs6 There is a relationship between the perception of CSR in the practice of enterprises and the characteristics of consumers.

Hs7 There is a relationship between the consideration and perception of CSR during the purchasing process and the characteristics of the respondents.

Considering the fact that Poland is classified as a developing market, and the years of the centrally controlled economy did not allow for a development similar to that in Western countries, it was assumed that the knowledge of the CSR concept is conditioned by the socio-demographic characteristics of consumers (Hs4), in particular it depends on: age, education, or status of the respondent. On the basis of empirical research, the statistical hypothesis formulated in this way was confirmed only in two areas. Namely, there is a statistically significant relationship between the declared knowledge about CSR and gender (very weak correlation) and between the declared knowledge about CSR and education (weak correlation). In the case of the remaining variables, no statistically significant correlations were found. The hypothesis in this section has been rejected.

It was also assumed that a positive assessment of CSR in practice results from certain characteristics of the respondents (Hs5). In this case, a statistically significant relationship exists between a positive opinion on the compliance of CSR with the company's interests and gender, age, education, place of residence, and the status of respondents (in all cases a weak correlation was found) and between a positive opinion on the validity of using CSR in business and gender, age, education, place of residence, income, and status of the respondents (in all cases the correlation found is weak).

There is also a statistically significant relationship between the belief that CSR has a positive impact on the company's image and the age, education, place of residence, income, and status of respondents (weak correlations), between the belief that the social involvement of companies has a positive impact on consumer loyalty to the company's brand/brands and age, education, place of residence, income, and status (weak correlations), and between the conviction about the positive impact of CSR on the company's financial results and education and place of residence (weak correlations). This means, for example, that younger people living in large cities are prone to higher assessments of the impact of CSR on the turnover of enterprises. In the case of the remaining variables, a statistically significant relationship does not exist (Table 5.11).

The study also assumed that there is a relationship between the perception of CSR in the market practice of enterprises and the characteristics of consumers (Hs6). The results of the conducted research allow for the determination of a statistically significant relationship in the case of the respondents' belief in undertaking CSR activities and the gender, age, and income of respondents (weak correlation), as well as between the assessment of the degree of implementation of CSR principles in Polish enterprises and gender, age, education, place of residence, and the status of the respondents (in all cases a weak correlation was found). This means that older people, with higher education, living in smaller towns assess the degree of CSR implementation in enterprises operating in Poland lower than young people, from large cities or with low education. No statistically significant relationship was found between the assessment of the degree of implementation of CSR principles in enterprises operating on the Polish market and the respondent's income.

*Table 5.11* Awareness and perception of CSR by consumers and their sociodemographic features – Pearson correlation coefficients (In the absence of a statistically significant relationship, the responses were omitted. Own study)

| *Variable A* | *Variable B* | *Pearson's CHI2* | *p-value* | *V Cramer's coefficient* | *Coefficient ϕ* |
|---|---|---|---|---|---|
| Knowledge of the concept of CSR | Gender | 4.110 | 0.043 | | -0.090 |
| | Education | 16.773 | 0.001 | 0.185 | |
| Compliance of CSR with the interests of enterprises | Gender | 11.083 | 0.011 | 0.149 | |
| | Age | 50.080 | < 0.001 | 0.182 | |
| | Education | 30.302 | 0.001 | 0.143 | |
| | Domicile | 21.999 | 0.009 | 0.121 | |
| | Status | 27.786 | 0.001 | 0.137 | |
| The legitimacy of applying CSR in business | Gender | 19.100 | 0.001 | 0.195 | |
| | Age | 42.005 | 0.001 | 0.167 | |
| | Education | 47.127 | < 0.001 | 0.179 | |
| | Domicile | 46.060 | < 0.001 | 0.118 | |
| | Income | 17.674 | 0.039 | 0.110 | |
| | Status | 25.691 | 0.002 | 0.131 | |
| Assessment of the impact of CSR on the company's image | Gender | 24.875 | 0.001 | 0.223 | |
| | Age | 47.648 | < 0.001 | 0.178 | |
| | Education | 47.529 | < 0.001 | 0.180 | |
| | Domicile | 27.872 | 0.001 | 0.136 | |
| | Income | 19.627 | 0.020 | 0.116 | |
| | Status | 22.486 | 0.007 | 0.123 | |
| Assessment of the impact of CSR on the loyalty of consumers to the company's brand/ brands | Age | 43.038 | < 0.001 | 0.169 | |
| | Education | 52.103 | < 0.001 | 0.188 | |
| | Domicile | 18.182 | 0.033 | 0.110 | |
| | Income | 17.342 | 0.044 | 0.110 | |
| | Status | 32.468 | 0.001 | 0.148 | |
| Assessment of the impact of CSR on the company's turnover | Gender | 33.730 | < 0.001 | 0.260 | |
| | Education | 20.735 | 0.014 | 0.119 | |
| | Domicile | 36.046 | < 0.001 | 0.155 | |

- very weak correlation, - weak correlation, - moderate correlation

There is also a statistically significant relationship between the assessment of companies' involvement in sponsorship and charity activities and such characteristics of the respondents as gender, age, education, and respondent status (weak correlations in both cases). There is also a statistically significant correlation between consumers' belief that enterprises undertake special actions for their customers and the status of respondents (weak correlation), the perception of specific actions addressed to employees and the gender, age and income of respondents (weak correlations) and between the perception of companies' involvement in the development of local community and gender,

*Table 5.12* Perception of CSR activities by consumers and their sociodemographic features – Pearson correlation coefficients (In the absence of a statistically significant relationship, the responses were omitted. Own study)

| *Variable A* | *Variable B* | *Pearson's CHI2* | *p-value* | *V Cramer's coefficient* | *Coefficient ϕ* |
|---|---|---|---|---|---|
| Undertaking CSR activities by enterprises operating in Poland | Gender | 11.14 | 0.0008 | | 0.149 |
| | Age | 17.41 | 0.002 | 0.186 | |
| | Income | 24.242 | < 0.001 | 0.224 | |
| Assessment of the degree of implementation of CSR principles in enterprises operating in Poland | Gender | 13.344 | 0.004 | 0.163 | |
| | Age | 38.197 | 0.001 | 0.159 | |
| | Education | 24.398 | 0.003 | 0.129 | |
| | Domicile | 17.532 | 0.041 | 0.110 | |
| | Status | 20.975 | 0.013 | 0.112 | |
| Assessment of companies' involvement in sponsorship | Gender | 9.405 | 0.024 | 0.137 | |
| | Age | 33.275 | 0.001 | 0.144 | |
| | Education | 25.683 | 0.002 | 0.132 | |
| | Status | 77.382 | < 0.001 | 0.228 | |
| Assessment of companies' involvement in charity activities | Gender | 11.969 | 0.018 | 0.154 | |
| | Age | 41.940 | 0.001 | 0.140 | |
| | Education | 22.501 | 0.032 | 0.124 | |
| | Status | 72.597 | < 0.001 | 0.221 | |
| Taking specific actions for the benefit of customers | Status | 14.700 | 0.002 | 0.172 | |
| Taking specific actions for the benefit of employees | Gender | 6.232 | 0.013 | | 0.111 |
| | Age | 5.221 | 0.265 | 0.102 | |
| | Income | 7.921 | 0.048 | 0.128 | |
| Taking special actions in relation to the local community | Gender | 18.281 | < 0.001 | | 0.191 |
| | Education | 23.021 | < 0.001 | 0.217 | |
| | Status | 14.523 | 0.002 | 0.171 | |

☐ - very weak correlation, ☐ - weak correlation, ■ - moderate correlation

education, and status of respondents (weak correlations). The research did not confirm a statistically significant relationship, e.g. between the perception of enterprises' activities for environmental protection and the characteristics of respondents (Table 5.12).

It was also found that there is a statistically significant relationship between considering the social commitment of companies during purchases and gender, age, education, income, and the status of the respondents. In either case, the correlation between the variables is weak. There is also a relationship between the perception of CSR in the market activities of enterprises and the characteristics of the respondents. Such a relationship was found between the perception of CSR in product advertisements and education, place of residence and the status of respondents (weak correlation), between the perception of advertisements for CSR initiatives and the age, place of residence, and status of respondents (weak correlations), and between the perception of CSR activities in the process of providing services and the age and status of respondents (weak correlations) (Table 5.13). However, there is no statistically significant relationship between the perception of CSR activities during purchases and the characteristics of the respondents.

As the above results show, there are relationships between the answers given and the characteristics of the respondents. However, there are no recurring sociodemographic variables of the respondents that show a constant relationship with consumer behaviour related to CSR. Therefore, the research does not allow for the identification of a model consumer who consciously considers CSR when making purchases. The only variable that clearly determines the behaviour towards CSR among the respondents is the knowledge of the CSR concept. People declaring contact with the concept of CSR not only positively assess and perceive the social commitment of enterprises, but more often than others make purchases considering CSR. This means, inter alia, that the increased awareness of CSR among consumers may increase the participation of this factor in the purchasing decision process. CSR can therefore become a sought-after purchasing element as consumer awareness of the concept grows. Similar conclusions concern the relationship between a positive attitude to CSR and the behaviour of consumers in the market. According to the research, people declaring a positive attitude towards CSR not only perceive CSR activities in the practice of enterprises, but also declare their inclusion in decision-making processes when purchasing goods and services.

*Table 5.13* Noticing and considering CSR during shopping versus sociodemographic features of consumers – Pearson correlation coefficients (In the absence of a statistically significant relationship, the responses were omitted. Own study)

| *Variable A* | *Variable B* | *Pearson's CHI2* | *p-value* | *V Cramer's coefficient* |
|---|---|---|---|---|
| Including CSR while purchasing | Gender | 25.609 | < 0.001 | 0.226 |
| | Age | 36.005 | 0.001 | 0.155 |
| | Education | 29.656 | 0.001 | 0.142 |
| | Income | 21.800 | 0.010 | 0.123 |
| | Status | 26.138 | 0.002 | 0.132 |
| Noticing CSR in product advertisements | Education | 14.650 | 0.002 | 0.173 |
| | Domicile | 13.902 | 0.003 | 0.167 |
| | Status | 11.939 | 0.008 | 0.155 |
| Noticing CSR in the advertising of CSR initiatives | Age | 9.586 | 0.0480 | 0.138 |
| | Domicile | 24.146 | < 0.001 | 0.220 |
| | Status | 8.141 | 0.043 | 0.128 |
| Noticing CSR in the process of providing services | Age | 13.092 | 0.011 | 0.161 |
| | Status | 13.884 | 0.003 | 0.167 |

☐ - very weak correlation, ☐ - weak correlation, ■ - moderate correlation

In order to define the specificity of the behaviour of enterprises on the Polish market, efforts were also made to determine: (1) how enterprises approach social responsibility, (2) to what extent they apply CSR as an element of the enterprise strategy and (3) what is their attitude to CSR as an area of generating value for stakeholders and the company itself. The results of the published social reports of enterprises or RBF publications indicate numerous involvements of enterprises in charity actions or taking specific actions, often dedicated to specific groups of recipients (RBF 2018: 22–168). Such an approach of enterprises could, in part, confirm not only their involvement in social problems, but also a conscious selection of supported groups, and thus at least partial compliance with the assumptions of creating common value. Therefore, it was assumed that enterprises operating in Poland are not only aware of CSR, but also consider activities in this area in their daily activities (Ha3). The thesis adopted in this way is also confirmed by numerous projects implemented on the Polish market, the purpose of which was to support enterprises in the field of CSR. One of them was the project entitled Increasing the competitiveness of regions through CSR implemented by the Polish Agency for Enterprise Development in 2011–2017 financed under the Swiss-Polish Cooperation Program (PARP 2018), where one of the adopted goals was to increase CSR awareness among enterprises.

By analogy, in the case of the group of the so-called entrepreneurs, efforts were made to establish the perception of CSR by respondents on behalf of enterprises. In this case, it was also assumed that it would be appropriate to refer to the respondents who had come across the concept of CSR, which means that they know the essence of CSR. As in the case of consumers, the mere awareness of the concept or a positive attitude towards it does not mean that the principles of CSR are considered in economic practice. Enterprises knowing the assumptions of the concept may not agree with its goals or effects for business, and in the event of a negative assessment, they will not be interested in implementing CSR in practice. It is also assumed that a positive assessment of CSR by managers also does not have to result in the implementation of the concept into the strategies of enterprises which, for other reasons, may not be interested in applying the principles of social responsibility in their activities. Meanwhile, considering the responses of people who did not come into contact with the term CSR when their first contact with the term took place while completing the questionnaire, would be a major mistake in the study. It does not mean that the enterprises on whose behalf the respondents gave a negative answer, i.e. indicated that they had not had contact with the concept of CSR before, do not undertake activities that are part of the area of corporate social involvement. Very often, despite the lack of knowledge of the assumptions of the discussed concept, they undertake actions at the level of legal responsibility (improvement of areas regulated by law, e.g. regarding working conditions) or engage in sponsorship or charity activities. Hence, it is legitimate to include their responses in the research. However, in the opinion of the author, these people are not able to precisely indicate which CSR activities are undertaken by the enterprises they represent.

In connection with these findings, in order to verify the adopted research hypothesis Ha3, the following statistical hypotheses were adopted:

Hs8 Knowledge of the assumptions of CSR influences the positive assessment of the CSR concept and taking actions in the area of social responsibility.
Hs9 A positive assessment of the assumptions of the CSR concept has a positive impact on the social commitment of enterprises.

When analyzing the behaviour of companies that know the concept of CSR, a statistically significant relationship was shown, among others, between the declared knowledge of CSR and the indication of the application of CSR principles in the enterprise in which the respondent works (moderate correlation). The results obtained are, however, a big surprise. According to the analysis, the knowledge of CSR is inversely correlated with the declaration of applying the principles of social responsibility in practice. This, however, can be interpreted in two ways, i.e. (1) companies, knowing the assumptions of CSR, are not convinced to apply them in practice or (2) knowledge of the assumptions of the CSR concept allows for a more critical assessment of activities undertaken by the enterprise and noticing areas where the desired actions are not implemented. No statistically significant relationship was found between the declared knowledge of CSR and the application in enterprises of the basic principles of social responsibility established by the Global Compact.

In the case of involvement in sponsorship and charity activities, a statistically significant relationship occurs only in the case of the relationship of CSR knowledge and the use of sponsorship supporting specific projects and when using financial sponsorship. In both cases, the correlation is weak and the relationship is inverse. There is also a statistically significant relationship between the knowledge of CSR and the lack of any charity activities – a correlation confirming a positive relationship between the knowledge of CSR and not taking up this type of support, as well as supporting institutions and charitable activities undertaken over a long period of time, which also means that respondents who declared their knowledge of CSR definitely indicate a lack of involvement in this type of charity. In all three cases, the correlation is weak.

However, the research made it possible to find a positive correlation between the knowledge of CSR and the possession of documentation related to CSR, i.e. codes, policies, or social reports (moderate correlation). This means that persons confirming their knowledge of CSR more often indicated that the represented enterprises possessed documents.

In the case of the analysis of the relationship between actions taken for the benefit of stakeholders and the knowledge of CSR, a statistically significant relationship was confirmed only in the case of informing the media about undertaking CSR activities (weak correlation) and in the case of timely payment of amounts due to the state (weak correlation). In both cases, the opposite relationships were found, which means that the respondents confirmed the lack of cooperation with the media in the indicated area, but also some shortcomings in the area of responsibility towards public administration (Table 5.14).

In order to deepen the explanations, attempts were also made to verify the relationship between the declared attitude towards CSR, defined by the attitude as to the convergence of CSR assumptions with the interests of the enterprise, and the social commitment of enterprises in practice. The aim of the problem defined in this way was to check how the attitude towards CSR influences the market activities of enterprises, including those targeted at stakeholders other than customers. It was assumed that positive beliefs as to the compliance of CSR with the interests of the enterprise have a positive impact on the actions taken by the enterprise in practice (Hs8).

Statistical analysis of the data, unfortunately, did not confirm a statistically significant relationship between the variables in the case of most of the responses. A statistically significant correlation exists only in the case of the attitude to CSR described above and the declared undertaking of CSR activities in the enterprise (weak correlation), declared support for and observance of human rights by the enterprise (moderate correlation), conducting a dialogue with the local community (weak correlation), and the use of in-kind sponsorship by the enterprise (weak correlation) (Table 5.15).

*Table 5.14* Possession of documentation related to CSR and the characteristics of enterprises – Pearson correlation coefficients (In the absence of a statistically significant relationship, the responses were omitted. Own study)

| *Variable A* | *Variable B* | *Pearson's CHI2* | *p-value* | *V Cramer's coefficient* | *Coefficient* $\phi$ |
|---|---|---|---|---|---|
| Knowledge of the CSR concept | Taking action in practice | 16.389 | < 0.001 | | -0.331 |
| | Project sponsorship | 4.025 | 0.045 | | -0.164 |
| | Financial sponsorship | 4.336 | 0.037 | | -0.170 |
| | No involvement in charity | 5.827 | 0.016 | | 0.197 |
| | Charitable support of the institution | 10.508 | 0.001 | | -0.265 |
| | Charitable support in the long term | 8.336 | 0.004 | -0.236 | |
| | Possession of CSR documentation | 22.962 | 0.001 | 0.391 | |
| | Informing the media about CSR activities | 10.508 | 0.001 | | -0.265 |
| | Timely payment of obligations to the state | 8.953 | 0.003 | | -0.244 |

▭ - very weak correlation, ▭ - weak correlation, ■ - moderate correlation

*Table 5.15* Positive assessment of the CSR concept and the application of CSR in practice (In the absence of a statistically significant relationship, the responses were omitted. Own study)

| *Variable A* | *Variable B* | *Pearson's CHI2* | *p-value* | *V Cramer's coefficient* |
|---|---|---|---|---|
| Positive assessment of CSR concept | Undertaking CSR activities in practice | 8.537 | 0.036 | 0.239 |
| | Supporting and respecting human rights | 17.919 | 0.001 | 0.346 |
| | In-kind sponsoring | 11.465 | 0.009 | 0.276 |
| | Dialogue with the local community | 9.435 | 0.024 | 0.251 |

▭ - very weak correlation, ▭ - weak correlation, ■ - moderate correlation

The responses obtained do not clearly confirm that a positive attitude towards CSR results in corporate responsibility and increased commitment to creating value for various stakeholders. Although there is a positive correlation between the attitude to CSR and taking actions in the area of CSR in the enterprise, the research did not confirm a statistically significant relationship in the case of other variables, including in terms of dealing with individual stakeholders of enterprises.

Another assumption made in relation to the group of enterprises was that the awareness of CSR and the conduct in accordance with its principles are conditioned by the characteristics of enterprises (Ha4). In relation to the auxiliary hypothesis formulated in this way, the following detailed hypotheses were adopted:

Hs10 There is a relationship between the knowledge of CSR and the perception of CSR and the characteristics of enterprises.
Hs11 There is a relationship between the responsible behaviour of enterprises and their characteristics.

In this case, it was assumed that having knowledge about CSR is related to the size, range of activities, and the form of supervision of the company. According to the experience of the Polish market, social involvement in large enterprises of an international nature is more often confirmed than in the case of small, local companies.

In an attempt to determine the conditions for the implementation and application of CSR on the Polish market, the statistical hypothesis Hs11 was verified. On the basis of the research, a statistically significant relationship was found between the declared knowledge about CSR and the knowledge of the company's brands on the market, the size of employment, the size of the company, the company's annual revenue, and the range of its activities. There is a moderate correlation in the case of such variables as the size of employment, the size of the enterprise, and the amount of revenues of the enterprise. There is also a relationship between the opinion on the validity of using CSR in business and the financial condition of the enterprise (weak correlation). In this case, however, it means that the legitimacy of applying CSR in practice is more often emphasised by enterprises with lower revenues. Perhaps they perceive social responsibility as an element that can improve the company's competitiveness on the market. There was also a correlation between the perceived impact of CSR on the company's image and the company's financial condition, the perceived impact of CSR on customer loyalty to the company's brand and the number and awareness of brands, and between the perceived impact of CSR on the company's turnover and the awareness of its brands. In all these cases, the identified correlation is weak (Table 5.16). However, no statistically significant relationship was found between the positive opinion on the compliance of CSR with the interests of the enterprise and any features describing the enterprise.

There is also a statistically significant correlation between the enterprise taking CSR activities and the number of brands owned (weak correlation), enterprise size (weak correlation), enterprise revenues (weak correlation), range of enterprise activity (moderate correlation), and the declared type of business activity (production, trade, services; weak correlation). This means that small enterprises with a local character and low annual revenues,

*Table 5.16* Knowledge and perception of CSR by entrepreneurs and the characteristics of enterprises (In the absence of a statistically significant relationship, the responses were omitted. Own study)

| *Variable A* | *Variable B* | *Pearson's CHI2* | *p-value* | *V Cramer's coefficient* |
|---|---|---|---|---|
| Knowledge of the concept of CSR | Knowledge of brands | 10.000 | 0.019 | 0.258 |
| | Employment size | 24.217 | < 0.001 | 0.402 |
| | The size of the enterprise | 23.58 | < 0.001 | 0.397 |
| | Revenue | 14.687 | 0.002 | 0.313 |
| | Range of activity | 10.419 | 0.034 | 0.264 |
| The legitimacy of applying CSR in business | Financial condition | 17.46 | 0.043 | 0.196 |
| Assessment of the impact of CSR on the company's image | Financial condition | 17.936 | 0.036 | 0.200 |
| Assessment of the impact of CSR on the loyalty of consumers to the company's brand/brands | Number of brands | 21.250 | 0.002 | 0.266 |
| | Knowledge of brands | 14.971 | 0.020 | 0.223 |
| Assessment of the impact of CSR on the company's turnover | Knowledge of brands | 19.053 | 0.025 | 0.206 |

- very weak correlation, - weak correlation, - moderate correlation

declaring having one brand, more often include activities in the area of community involvement in their activities. Perhaps in this case it is this local, neighbourly character that determines the way of treating the market and the company's stakeholders. The small scale of operations allows these companies to focus on real values, which are perceived in this way by both customers and other interest groups, with particular emphasis on employees and the local community.

A statistically significant correlation was also confirmed between the degree of implementation of CSR principles in enterprises and their financial condition, brand awareness, and the form of enterprise ownership. In all cases, there is a weak correlation. A higher degree of CSR implementation can therefore be found rather in companies with a favourable financial situation, with well-known brands. These enterprises most likely feel obliged to act in a more responsible manner, and the favourable financial situation allows them to undertake additional activities for the benefit of their stakeholders, without the need to guarantee an increase in revenues in a short period of time as a result of undertaken actions.

There is also a statistically significant relationship between the involvement of enterprises in sponsorship and their financial condition (weak correlation), knowledge of the owned brands on the market (weak correlation), the size of employment (moderate correlation), the size of the enterprise (weak correlation), and the declared type of business activity (weak correlation). This leads to quite obvious conclusions. Large enterprises with a favourable financial condition with well-known brands are more often interested in sponsoring activities. Such conclusions confirm, inter alia, by results of the report on the sports sponsorship market from 2018. According to the report, the industries that incurred the largest expenses for the purchase of sponsorship rights in the analysed period are energy (19% of total expenditure) and the fuel industry (17%), i.e. entities with an established position on the market and at least recognisable brands (Sponsoring Insight: 13).

There is also a statistically significant relationship between companies' involvement in charity activities and the length of their operation on the market. In this case, charitable actions are more willingly undertaken by companies with a shorter history (Table 5.17).

The research also verified the declared approach to individual stakeholders of the company, assuming that it is related to the variables describing the examined entities. In the case of activities aimed at consumers, statistical analysis of data allowed, inter alia, to confirm the existence of a relationship between the declaration ofbeing honest with customers (being "fair") and the form of ownership of the enterprise (moderate correlation) and between the declaration of enterprises that they provide valuable products and the number of brands owned, the scope of the company's activity and the declared type of business activity (weak correlations).

In the case of activities aimed at investors, there is a relationship between maintaining constant contact, which is based on informing about the

*Table 5.17* Involvement in CSR and the characteristics of enterprises (In the absence of a statistically significant relationship, the responses were omitted. Own study)

| *Variable A* | *Variable B* | *Pearson's CHI2* | *p-value* | *V Cramer's coefficient* |
|---|---|---|---|---|
| Undertaking CSR activities | Number of brands | 11.198 | 0.011 | 0.273 |
| | The size of the enterprise | 11.674 | 0.008 | 0.279 |
| | Revenue | 9.729 | 0.02 | 0.255 |
| | Range of activity | 14.359 | 0.006 | 0.309 |
| | The nature of the enterprise | 9.654 | 0.022 | 0.254 |
| The degree of implementation of CSR principles in the enterprise | Financial condition | 25.602 | 0.002 | 0.239 |
| | Knowledge of brands | 24.721 | 0.003 | 0.234 |
| | Form of the property | 12.758 | 0.047 | 0.206 |
| The company's involvement in sponsorship | Financial condition | 12.266 | 0.006 | 0.286 |
| | Knowledge of brands | 10.139 | 0.017 | 0.260 |
| | Employment size | 19.448 | < 0.001 | 0.360 |
| | The size of the enterprise | 12.990 | 0.005 | 0.294 |
| | Range of activity | 10.189 | 0.037 | 0.261 |
| The company's involvement in charity activities | Time of existence in the market | 9.305 | 0.026 | 0.249 |

[ ] - very weak correlation, [ ] - weak correlation, [ ] - moderate correlation

development and activities undertaken in the company, and variables such as: financial condition of the company, the number of brands owned and corporate governance (weak correlations), as well as the size of employment, enterprise size, revenues, and declared type of business activity (moderate correlations). This means that smaller enterprises with lower revenues maintain constant contact with investors.

The research also confirmed the relationship between the declared, constant contact with suppliers and such variables as: the financial condition of the enterprise (weak correlation), the size of employment (moderate correlation), the size of the enterprise (weak correlation), the amount of revenues (weak correlation), and the scope of the company's operations (weak correlation). There is a weak correlation in all cases, except for employment, where there is a moderate correlation.

No statistically significant relationship was found, e.g. between educating suppliers in the area of CSR and the characteristics of enterprises. However, the existence of a significant relationship between the declared CSR verification of subcontractors and suppliers and the financial condition of enterprises (weak correlation) and the conduct of activities by enterprises in several industries (weak correlation) was confirmed.

During the research, the approach to the media and its relationship with the characteristics of enterprises were also verified. In this case, a statistically significant relationship exists only between informing the media about actions taken in the area of social responsibility and the assessment of the awareness of the company's brands on the market (weak correlation) and the size of the company's revenues (moderate correlation).

The relationship between the timely payment of liabilities by enterprises and the number of brands owned, the size of the enterprise, and the scope of the enterprise's operations was also confirmed. In all these cases, there is a weak correlation.

There is also a relationship between activities undertaken for the benefit of the local community and the characteristics of the surveyed enterprises. As a result of the analysis, no statistically significant relationship was found, e.g. between the declared limitation of the negative impact of the company's operations on the natural environment and the characteristics of enterprises. However, there is a statistically significant relationship between the declared promotion of pro-ecological behaviour and the financial condition of the company (weak correlation), the size of employment (weak correlation), the size of the company (weak correlation), corporate governance (weak correlation), the amount of revenues (moderate correlation), the scope of the company's operations (weak correlation), and diversification of the company's activity (weak correlation). There is also a weak correlation between the declared dialogue with the local community and the size of employment.

No statistically significant relationship was found between the approach to employees and the characteristics of enterprises (Table 5.18).

There is also a statistically significant correlation between the involvement of enterprises in environmental protection activities (the indicator is the percentage of profits that enterprises allocate to environmental protection) and such characteristics as: financial condition of the enterprise (weak correlation), employment volume (moderate correlation), company size (moderate correlation), type of corporate governance (weak correlation), revenues (weak correlation), scope of activity (moderate correlation), time of the company's operation on the market (weak correlation), number of industries in which the company operates (weak correlation), and the declared type of business activity (weak correlation) (Table 5.19). In this case, this means that the expenses for environmental protection are incurred primarily by large enterprises that have been operating on the market for more than ten years, of an international or global nature, often with foreign supervision, and with high annual revenues.

An important element of verifying the social involvement of enterprises is also having documentation related to CSR by them. Most often, these are social reports presenting the results of enterprises' activity in the social sphere. Such documents also include corporate codes of ethics and CSR policy. In this case, it was also assumed that the possession of such documentation is related to the characteristics of the examined enterprises.

The research confirmed the relationship between the possession of specific documents and the characteristics of enterprises in all cases, i.e. between the

*Table 5.18* Undertaking activities directed at particular groups of stakeholders and the characteristics of enterprises (In the absence of a statistically significant relationship, the responses were omitted. Own study)

| *Variable A* | *Variable B* | *Pearson's CHI2* | *p-value* | *V Cramer's coefficient* | *Coefficient* $\phi$ |
|---|---|---|---|---|---|
| Honesty towards customers/ "being" fair/ | Number of brands | 9.170 | 0.027 | 0.247 | |
| | Range of activity | 10.984 | 0.027 | 0.271 | |
| | The nature of the enterprise | 12.300 | 0.006 | 0.286 | |
| Providing valuable products | Number of brands | 9.170 | 0.027 | 0.247 | |
| | Range of activity | 10.984 | 0.027 | 0.271 | |
| | The nature of the enterprise | 12.300 | 0.006 | 0.286 | |
| Systematic informing of investors about the development and activities undertaken in the company | Financial condition | 11.150 | 0.011 | 0.273 | |
| | Number of brands | 7.881 | 0.048 | 0.229 | |
| | Employment size | 24.180 | $< 0.001$ | 0.401 | |
| | The size of the enterprise | 19.127 | $< 0.001$ | 0.357 | |
| | Corporate governance | 6.558 | 0.038 | 0.209 | |
| | Revenue | 18.892 | $< 0.001$ | 0.355 | |
| | Range of activity | 19.249 | $< 0.001$ | 0.358 | |
| Systematic informing of suppliers about the development and activities undertaken in the company | Financial condition | 10.353 | 0.016 | 0.263 | |
| | Employment size | 3.973 | 0.003 | 0.305 | |
| | The size of the enterprise | 10.104 | 0.018 | 0.260 | |
| | Revenue | 11.240 | 0.011 | 0.274 | |
| | Range of activity | 12.632 | 0.013 | 0.290 | |
| Verification of subcontractors/ suppliers in terms of CSR | Financial condition | 8.290 | 0.040 | 0.235 | |
| | Number of industries | 4.679 | 0.017 | | -0.195 |
| Informing the media about the company's CSR activities | Knowledge of brands | 10.657 | 0.014 | 0.267 | |
| | Revenue | 16.980 | 0.001 | 0.336 | |
| Timely payment of obligations (e.g. taxes) | Number of brands | 10.734 | 0.013 | 0.267 | |
| | The size of the enterprise | 11.314 | 0.010 | 0.275 | |
| | Range of activity | 10.804 | 0.029 | 0.268 | |
| Promoting pro-ecological behaviour by the company | Financial condition | 7.898 | 0.048 | 0.229 | |
| | Employment size | 11.901 | 0.008 | 0.282 | |
| | The size of the enterprise | 11.680 | 0.009 | 0.279 | |
| | Corporate governance | 6.138 | 0.046 | 0.202 | |
| | Revenue | 13.693 | 0.003 | 0.302 | |
| | Range of activity | 13.244 | 0.010 | 0.297 | |
| | Number of industries | 4.582 | 0.032 | | -0.174 |
| Dialogue with the local community | Employment size | 10.020 | 0.018 | 0.258 | |

[ ] - very weak correlation, [ ] - weak correlation, [ ] - moderate correlation

*Table 5.19* Undertaking activities aimed at environmental protection and the characteristics of enterprises (In the absence of a statistically significant relationship, the responses were omitted. Own study)

| *Variable A* | *Variable B* | *Pearson's CHI2* | *p-value* | *V Cramer's coefficient* |
|---|---|---|---|---|
| Percentage (%) of annual profits allocated to environmental protection | Financial condition | 18.230 | 0.006 | 0.247 |
| | Employment size | 37.072 | < 0.001 | 0.352 |
| | The size of the enterprise | 40.666 | < 0.0001 | 0.368 |
| | Corporate governance | 16.666 | 0.002 | 0.236 |
| | Revenue | 22.973 | 0.001 | 0.277 |
| | Range of activity | 42.718 | < 0.001 | 0.377 |
| | Time of existence in the market | 13.554 | 0.035 | 0.213 |
| | Number of industries | 7.640 | 0.022 | 0.226 |
| | The nature of the enterprise | 14.167 | 0.028 | 0.217 |

- very weak correlation, - weak correlation, - moderate correlation

declared possession of a code of ethics and the financial condition of the enterprise (weak correlation), the number of brands owned (weak correlation), the size of employment (weak correlation), the size of the enterprise (weak correlation), corporate governance (moderate correlation), the size of the company's revenues (weak correlation), and the scope of the company's operations (weak correlation), between having a CSR policy and the size of employment (moderate correlation), the size of the company (moderate correlation), the size of the company's revenues (moderate correlation), the range of the company's activity (weak correlation), and the declared type of activity of the company (weak correlation), and between the declared preparation of social reports and the size of employment (weak correlation), the size of the enterprise (weak correlation), the type of ownership supervision (moderate correlation), the size of the company's revenues (moderate correlation), the scope of the company's activity (weak correlation), the duration of the company's existence on the market (weak correlation), and the declared type industry (weak correlation) (Table 5.20).

Comparing the obtained results, it can be said that CSR documentation is much more common in large enterprises, with high annual revenues, of an international or global nature.

Despite numerous correlations between the variables determining the attitude of enterprises to CSR, as in the group of consumers, it is difficult to build a model enterprise that knows the concepts of CSR, assesses it positively, and consciously implements the Global Compact principles in practice, creating values for consumers and other stakeholders. It should be emphasised, however, that the Polish market is catching up in terms of responsibility in relation to the more developed countries of Western Europe or the United States. A summary of the statistical analysis is provided in Table 5.21.

*Table 5.20* Possession of documentation related to CSR and the characteristics of enterprises (In the absence of a statistically significant relationship, the responses were omitted. Own study)

| *Variable A* | *Variable B* | *Pearson's CHI2* | *p-value* | *V Cramer's coefficient* |
|---|---|---|---|---|
| Having a code of ethics | Financial condition | 35.244 | 0.001 | 0.280 |
| | Number of brands | 22.408 | 0.033 | 0.223 |
| | Employment size | 38.244 | 0.001 | 0.292 |
| | The size of the enterprise | 35.187 | 0.001 | 0.280 |
| | Corporate governance | 27.967 | 0.001 | 0.305 |
| | Revenue | 32.400 | 0.001 | 0.268 |
| | Range of activity | 28.429 | 0.028 | 0.218 |
| Having a CSR policy | Employment size | 16.644 | 0.001 | 0.333 |
| | The size of the enterprise | 24.330 | < 0.001 | 0.403 |
| | Revenue | 14.404 | 0.002 | 0.310 |
| | Range of activity | 11.400 | 0.022 | 0.276 |
| | The nature of the enterprise | 10.446 | 0.015 | 0.264 |
| Preparation of social reports | Employment size | 10.189 | 0.017 | 0.261 |
| | The size of the enterprise | 11.657 | 0.008 | 0.279 |
| | Corporate governance | 15.098 | 0.001 | 0.317 |
| | Revenue | 16.774 | 0.001 | 0.334 |
| | Range of activity | 10.215 | 0.037 | 0.261 |
| | Time of existence in the market | 10.833 | 0.013 | 0.269 |
| | The nature of the enterprise | 10.120 | 0.018 | 0.260 |

- very weak correlation, - weak correlation, - moderate correlation

*Table 5.21* Summary of the statistical analysis of the research results – matrix of auxiliary and statistical hypotheses (Own study)

| *An auxiliary hypothesis* | *Correlation* |
|---|---|
| Ha1. Consumers who know the basic assumptions of the CSR concept positively assess the activities in the area of social responsibility undertaken by enterprises and, seeing their value, take CSR into account when making purchases. | Hs1. Knowledge of the CSR concept influences the perception and assessment of activities in the area of social responsibility.<br>The hypothesis was confirmed in terms of:<br>1 the relationship between the awareness of the concept of CSR by consumers and their conviction that CSR is in line with the interests of the enterprise, about the legitimacy of using CSR in business, and about the positive impact of CSR on the loyalty of consumers to the brand/brands of the enterprise and the volume of the company's turnover;<br>2 the relationship between consumers' awareness of the concept of CSR and their perception of companies' involvement in sponsorship, charity activities and taking specific actions for the benefit of customers and employees; |

(*Continued*)

*Table 5.21* Continued

| *An auxiliary hypothesis* | *Correlation* |
| --- | --- |
| | Hs2 Knowledge of the CSR concept influences the perception and consideration of corporate social involvement during purchases.<br>1 The hypothesis was confirmed in terms of:<br>2 the relationship between CSR awareness and taking CSR into account when purchasing;<br>3 the relationship between CSR awareness and the perception of CSR during purchases, in advertising of products, in advertising of CSR initiatives and in the process of providing services;<br>Hs3 Including CSR during purchases results from a positive assessment of the CSR concept and practice.<br>Confirmed hypothesis regarding the relationship:<br>1 between including CSR while purchasing and the belief that the use of CSR is in line with the interests of enterprises and the application of the concept of corporate social responsibility in practice is justified;<br>2 between including CSR while purchasing and the belief that CSR has a positive impact on the brand image, customer loyalty to the brand/brands and the company's turnover;<br>3 between including CSR while purchasing and evaluating the application of CSR in practice, the degree of implementation of CSR in enterprises operating in Poland, the involvement of enterprises in sponsorship and charity activities;<br>4 between including CSR while purchasing and recognising the commitment of enterprises to environmental protection,<br>5 between taking CSR into account when purchasing and the perception of special treatment of customers, employees and the local community by enterprises;<br>6 between including CSR while purchasing and seeing CSR in purchasing, in advertising CSR initiatives and in the process of providing services. |
| Ha2. The perception of CSR as a value and its consideration by consumers when making purchases is conditioned by their socio-demographic features. | Hs4 There is a relationship between the knowledge of the CSR concept and the characteristics of consumers.<br>Confirmed hypothesis regarding the relationship between knowledge of social responsibility and gender and education.<br><br>Hs5 There is a relationship between the perception of CSR and the characteristics of consumers.<br>Confirmed hypothesis in terms of:<br>1 the relationship between the opinion on the compliance of CSR with the interests of the enterprise and such characteristics of the respondents as: gender, age, place of residence, status; |

2 the relationship between the opinion on the validity of using CSR in business and such characteristics of respondents as: gender, age, place of residence, income, and status;
3 the relationship between the assessment of the impact of CSR on the company's image and such characteristics of the respondents as: gender, age, education, place of residence, income and status;
4 the relationship between the assessment of the impact of CSR on the loyalty of consumers towards the company's brand/brands and such characteristics of the respondents as: age, education, place of residence, income, and status;
5 the relationship between the assessment of the impact of CSR on the company's turnover and such characteristics of the respondents as: gender, education and place of residence;

Hs6 There is a relationship between the perception of CSR in the practice of enterprises and the characteristics of consumers.

Confirmed hypothesis in terms of:

1 the relationship between CSR activities undertaken by enterprises operating in Poland and the gender, age, and income of respondents;
2 the relationship between the assessment of the degree of implementation of CSR principles in enterprises operating in Poland and the gender, age, education, place of residence, and status of respondents;
3 the relationship between the assessment of companies' involvement in sponsorship and the gender, age, education, and status of respondents;
4 the relationship between the assessment of companies' involvement in charity activities and the gender, age, education, and status of respondents;
5 the relationship between the perceived undertaking by enterprises of specific actions for the benefit of customers and the status of respondents;
6 the relationship between the perceived undertaking by enterprises of specific actions for the benefit of employees and the gender, age, and income of the respondents;
7 the relationship between the perceived undertaking by enterprises of special actions in relation to the local community and the gender, education, and status of respondents.

Hs7 There is a relationship between the consideration and perception of CSR during the purchasing process and the characteristics of the respondents.

(*Continued*)

*Table 5.21* Continued

| *An auxiliary hypothesis* | *Correlation* |
|---|---|
| | Confirmed hypothesis in terms of:<br>1 the relationship between including CSR while purchasing and the gender, age, education, income, and status of respondents;<br>2 the relationship between the perception of CSR in product advertisements and the education, place of residence, and status of respondents;<br>3 the relationship between the perception of CSR in the advertising of CSR initiatives and the age, place of residence, and status of respondents;<br>4 the relationship between the perception of CSR in the process of providing services and the age and status of respondents. |
| Ha3. Enterprises familiar with the basic assumptions of CSR positively evaluate the concept of CSR and apply its principles in their business activities. | Hs8 Knowledge of the assumptions of CSR influences the positive assessment of the CSR concept and taking actions in the area of social responsibility.<br>The hypothesis confirmed in terms of the relationship between the declared knowledge (contact with the concept) of CSR and the application of CSR principles in the company, the use of financial sponsorship, support for projects in the form of sponsorship, long-term charity activities addressed to institutions, possession of CSR documentation, informing the media about CSR activities and timely settlement of liabilities;<br>Hs9 A positive assessment of the assumptions of the CSR concept has a positive impact on the social commitment of enterprises.<br>The hypothesis confirmed in terms of the relationship between a positive assessment of the CSR concept and taking CSR activities in practice, supporting and respecting human rights, using material sponsorship and conducting a dialogue with the local community. |
| Ha4. CSR awareness in enterprises and compliance with its principles are determined by the characteristics of enterprises | Hs10 There is a relationship between the knowledge of CSR and the perception of CSR, and the characteristics of the company.<br>Confirmed hypothesis in terms of:<br>1 the relationship between the knowledge of CSR and the knowledge of the company's brands on the market, the size of employment, the size of the company, the amount of revenues, and the range of the company's operations;<br>2 the relationship between the belief in the positive impact of CSR on the image of the enterprise and the financial condition of enterprises;<br>3 the relationship between the opinion on the validity of using CSR in business and the financial condition of the enterprise; |

4 between the belief that CSR has a positive impact on customer loyalty towards the company's brand/brands and the number of brands owned by the company;
5 between the conviction about the positive impact of CSR on the company's turnover and the knowledge of the company's brands;

Hs11 There is a relationship between responsible behaviour of enterprises and the characteristics of the enterprise.

Confirmed hypothesis in terms of:

1 the relationship between the undertaking of CSR activities and the number of brands owned, the size of the enterprise, the amount of revenues, range, and type of activity (production, trade, services);
2 the relationship between the degree of implementation of CSR activities in enterprises and their financial condition, brand awareness on the market, and form of ownership;
3 the relationship between the company's involvement in sponsorship and its financial condition, brand awareness, employment, size of the enterprise and the type of business;
4 the relationship between the involvement of enterprises in charitable activities and the time of their operation on the market;
5 the relationship between the involvement of enterprises in environmental protection activities and their financial condition, employment, size of enterprises, type of corporate governance, the amount of revenues, range, duration of operation, the number of industries served and the type of business;
6 the relationship between the declaration of being "fair" and the form of ownership;
7 the relationship between the declared supply of valuable products and the number of brands, range and type of activity;
8 the relationship between the declared maintenance of constant contact with investors and the financial condition, the number of brands, the size of employment, the size of the enterprise, corporate governance, the amount of revenues, and the type of activity;
9 the relationship between the declared maintenance of constant contact with suppliers and the financial condition, the size of employment, the size of the enterprise, the amount of revenues, and the scope of activity;
10 the relationship between the approach to the media and the assessment of brand awareness of the enterprise;

(*Continued*)

*Table 5.21* Continued

| *An auxiliary hypothesis* | *Correlation* |
|---|---|
| | 11 the relationship between the timely payment of receivables and the number of brands, the size of the enterprise, and the range of operations;<br>12 the relationship between the promotion of pro-ecological behaviour and the financial condition, the size of employment, the size of enterprises, corporate governance, the amount of revenues, range and diversification of activities;<br>13 the relationship between the preparation of social reports and the size of employment, the size of the enterprise, the type of supervision, the amount of revenues, the range of activities, duration, and type of activity of the enterprise;<br>14 the relationship between having a code of ethics and the financial condition, the number of brands, the size of employment, the size of the enterprise, corporate governance, the amount of revenues, and the range of activities;<br>15 the relationship between having a CSR policy and the size of employment, enterprise size, revenues, range, and type of activity. |

## Notes

1 The results do not add up to 100 because respondents could choose more than one answer. The question was answered by the respondents who agreed with the legitimacy of applying CSR by enterprises.
2 The results do not add up to 100 because respondents could choose more than one answer.
3 The results do not add up to 100 because respondents could choose more than one answer.
4 Żywiec Group (Grupa Żywiec) is part of the HEINEKEN Group.
5 SABMiller has been the owner of Kompania Piwowarska since 2009. In 2017, Kompania Piwowarska changed its owner and is part of the Japanese Asahi Group Holdings.
6 The results do not add up to 100 because respondents could choose more than one answer.
7 Ibidem.
8 Ibidem.
9 In Poland, the obligation of Workers' Councils was established by the Act of 7 April 2006 on informing and consulting employees (Journal of Laws of 2006 No. of 2006, No. 79, item 550). The activity of trade unions in Poland is regulated by the Act of May 23, 1991 on trade unions (Journal of Laws No. 1991, No. 55, item 234).
10 When building the questionnaire, the author suggested actions taken, for example, by the Danone Group on the Polish market. From April 1, 2011, all Danone employees under an employment contract were covered by private medical care. Employees could also buy additional services: care for relatives and dental care. A Hospital Fund was also launched, the purpose of which was to finance medical

treatments of employees that could not be performed under the National Health Fund or the waiting period was too long (there was a real threat to the health and life of the employee). Facilities for pregnant women and young mothers have also been introduced. These women could benefit, inter alia, from one month of additional leave and a six-hour working day for the first two months. Source: Report on Social and Environmental Responsibility 2006–2009 (Danone 2017).

11 The idea of "Zero Waste" is one of the visionary concepts in solving waste problems. As defined by the Zero Waste International Alliance (ZWIA), Zero Waste is the preservation of all resources through responsible production, consumption, reuse and recovery of products, packaging and materials without burning and without discharges to land, water or air that endanger the environment or human health. The basic principles of the Zero Waste (5R) idea are refuse, reduce, reuse, recycle, and rot. This idea is widely used in enterprises, city management, and even promoted as a lifestyle (ZWIA 2018, online). ANIMAL (2018). The definition of Zero Waste adopted by the Zero Waste Planning Group: http://zwia.org/standards/zw-definition/ (09/12/2018).

12 These conclusions are based on indications with a very high probability (in the assessment of the respondents) of the occurrence of particular benefits. Moreover, the respondents could determine the chances of the occurrence of particular effects by selecting the following answers: big, medium, small and very small.

13 As the basis for these conclusions, as in the group of consumers, indications of a very high probability (in the assessment of the respondents) of the occurrence of particular benefits were adopted. Moreover, the respondents could determine the chances of the occurrence of particular effects by selecting the following answers: big, medium, small and very small.

# Conclusion

Changes in the environment of enterprises, both in the area of expectations formulated by society and in the area of technology, force a critical look at the current functioning of the enterprise. Both the current method of delivering value and shaping relations with the widely understood environment of the enterprise still require improvement. The concepts proposed as a remedy for business problems, so clearly visible during the economic crisis, are: (1) strengthening in the area of business ethics and (2) the concept of CSR, which has dominated the literature in the field of searching for factors enabling the growth of the company's value in the long term.

CSR is certainly a multi-dimensional issue. The multiplicity of shots as well as the complexity and ambiguity of the problem make it difficult to assess the effectiveness of CSR. However, we can talk about social responsibility or social commitment when the company goes beyond its basic activity aimed at achieving economic goals and complying with the law. Thus, CSR occurs when they engage in undertakings aimed at social welfare, considering the business goals they set for themselves.

Despite difficulties in estimating the benefits of corporate social involvement and criticism of CSR, CSR is becoming more and more popular. More and more often we hear about taking additional actions aimed at customers, employees, or the local community, actions that differ from the solutions adopted on the market. Companies are not only involved in supporting specific groups or projects, but are also interested in the quality of cooperation with recipients. One of the elements that allow them to build long-term relationships is based on the value that will be perceived as such by the company's stakeholders. The justification of such defined actions is, however, their connection with the planned financial goals of the enterprise.

The concept that combines, on the one hand, social expectations for a more responsible, sustainable approach to the implementation of economic activities, and, on the other hand, business expectations regarding the implementation of activities that will contribute to an increase in shareholder value, and therefore will be economically justified, is the concept of Creating Shared Value (CSV). Enterprises not only create value for stakeholders, but by strategically approaching the selection of the area of social involvement,

DOI: 10.4324/9781003317364-7

they can multiply this value. The strategic selection of the support area may provide benefits not only to stakeholders, the society, but also the enterprise itself.

Value creation by enterprises is not only the right choice of additional activities that will draw the society's attention to the company's social commitment, but above all a change in the approach to content shaped by business, i.e. product, price, distribution, and promotion. The marketing activities of companies determine the effectiveness of their functioning on the market. The way of creating a product or other elements of the marketing-mix is important from the point of view of the effectiveness of the market strategy. Meanwhile, the changes taking place in the area of technology and approach to business stakeholders force changes also in the area of broadly understood marketing. The actions taken so far have been ineffective, and failure by enterprises to consider progress in this area will condemn them to non-existence. It is imperative to consider value creation for customer in the current market service and to shift market action in this direction. The limitation to communicating CSR initiatives or undertaking activities in an image-related manner, consisting in an ad hoc, most often current response to the most widely publicised social problems, is no longer sufficient. The company's activities must be associated with value.

Value-based marketing is the strategic selection of content that is relevant to customers and other stakeholders. Designing a product, promotion, and price should not only consider solutions that are accepted by customers, but must be perceived by them in terms of real value. A sales proposition constructed in this way will also create value for the enterprise itself. Value-based marketing is based in equal part on a set of marketing techniques and Shareholder Value Analysis (SVA), which more and more often see marketing opportunities to create profit in the long term (Doyle 2008: 21). The inclusion of the CSR concept in the marketing activities of companies will allow for a more complete creation of value for customers, stakeholders, and business owners.

Despite numerous evidences for such a position in the literature and the existing potential of the proposed activities, markets are not fully ready to perceive the value in the created marketing activities. This sentence does not mean, however, that creating value and corporate social commitment is not profitable. The conducted research shows, inter alia, that consumers positively assess CSR as such, but how they perceive CSR and how they rate the activities of enterprises in the area of CSR is primarily influenced by the knowledge of the concept or assumptions of the CSR concept. Consumers who declared prior contact with the concept much more often declare a positive reception of CSR, as well as considering CSR when shopping.

The presented research did not confirm the relationship between the declared attitudes of consumers towards CSR and their sociodemographic variables. This means that, although there are statistically significant associations between some responses and responders, there is no clear-cut consumer

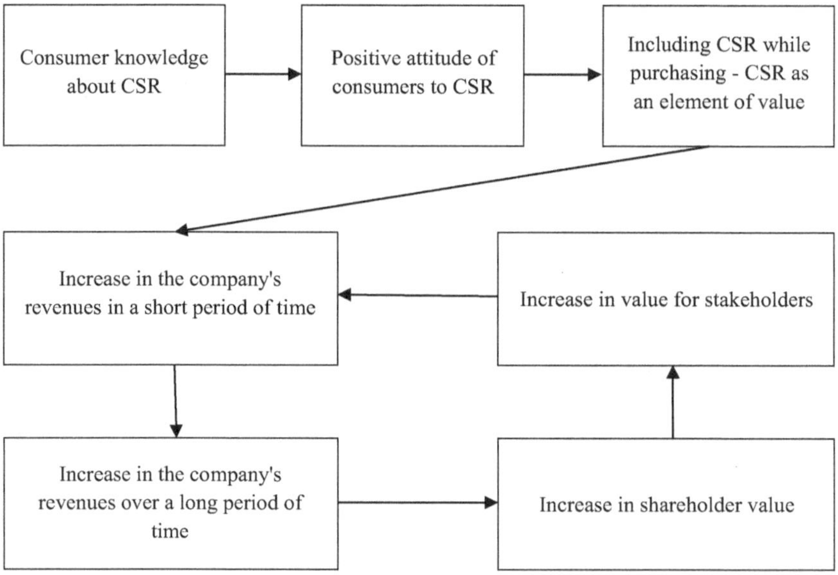


*Figure 6.1* Place of CSR in creating value for the company's stakeholders and shareholders (Own study)

model that is more sensitive to corporate social responsibility. These conclusions confirm the Polish market research in the area of acceptance and consideration of CSR by buyers, indicating a low knowledge of the concept and the lack of common features of people who take the CSR aspect into account when purchasing. However, it also means that the only factor that drives CSR when purchasing in developing countries is the knowledge of the buyers.

Increased awareness of CSR in the society may, therefore, increase consumer interest in the aspect of corporate social involvement during shopping. These conclusions seem to confirm the results of research carried out in more developed countries in Western Europe and the United States, where a higher level of CSR awareness among consumers and a higher level of considering CSR during market choices is observed. An example of a model built on the basis of confirmed assumptions is presented in Figure 6.1.

Considering CSR in a strategic way may therefore affect not only the increase in revenues in the short term, but also in the increase in revenues in the long term, increase in value for shareholders, and increase in value for other stakeholders (increased investment certainty, guarantee of work, etc.).

Unfortunately, as research has confirmed, companies operating on the Polish market do not include CSR in their market strategies to a large extent. The reason for this state of affairs is most likely the lack of customer requirements in this area. Managers, despite having knowledge of CSR and a positive attitude to the assumptions of the concept, most often declare the implementation of CSR principles at the level of legal responsibility, i.e. at a level not sufficient to qualify their enterprises as socially responsible. The knowledge of CSR assumptions does not affect the above-average undertaking of activities in this area in the practice of enterprises. The above-mentioned positive attitude to social responsibility also is not such a factor.

The research also did not confirm a clear relationship between the declared responsibility and shaping activities dedicated to specific groups of stakeholders and the characteristics of companies. However, surprisingly, such an attitude was more often declared by few local companies than large international companies. The only factor that would motivate enterprises to increase responsibility and create value for stakeholders is the demand for this type of activity. The lack of interest from the market does not encourage business to take additional action. However, this approach is highly risky. Education in the area of social responsibility means that more and more customers take this factor into account when shopping.

# Bibliography


Aaker, D. (1991). *Managing Brand Equity. Capitalizing on the Value of a Brand Name.* New York: The Free Press.

Abela, A.V., Murphy, P.E. (2008). Marketing with Integrity: Ethics and the Service-Dominant Logic for Marketing. *Journal of the Academy of Marketing Science*, 36(1): 39–53.

Ackerman, R., Bauer, B. (1976). *Corporate Social Responsiveness. The Modern Dilemma.* Reston, VA: Reston Publishing.

Ahlstedt, L., Jahnukainen, I. (1971). *Yritysorganisaatio yhteistoiminnan ohjausjaerjestelmaenae.* Helsinki: Weilin + Goeoes.

Ahmed, P.K., Machold, S. (2004). The Quality and Ethics Connection: Toward Virtuous Organizations. *Total Quality Management and Business Excellence*, 15(4): 527–545.

Akroush, M. (2010). Transactional Marketing and Relationship Marketing Paradigms: A Structural Equation Modeling Approach. *International Journal of Electronic Customer Relationship Management*, 4(2): 125–160.

Alkhafaji, A.F. (1989). *A Stakeholder Approach to Corporate Governance: Managing in a Dynamic Environment.* Westport, CT: Quorum Books.

Altkorn, J., Kramer, T. (1998). *Leksykon marketingu.* Warsaw: PWE.

AMA. (2018), https://www.ama.org/.

Ambler, T., Barrow, S. (1996). The Employer Brand. *Journal of Brand Management*, 4(3): 185–206.

Anderson, E.W., Fornell, C., Lehmann, D.R. (1994). Customer Satisfaction, Market Share and Profitability: Findings from Sweden. *Journal of Marketing*, 58(3): 53–66.

Ansoff, H.I. (1965). *Corporate Strategy: An Analytic Approach to Business for Growth and Expansion.* New York, NY: McGraw Hill.

Arystoteles (1996). Etyka nikomachejska. Tłum. In: Gromska, D. (ed) *Arystoteles. Dzieła wszystkie*, T. 5, ks. II, 6, 1107a. Warsaw: PWN.

Assibong, P.A., Wogu, I.A.P., Sholarin, M.A., Misra, S., Damaševičius, R., Sharma, N. (2020). The Politics of Artificial Intelligence Behaviour and Human Rights Violation Issues in the 2016 US Presidential Elections: An Appraisal. In: Sharma, N., Chakrabarti, A., Balas, V. (eds) *Data Management, Analytics and Innovation.* Advances in Intelligent Systems and Computing, vol 1016. Singapore: Springer, https://doi.org/10.1007/978-981-13-9364-8_22.

Ayuso, S., Rodriguez, M.A., Ricart, J.E. (2006). Responsible Competitiveness at the "Micro" Level of the Firm Using Stakeholder Dialogue as a Source for New Ideas:

A Dynamic Capability Underlying Sustainable Innovation. *Corporate Governance*, 6(4): 475–490.

Backhaus, K., Tikoo, S. (2004). Conceptualizing and Researching Employer Branding School of Business. *Career Development International*, 9(4/5): 501–517.

Ballantyne, D. (2004). Dialogue and Its Role in the Development of Relationship Specific Knowledge. *Journal of Business and Industrial Marketing*, 19(2): 114–123.

Baran, G. (2010). Raportowanie jako ważny element powiązania społecznej odpowiedzialności ze strategią organizacji. In: Nalepka, A., Ujwary-Gil, A. (eds) *Organizacje komercyjne i niekomercyjne wobec wzmożonej konkurencji oraz wzrastających wymagań konsumentów*. Nowy Sącz: Wyższa Szkoła Biznesu – National-Louis University w Nowym Sączu: 172–187.

Barley, S.R. (2007). Corporations, Democracy, and the Public Good. *Journal of Management Inquiry*, 16(3): 201–215.

Barnard, C. (1938). *The Functions of the Executive*. Cambridge, MA: Harvard University Press.

Bartkowiak, G. (2011). *Społeczna odpowiedzialność biznesu w aspekcie teoretycznym i empirycznym*. Warsaw: Difin.

Baughn, C.C., Buchanan, M.A. (2001). Cultural Protectionism. *Business Horizons*, 44(6): 5–15.

Bazillier, R., Vauday, J. (2009). The Greenwashing Machine: Is CSR More than Communication. *LEO Working Papers No 1617*. Orleans: University of Orleans.

Beauchamp, T.L., Bowie, N.E. (1983). *Ethical Theory and Business*, Englewood Cliffs, NJ: Prentice Hall, Inc.

Becker-Olsen, K.L., Cudmore, B.A., Hill, R.P. (2006). *The Impact of Perceived Corporate Social Responsibility on Consumer Behavior.* Journal of Business Research, 59(1): 46–53.

Beckford, J. (1998). *Quality. A Critical Introduction*. London & New York, NY: Routledge.

Beckford, J. (2001). *Quality. A Critical Introduction*. London: Routledge.

Belk, R.W. (1988). Possessions and the Extended Self. *Journal of Consumer Research*, 15(2): 139–168.

Berger, J., Heath, C. (2007). Where Consumers Diverge from Others: Identity-Signaling and Product Domains. *Journal of Consumer Research*, 34(2): 121–134.

Berle, A.A. (1931). Corporate Powers as a Power of Trust. *Harvard Law Review*, 44(7): 1049–1074.

Berle, A.A. (1932). For Whom Are Corporate Managers Trustees: A Note. *Harvard Law Review*, 45(8): 1365–1372.

Berle, A.A. (1954). *The 20th Century Capitalist Revolution*. New York, NY: Harcourt, Brace.

Berle, A.A., Means, G.C. (1932). *The Modern Corporation and Private Property*. New York, NY: Macmillan.

Berry, L.L., Parasuraman, A. (1991). *Marketing Services. Competing Through Quality*. New York, NY: The Free Press.

Bhattacharya, C.B., Sen, S. (2003). Consumer–Company Identification: A Framework for Understanding Consumers' Relationship with Companies. *Journal of Marketing*, 67(2): 76–88.

Bhattacharya, C.B., Sen, S. (2004). Doing Better at Doing Good: When, Why, and How Consumers Respond to Corporate Social Initiatives. *California Management Review*, 47(1): 9–24.

*Bible*, https://biblia.com/bible/esv/luke/12/15, https://biblehub.com/mark/10-25.htm.

Bird, T., Waters, J.A. (1989). The Moral Muteness of Managers. *California Management Review*, 32(1): 73–88.

Bobbink, M., Hartmann, A., Dewulf, G. (2016) Sustaining Extended Enterprise Performance: A Value Co-creation Perspective. *Journal of Organization Design*, 5: 3.

Bobola, A. (2016). CSR w programach kształcenia przyszłych menedżerów – przyczynek empiryczny. In: Popławski, W.T., Kaczorowska-Spychalska, D. (eds) *Nowe trendy w zarządzaniu – wybrane uwarunkowania innowacyjności i konkurencyjności*. Przedsiębiorczość i Zarządzanie. T. XVII. Z. 7(3). Łódź-Warsaw: Wydawnictwo SAN: 257–274.

Bockstette, V., Stamp, M. (2011). *Creating Shared Value: A How-to Guide for the New Corporate (R)evolution*. FSG, https://bibliotecadigital.ccb.org.co/bitstream/handle/11520/20968/Shared_Value_Guide.pdf?sequence=1&isAllowed=y.

Booms, B.H., Bitner, M.J. (1981). Marketing Strategies and Organization Structures for Service Firms. In: Donnelly, J.H, George, W.R. (eds) *Marketing of Services*. Chicago, IL: American Marketing Association: 47–51.

Borden, N.H. (1964). The Concept of the Marketing Mix. *Journal of Advertising Research*, 4: 2–7.

Borys, T. (2015). Typologia jakości życia i pomiar statystyczny. *Wiadomości statystyczne*, 7(650): 1–18.

Bowen, H. (1953). *The Social Responsibilities of Buisnessman*. New York, NY: Harper.

Bowen, F., Aragon-Correa, J.A. (2014). Greenwashing in Corporate Environmentalism Research and Practice: The Importance of What We Say and Do. *Organization & Envinronment*, 27(2): 107–112.

Bowie, N. (1988). The moral obligations of multinational corporations. In: Luper-Foy S. (ed), *Problems of international justice*, Boulder, CO: Westview Press: 97–113.

Brammer, S., Millington, A. (2005). Corporate reputation and philanthropy: An empirical analysis. *Journal of Business Ethics*, 61(1): 29–44.

Brand Finance (2021). Global 500 2021 Ranking, https://brandirectory.com/rankings/global/2021/table.

Brenner, S.N. (1993). The stakeholder theory of the firm and organizational decision making: Some propositions and a model. In: Pasquero J., Collins, D. (eds), *Proceedings of the Fourth Annual Meeting of the International Association for Business and Society*, San Diego: 205–210.

Brenner, S.N. (1995). Stakeholder theory of the firm: Its consistency with current management techniques. In: Näsi, J. (ed), Understanding stakeholder thinking. Helsinki: LSR-Julkaisut Oy: 75–96.

Brilman, J. (2002). *Nowoczesne koncepcje i metody zarządzania*. Warsaw: PWE.

Brown, T.J., Dacin, P.A. (1997). The Company and the Product: Corporate Associations and Consumer Product Responses. *Journal of Marketing*, 61(1): 68–85.

Bukowska, U. (2008). Proces zarządzania interesariuszami. *Zeszyty Naukowe Uniwersytetu Ekonomicznego w Krakowie*, 784: 90–99

Bunge, M. (1988). *Treatise on Basic Philosophy*. T. 8: Ethics. Dordrecht: D. Reidel Publishing Company.

Burke, L., Logsdon, J.M. (1996). How Corporate Social Responsibility Pays off. *Long Range Planning*, 29(4): 495–502.

Canadian International Development Agency (1997). *The Sustainable Development Framework*. Ottawa, ON: Canadian International Development Agency.

Carlisle, Y.M., Faulkner, D.O. (2005). The Strategy of Reputation. *Strategic Change*, 14(8): 413–422.

Carnegie, A. (1889). Wealth. *North American Review*, 148(391): 653–665.

Carroll, A.B. (1979). A Three-Dimensional Conceptual Model of Corporate Performance. *Academy of Management Review*, 4(4): 497–505.

Carroll, A.B. (1987). In Search of the Moral Manager. *Business Horizons*, 30(2): 7–15.

Carroll, A.B. (1989). *Business and society: Ethics and stakeholder management*. Cincinnati: South-Western.

Carroll, A.B. (1991). The Pyramid of Corporate Social Responsibility: Toward the Moral Management of Organizational Stakeholders. *Business Horizons*, 34(4): 39–48.

Carroll, A.B. (1993). *Business and Society: Ethics and Stakeholder Management*, 2nd ed. Cincinnati, OH: College Division South-Western Publishing Co.

Carroll, A.B. (1999). Corporate Social Responsibility. Evolution of Definitional Construct. *Business and Society*, 38(3): 268–295.

Carroll, A.B., Buchholtz, A.K. (2003). *Business & Society. Ethics and Stakeholder Management*. Mason, IA: Thompson Learning, South-Western College.

Carroll, A.B., Buchholtz, A.K. (2009). *Business and Society. Ethics and Stakeholders Management*. 7th ed. Mason, OH: South-Western Cengage Learning.

Carroll, A.B., Shabana, K.M. (2010). The Business Case for Corporate Social Responsibility: A Review of Concepts, Research and Practice. *International Journal of Management Reviews*, 12(1): 85–105.

Carson, R. (1962). *Silent Spring*. Boston, MA: Houghton Mifflin Harcourt.

Castells, M. (2000). The Rise of the Network Society, 2nd ed. Malden, MA: Wiley-Blackwell.

CGA-Canada: Certified General Accountants Association of Canada (2005). Measuring up: A Study on Corporate Sustainability Reporting in Canada, http://www.cga-canada.org/en-ca/ResearchReports/ca_rep_2005-06_sustainability.pdf.

Chand, M., Fraser, S. (2006). The Relationship Between Corporate Social Performance and Corporate Financial Performance: Industry Type as a Boundary Condition. *The Business Review*, 5(1): 240–245.

Chen, Y.S. (2010). The Drivers of Green Brand Equity: Green Brand Image, Green Satisfaction, and Green Trust. *Journal of Business Ethics*, 93(2): 307–319.

Chodyński, A. (2011). *Odpowiedzialność ekologiczna w proaktywnym rozwoju przedsiębiorstw*. Cracow: Krakowska Akademia im. Andrzeja Frycza Modrzewskiego.

Chryssides, G.D., Kaler, J.H. (1999). *Wprowadzenie do etyki biznesu*. Warsaw: PWN.

Clark, J.M. (1916). The Changing Basic of Economic Responsibility. *Journal of Political Economy*, 24: 209–229.

Clarke, I., Micken, K.S., Hart, H.S. (2002). Symbols for Sale… At Least for Now: Symbolic Consumption in Transition Economies. *Advances in Consumer Research*, 29(1): 25–30.

Clarkson, M.B. (1994). *A risk based model of stakeholder theory. Proceedings of the Second Toronto Conference on Stakeholder Theory*. Toronto: Centre for Corporate Social Performance & Ethics, University of Toronto.

Clarkson, M.B. (1995). A stakeholder framework for analyzing and evaluating corporate social performance. *Academy of Management Review*, 20(1): 92–117.

Cohen, B., Smith, B., Mitchell, R. (2008). Toward a Sustainable Conceptualization of Dependent Variables in Entrepreneurship Research. *Business Strategy and the Environment*, 17(2): 120–136.

Commitee for Economic Development (1971). *Social Responsibilities of Business Corporations*. New York, NY: CED.

Constantinides, E. (2002). The 4S Web-Marketing Mix Model. *Electronic Commerce Research and Applications*, 1(1): 57–76.

Constantinides, E. (2006). The Marketing Mix Revisited: Towards the 21st Century. *Marketing. Journal of Marketing Management*, 22 (3): 407–438.

Cornell, B., Shapiro, A. (1987). Corporate Stakeholders and Corporate Finance. *Financial Management*, 16, 5–14.

Culliton, J.W. (1948). *The Management of Marketing Costs*. Boston: Division of Research, Graduate School of Business Administration, Harvard University.

Daim, T.U., Wang, X., Cowan, K. (2016). Technology Roadmap for Smart Electric Vehicle-to-Grid (V2G) of Residential Chargers. *Journal of Innovation and Entrepreneurship*, 5(15): 1–13.

Danone (2017). www.danone.pl/news?newsId=8841.

Davis, K., Blomstrom, R.L. (1975). *Business and Society: Environment and Responsibility*, 3rd ed. New York, NY: McGraw Hill.

Day, G., Montgomery, D. (1999). Charting New Direction for Marketing. *Journal of Marketing*, 63: 3–13.

De Chernatony, L. (2003). *Marka. Wizja i tworzenie marki*. Gdańsk: GWP.

De Chernatony, L., McDonald, M. (1998). *Creating Powerful Brands*. Oxford: Butterworth-Heinemann.

De George, R.T. (1982). *Business Ethics*, 2nd ed. New York, NY: Macmillan Publishing.

De George, R.T. (1993). *Competing with Integrity in International Business*. New York, NY: Oxford University Press.

De George, R.T. (1995). *Business Ethics*. Englewood Cliffs, NJ: Prentince Hall.

Des Jardis, J.R., McCall, J.J. (1985). *Contemporary Issues in Business Ethics*. Belmont, CA: Reston Publishing Company.

Devaraj, S., Krajewski, L., Wei, J.C. (2007). Impact of eBusiness Technologies on Operational Performance: The Role of Production Information Integration in the Supply Chain. *Journal of Operations Management*, 25(6): 1199–1216.

Dhaliwal, D.S., Li, O.Z., Tsang, A., Yang, Y.G. (2011). Voluntary Nonfinancial Disclosure and the Cost of Equity Capital: The Initiation of Corporate Social Responsibility Reporting. *The Accounting Review*, 86(1): 59–100.

Dhaliwal, D.S., Radhakrishnan, S., Tsang, A., Yang, Y.G. (2012). Nonfinancial Disclosure and Analyst Forecast Accuracy: International Evidence on Corporate Social Responsibility Disclosure. *The Accounting Review*, 87(3): 723–759.

Dobiegała-Korona, B. (2008). Zarządzanie wartościami dla klienta (wybrane aspekty). In: Grudzewski, W.M., Hejduk, I.K. (eds) *W poszukiwaniu nowych paradygmatów zarządzania*. Warsaw: SGH: 29–53.

Dobiegała-Korona, B. (2014). Innowacje w budowie wartości przedsiębiorstwa. *Zeszyty Naukowe Wyższej Szkoły Humanitas. Zarządzanie*, 1: 24–40.

Dodd, E.M. (1932). For Whom Are Corporate Managers Trustees? *Harvard Law Review*, 45(7): 1145–1163.

Donaldson, T., Dunfee, T.W. (2002). Ties that Bind in Business Ethics: Social Contracts and Why They Matter. *Journal of Banking & Finance*, 26(9): 1853–1865.

Donaldson, T., Preston, L.E. (1995). The Stakeholder Theory of the Corporation: Concepts, Evidence, and Implications. *Academy of Management Review*, 20(1): 65–91.

Doyle, P. (2000). *Value-Based Marketing: Marketing Strategies for Corporate Growth and Shareholder Value.* New York: John Wiley & Sons.

Doyle, P. (2008). *Value-Based Marketing. Marketing Strategies for Corporate Growth and Shareholder Value.* 2nd ed. Chichester: John Wiley & Sons, Ltd.

Driscoll, C., Starik, M. (2004). The Primordial Stakeholder: Advancing the Conceptual Consideration of Stakeholder Status for the Natural Environment. *Journal of Business Ethics*, 49(1): 55–73.

Drucker, P.F. (1954). *Practice of Management.* New York, NY: Harper & Row.

Drucker, P.F. (1955). "Management science" and the manager. *Management Science*, 1(2):115–126.

Drucker, P.F. (1974). *Management: Tasks, Responsibilities, Practices.* London: Heinemann.

Drucker, P.F. (1984). The New Meaning of Corporate Social Responsibility. *California Management Review*, 26(2): 53–63.

Drucker, P.F. (1984a). A New Look at Corporate Social Responsibility. *The McKinsey Quarterly*, 4: 17–28.

Drucker, P.F. (1986). *Management. Task, Responsibilities, Practices.* New York, NY: Truman Talley Books. E.P. Dutton.

Drucker, P.F. (1994). *Praktyka zarządzania.* Cracow: AE w Krakowie.

Drucker, P.F. (1995). *Zarządzanie w czasach burzliwych. Nowe wyzwania – nowe horyzonty.* Cracow: Biblioteka Nowoczesności, AE Cracow „Czytelnik".

Drucker, P.F. (1997). Kłopoty z "etyką biznesu". In: Ryan, L.V., Sójka, J. (eds) *Etyka biznesu: z klasyki współczesnej myśli amerykańskiej.* Poznań: W drodze.

Drucker, P.F. (2010). *The Changing World of the Executive.* Boston, MA: Harvard Business School Publishing.

Du, S., Bhattacharya, C.B., Sen, S. (2007). Reaping Relational Rewards from Corporate Social Responsibility: The Role of Competitive Positioning. *International Journal of Research in Marketing*, 24(3): 224–241.

Dyllick, T., Hockerts, K. (2002). Beyond the Business Case for Corporate Sustainability. *Business Strategy and the Environment*, 11(2): 130–141.

Eells, R. (1959). Social Responsibility: Can Business Survive the Challenge? *Business Horizons*, 2(4): 33–41.

Eells, R. (1960). *The Meaning of Modern Business.* New York, NY: Columbia University Press.

Eells, R., Walton, C. (1961). *Conceptual Foundations of Business.* III. Homewood, IL: Richard D. Irwin.

Eells, R., Walton, C. (1974). *Conceptual Foundations of Business.* 3rd ed. Burr Ridge, IL: Irwin.

EFQM (2013). Model Doskonałości EFQM, https://www.efqm.org/.

Elkington, J. (1994). Towards the Sustainable Corporation: Win-Win-Win Business Strategies for Sustainable Development. *California Management Review*, 36(2): 90–100.

Elkington, J. (1998). *Cannibals with Forks: The Triple Bottom Line of 21st Century Business.* Gabriola Island, Stony Creek: New Society Publishers.

Ellen, P.S., Mohr, L.A., Webb, D.J. (2006). Building Corporate Associations: Consumer Attributions for Corporate Socially Responsible Programs. *Journal of the Academy of Marketing Science*, 34(2): 147–157.

Environmental Protection Agency (1998). *Environmental labeling issues, policies and practices worldwide. Report for the Pollution Prevention Division.* US EPA.

European Commission (2001). *Green Paper: Promoting a European Framework for Corporate Social Responsibility*, COM (2001) 366 final. Brussels 18.07.2001.

European Commission (2010). *EUROPE 2020. A strategy for smart, sustainable and inclusive growth*. Brussels, 3.3.2010, COM(2010) 2020 final, https://op.europa.eu/en/publication-detail/-/publication/6a915e39-0aab-491c-8881-147ec91fe88a/language-pl/format-PDF.

European Commission (2011). A renewed EU strategy 2011–14 for Corporate Social Responsibility,https://www.eurocommerce.eu/media/7237/position-csr-renewed_csr_strategy_2011-14-07.03.2012.pdf.

European Commission (2011a). Communication from The Commission to The European Parliament, The Council, The European Economic And Social Committee And The Committee Of The Regions. A renewed EU strategy 2011–14 for Corporate Social Responsibility. Brussels, 25.10.2011. COM (2011) 681 final, https://eur-lex.europa.eu/LexUriServ/LexUriServ.do?uri=COM:2011:0681:FIN:en:PDF.

European Commission (2013). European Parliament resolution of 6 February 2013 on corporate social responsibility: accountable, transparent and responsible business behavior and sustainable growth, https://www.europarl.europa.eu/doceo/document/TA-7-2013-0049_EN.html.

European Commission (2013a). European Parliament resolution of 6 February 2013 on Corporate Social Responsibility: Promoting society's interests and a route to sustainable and inclusive recovery (2012/2097(INI)), https://eur-lex.europa.eu/legal-content/EN/TXT/?toc=OJ%3AC%3A2016%3A024%3AFULL&uri=uriserv%3AOJ.C_.2016.024.01.0033.01.ENG.

Evan, W.M., Freeman, R.E. (1988). A stakeholder theory of the modern corporation: Kantian capitalism. In: Beauchamp T.L., Bowie N. (eds), Ethical theory and business, Englewood Cliffs, NJ: Prentice-Hall: 75–84.

Ferrell, O.C., Gresham, L.G. (1985). A Contingency Framework for Understanding Ethical Decision Making in Marketing. *Journal of Marketing*, 49(3): 87–96.

Filek, J. (2008). Przyczyny małego zainteresowania ideą CSR w Polsce. In: Bąk, M., Kulawczuk, P. (eds) *Społeczna odpowiedzialność biznesu w małych i średnich przedsiębiorstwach,* Warsaw: Instytut Badań nad Demokracją i Przedsiębiorstwem Prywatnym: 61–74.

Filek, J. (2009). Czy społeczna odpowiedzialność biznesu jest nową wersją umowy społecznej? *Prakseologia*, 149: 21–38.

Fisher, D., Smith, S. (2011). Co-creation is Chaotic: What it Means for Marketing When No One Has Control. *Marketing Theory*, 11(3): 325–350.

Flew, A. (1984). *Dictionary of Philosophy*. New York, NY: St. Martin's Press.

Fombrun, C., Gardberg, N.A., Barnett, M.L. (2000). Opportunity Platforms and Safety Nets: Corporate Citizenship and Reputational Risk. *Business and Society Review*, 105(1): 85–106.

Forehand, M.R., Grier, S. (2003). When is Honesty the Best Policy? The Effect of Stated Company Intent on Consumer Skepticism. *Journal of Consumer Psychology*, 13(3): 349–356.

Frederick, W.C. (1978). From CSRl to CSR2: *The maturing of business-and-society thought. Worlung paper.* Pittsburgh, PA: Graduate School of Business, University of Pittsburgh.

Frederick, W.C. (1994). From CSR1 to CSR2. The Maturing of Business-and-Society Thought. *Business & Society*, 33(2): 150–164.

Frederick, W.C., Davis, K., Post, J.E. (1988). *Business and Society. Public Strategy, Public Policy, Ethics*. New York, NY and Toronto: McGraw-Hill Publishing Company.

Freeman, R.E. (1984). *Strategic Management: A Stakeholder Approach*. Boston, MA: Pitman/Ballinger (Harper Collins).

Freeman, R.E. (1994). The politics of stakeholder theory: Some future directions. *Business Ethics Quarterly* 4: 409–421.

Freeman, R.E., Evan, W.M. (1990). Corporate Governance: A Stakeholder Interpretation. *Journal of Behavioural Economics*, 19(4): 337–359.

Freeman, R.E., Gilbert, D. R. (1987). Managing stakeholder relationships. In: Sethi S.P., Falbe C.M. (eds), *Business and society: Dimensions of conflict and cooperation*, Lexington, MA: Lexington Books: 397–423.

Freeman, R.E., Harrison, J.S., Wicks, A.C. (2007). *Managing for Stakeholders: Survival, Reputation, and Success*. New Haven, CT: Yale University Press.

Freeman, R.E., Harrison, J.S., Wicks, A.C., Parmar, B., de Colle, S. (2010). *Stakeholder Theory: The State of the Art*. New York, NY: Cambridge University Press.

Freeman, R.E., Philips, R.A. (2002). Stakeholder Theory: A Libertarian Defense. *Business Ethics Quarterly*, 12(3): 331–350.

Freeman, R.E., Reed, D.L. (1983). Stockholders and Stakeholders: A New Perspective on Corporate Governance. *California Management Review*, 25(3): 88–106.

Friedman, M. (1962). *Capitalism and Freedom*. Chicago, IL: University of Chicago Press.

Friedman, M. (1970). The Social Responsibility of Business is to Increase its Profits. *The New York Times Magazine*, 13 September, 32–33, 122–124.

Fryar, C.R. (1991). What's Different About Services Marketing? *The Journal of Marketing Services*, 5(4): 53–58.

Gałkowski, S. (2004). Cnoty i relatywizm. Alasdaira MacIntyre'a próba przekroczenia relatywizmu. *Diametros*, 2: 1–17.

Garbarski, L. (2012). Etyczne aspekty działań marketingowych. In: Gasparski, W. (ed) *Biznes, etyka, odpowiedzialność*. Warsaw: PWN: 64–78.

Garvin, D. (1984). What Does "Product Quality" Really Mean? *Sloan Management Review*, 26(1): 28–42.

Gasparski, W. (1997). Etyka biznesu – szkice do portretu. In: Dietl, J., Gasparski, W. (eds) *Etyka biznesu*. Warsaw: PWN.

Gasparski, W. (2004). Społeczna Odpowiedzialność Biznesu: argumenty przeciw i za. *Annales: Etyka w życiu gospodarczym*, 7(1): 39–49.

Gasparski, W. (2004a). *Wykłady z etyki biznesu*. Warsaw: Wydawnictwo Wyższej Szkoły Przedsiębiorczości i Zarządzania im. Leona Koźmińskiego.

Gasparski, W. (2012). Etyka biznesu. In: Gasparski, W. (ed) *Biznes, etyka, odpowiedzialność*. Warsaw: PWN: 79–88.

Gasparski, W., Lewicka-Strzałecka, A. (2001). *Etyka biznesu jako przedmiot nauczania*. Warsaw: Wydawnictwo Wyższej Szkoły Przedsiębiorczości i Zarządzania im. Leona Koźmińskiego.

Gębarowski, M. (2007). *Nowoczesne formy promocji*. Rzeszów: Oficyna Wydawnicza Politechniki Rzeszowskiej.

George, W.R. (1990) Internal Marketing and Organizational Behavior: A Partnership in Developing Customer-Conscious Employees at Every Level. *Journal of Business Research*, 20: 63–70.

George, W.R., Grönroos, C. (1989) Developing Customer Conscious Employees at Every Level – Internal Marketing. In: Congram, C.A., Friedman, M.L.

(eds) *Handbook of Marketing for the Services Industries*. New York, NY: AMACOM: 85–100.

Gilbert, J. (1992). *How to Eat an Elephant: A Slice by Slice Guide to Total Quality Management*. London: Tudor.

Gombeski, W. (1998). Better Marketing Through a Principles-Based Model. *Marketing Health Services*, 18(3): 43–48.

Google (2008). Google Project 10 to 100, https://web.archive.org/web/20090803133153, http://www.project10tothe100.com/why.html.

Griffin, R.W. (1998). *Podstawy zarządzania organizacjami*. Warsaw: PWN.

Griffin, R.W. (2004). *Podstawy zarządzania organizacjami*. Warsaw: PWN.

Grönroos, C. (1994). From Marketing Mix to Relationship Marketing: Towards a Paradigm Shift in Marketing. *Management Decision*, 32(2): 4–20.

Grönroos, C. (1994a). Quo Vadis, Marketing? Toward a Relationship Marketing Paradigm. *Journal of Marketing Management*, 10(5): 347–360.

Grönroos, C. (1996). Relationship Marketing: Strategic and Tactical Implications. *Management Decision*, 34(3): 5–14.

Grönroos, C. (2011). Value Co-creation in Service Logic: A Critical Analysis. *Marketing Theory*, 11(3): 279–301.

Grönroos, C., Voima, P. (2013). Critical Service Logic: Making Sense of Value Creation and Co-creation. *Journal of the Academy of Marketing Science*, 41(2): 133–150.

Grudzewski, W.M., Hejduk, I.K., Sankowska, A., Wańtuchowicz, M. (2009). *Zarządzanie zaufaniem w przedsiębiorstwie. Koncepcja, narzędzia, zastosowanie*, Cracow: Wolters Kluwer Polska – Oficyna Sp. z o. o.

Gummesson, E. (1994). Making Relationship Marketing Operational. *International Journal of Service Industry Management*, 5(5): 5–20.

Gundlach, G.T. (2007). The American Marketing Association's 2004 Definition of Marketing: Perspectives on Its Implications for Scholarship and the Role and Responsibility of Marketing in Society. *Journal of Public Policy & Marketing*. 26(2): 243–250.

Hąbek, P. (2015). *Sprawozdawczość przedsiębiorstw w zakresie ich społecznej odpowiedzialności. Ocena jakości raportów CSR*. Warsaw: CeDeWu Sp. z o.o.

Haigh, N., Griffiths, A. (2009). The Natural Environment as a Natural Stakeholder: The Case of Climate Change. *Business Strategy and Environment*, 18: 347–359.

Hakansson, H., Waluszewski, A. (2005). Developing a New Understanding of Markets: Reinterpreting the 4Ps. *Journal of Business and Industrial Marketing*, 20(3): 110–117.

Halal, W.E. (2001). The Collaborative Enterprise. A Stakeholder Model Uniting Profitability and Responsibility. *The Journal of Corporate Citizenship*, 2: 27–42.

Hamrol, A. (2005). *Zarządzanie jakością z przykładami*. Warsaw: PWN.

Handley, A., Chapman, C.C. (2012). *Content Rules*. Hoboken, NJ: John Wiley & Sons, Inc.

Harlow, W.F., Brantley, B.C., Harlow, R.M. (2011). BP Initial Image Repair Strategies After the Deepwater Horizon Spill. *Public Relations Review*, 37(1): 80–83.

Hart, S.L., Sharma, S. (2004). Engaging Fringe Stakeholders for Competitive Imagination. *Academy of Management Executive*, 18(1): 7–18.

Hawkes, J. (2001). *The Fourth Pillar of Sustainability: Culture's Essential Role in Public Planning*. Melbourne: Common Ground Publishing.

Heald, M. (1970). *The Social Responsibilities of Business: Company and Community, 1900–1960*. Cleveland, OH: The Press of Case Western Reserve University.

Hill, C.W.L., Jones, T.M. (1992) Stakeholder-Agency Theory. *Journal of Management Studies*, 29(2), 131-154. http://dx.doi.org/10.1111/j.1467-6486.1992.tb00657.x

Hinterhuber, A. (2004). Towards Value-Based Pricing—An Integrative Framework for Decision Making. *Industrial Marketing Management*, 33(8): 765–778.

Hoffman, W.M. (1986). What is Necessary for Corporate Moral Excellence? *Journal of Business Ethics*, 5(223): 233–242.

Hollensen, S. (2003). *Marketing Management. A Relationship Approach*. Harlow: FT Prentince Hall.

Hosmer, L.T. (1994). Why Be Moral? A Different Rationale for Managers. *Business Ethics Quartely*, 4(2): 191–204.

Howaniec, H. (2000). Komercyjne zawłaszczanie podświadomości. *Marketing w Praktyce*, 3: 60–61.

Howaniec, H. (2001). NLP w reklamie. *Marketing w Praktyce*, 3: 12–14.

Howaniec, H. (2008). Udział marki w tworzeniu wartości przedsiębiorstwa. In: Urbańczyk, E. (ed) *Zarządzanie przedsiębiorstwem. Studia i Prace Wydziału Nauk Ekonomicznych i Zarządzania*, 7: 485–494.

Howaniec, H. (2009). Miejsce ceny w podnoszeniu konkurencyjności przedsiębiorstwa. In: Howaniec, H., Waszkielewicz, W. (eds) *Marketing. logistyka i ludzie w zarządzaniu organizacjami*. Bielsko-Biala: Wydawnictwo Naukowe ATH: 173–184.

Howaniec, H. (2010). Marka społecznie odpowiedzialna – wpływ stosowania CSR na wartość marki. In: Brzozowska-Woś, M. (ed) *Marketing – ujęcie relacyjne*. Gdańsk: WZiE Politechnika Gdańska: 187–205.

Howaniec, H. (2013). Brand as the value for shareholders and stakeholders. In: Howaniec, H., Waszkielewicz, W. (eds) *Value-based marketing – selected problems*. Bielsko-Biala: University in Bielsko-Biala Publishing Hause: 61–71.

Howaniec, H. (2014). Marketing a kształtowanie wartości dla klienta. Realizacja marketingu wartości na przykładzie wybranych marek. In: Czubała, A., Hadrian, P., Wiktor, W. (eds) *Marketing w 25-leciu gospodarki rynkowej w Polsce*. Warsaw: PWE: 590–598.

Howaniec, H. (2014a). Wykorzystanie mediów społecznościowych w działaniach marketingowych przedsiębiorstw na polskim rynku. *Marketing i Rynek*, 11(CD): 170–180.

Howaniec, H. (2015). Postrzeganie CSR w Polsce w kontekście zaangażowania przedsiębiorstw w poszczególne grupy interesariuszy. In: Kaczmarek, J., Szymla, W. (eds) *Teoria i praktyka zarządzania w obliczu nowych wyzwań*. Cracow: Fundacja Uniwersytetu Ekonomicznego: 221–229.

Howaniec, H. (2015a). Social Responsibility of Enterprises – The Polish Practice. In: Howaniec, H., Waszkielewicz, W. (eds) *The Creation of Value and Responsibility in Activities of Organizations*. Krakow: AGH University of Science and Technology Press: 61–69.

Howaniec, H. (2016). CSR and Responsibility for the Local Community. In: Barcik, A., Howaniec, H., Malara, Z. (eds) *Selected Aspects of Management of Contemporary Enterprises*. Bielsko-Biala: University of Bielsko-Biala: 29–36.

Howaniec, H. (2016a). Percepcja społecznej odpowiedzialności biznesu wśród klientów, *Marketing i Rynek*, 7: 289–297.

Howaniec, H. (2016b). Wpływ społecznej odpowiedzialności biznesu na lojalność konsumentów wobec marki. *Nierówności Społeczne a Wzrost Gospodarczy*, 45(1): 32–40.

Howaniec, H. (2017). CSR and shaping of values for stakeholders. *Zeszyty Naukowe Politechniki Częstochowskiej Zarządzanie*, 27(1): 151–161.

Howaniec, H. (2017a). Zaangażowanie społeczne firmy a percepcja marki na przykładzie Nivea Beiersdorf. *Rynek – Społeczeństwo – Kultura*, 1(22): 102–108.

Howaniec, H. (2018). Employer branding and responsibility for employees in CSR practices in Poland. *Proceedings of the 2nd International Conference: Contemporary Issues in Theory and Practice of Management. Czestochowa University of Technology.* Czestochowa: Czestochowa University of Technology. Faculty of Management: 133–140.

Howaniec, H. (2018a). The Employer Branding as Part of the Value Creation in the Company. In: Dziura, M., Jaki, A., Rojek, T. (eds) *Enterprises and Economies in the Face of Contemporary Challenges. Management – Restructuring – Innovation.* Cracow: Cracow University of Economic: 167–175.

Howaniec, H., Okrzesik, O. (2015). *Współpraca nauka – biznes. Współpraca trójstronna jako przykład innowacji w procesie komercjalizacji badań i transferu technologii.* Bielsko-Biala: Centrum Innowacji i Transferu Technologii. Akademia Techniczno-Humanistyczna w Bielsku-Białej.

Howaniec, H., Waszkielewicz, W. (2007) *Corporate Social Responsibility and Protection of the Environment.* In: *Richnes and Diversity of GIS.* Zagreb: Hrvatski Informaticki Zbor – GIS Forum: 260–265.

Howaniec, H., Waszkielewicz, W. (2013). Marketing Concepts During Systemic Changes in Poland. In: Teczke, J., Terblanche, N. (eds) *Management Science in Transition Period in South Africa and Poland.* Cracow – Stellenbosch: International Management Foundation, Cracow University of Economics: 227–241.

Howaniec, H., Wróblewski, Ł. (2018). Support of Culture as a Part of Social Responsibility of Companies. In: Wróblewski, Ł., Dacko-Pikiewicz, Z., Liu, J.C.Y. (eds) *Cultural Management. From Theory to Practice.* London: London Stientific i WSB University, 156–169.

Hu, M. (2020). Cambridge Analytica's Black Box. *Big Data & Society*, 7(2): 1–6, https://doi.org/10.1177/2053951720938091.

Hunt, S.D., Vitell, S.J. (1986). A General Theory of Marketing Ethics. *Journal of Macromarketing*, 6(1): 5–16.

Husted, B.W., Salazar, J. (2006). Taking Friedman Seriously: Maximising Profits and Social Performance. *Journal of Management Studies*, 43(1): 75–91.

Iacobucci, D., Grayson, K.A. Ostrom, A.L. (1994). The Calculus of Service Quality and Customer Satisfaction: Theoretical and Empirical Differentiation and Integration. *Advances in Services Marketing and Management*, 3(C): 1–67.

Ingenbleek, P. (2014). The Theoretical Foundations of Value-Informed Pricing in the Service-Dominant Logic of Marketing. *Management Decision*, 52(1): 33–53.

ISO 8402 (1994). Quality management and quality assurance — Vocabulary.

ISO (2003). *ISO Horizon 2010. Standards for a Sustainable World.* Geneva: International Organization for Standardization.

ISO 26000 (2012). *Wytyczne dotyczące społecznej odpowiedzialności.* Warsaw: PKN.

Jackson, J. (1999). *Biznes i moralność.* Warsaw: PWN.

John Paul II, Laborem Exercens (On Human Work), September 14, 1981, Rome.

Jaruga, A., Kabalski, P., Szychta, A. (2010). *Rachunkowość Zarządcza.* Warsaw: Wolters Kluwer Polska Sp. z o.o.

Jeurissen, R. (2004). Institutional Conditions of Corporate Citizenship. *Journal of Business Ethics*, 53(1–2): 87–96.

Jones, T.M. (1980). Corporate Social Responsibility Revisited, Redefined. *California Management Review*, 22(3): 59–67.

Kall, J. (2001). *Silna marka. Istota i kierowanie*, Warsaw: PWE.

Kant, I. (1984). *Krytyka praktycznego rozumu*. Przeł. J. Gałecki, Warsaw: PWN.

Kant, I. (2013). *Uzasadnienie metafizyki moralności*. Kąty: Wydawnictwo Marek Derewiecki.

Kaplan, A.M., Haenlein, M. (2010). Users of the world, unite! Challenges and opportunities of Social Media. *Business Horizons*, 53: 59–68.

Kaptein, M. (1998). *Ethics Management: Auditing and Developing the Ethical Content of Organization*. Dordrecht: Kluwer.

Kauf, S. (2005). *Strategiczno-planistyczne aspekty integracji marketingu i logistyki*. Opole: Wydawnictw o Instytut Śląski Sp. z o.o.

Keller, K.L., Lehmann, D.R. (2006). Brands and Branding: Research Findings and Future Priorities. *Marketing Science*, 25(6): 740–759.

Kennedy, D.M. (1999). *Freedom from Fear*. Oxford: Oxford University Press.

Khan, M.T., Khan, N.A., Ahmed, S., Ali, M. (2012). Corporate Social Responsibility (CSR): Definition, Concepts and Scope (A Review). *Universal Journal of Management and Social Sciences*, 2(7): 41–52.

Kienzler, M. (2018). Value-Based Pricing and Cognitive Biases: An Overview for Business Markets. *Industrial Marketing Management*, 68(January): 86–94.

Kietliński, K., Reyes, V.M., Oleksyn, T. (2005). *Etyka w biznesie i zarządzaniu*. Cracow: Oficyna Ekonomiczna.

Kleemann, F., Voss, G., Rieder, K. (2008). Un(der)paid Innovators: The Commercial Utilization of Consumer Work Through Crowdsourcing. *Science, Technology & Innovation Studies*, 4(1): 5–26.

Klein, N. (2000). *No logo*. New York, NY: Picador.

Klein, J., Dawar, N. (2004). Corporate Social Responsibility and Consumers' Attributions and Brand Evaluations in a Product-Harm Crisis. *International Journal of Research in Marketing*, 21(3): 203–217.

Klimczak, B. (1999). Etyka gospodarcza. In: Gasparski, W., Lewicka-Strzałecka, A., Miller, D. (eds) *Etyka biznesu, gospodarki i zarządzania*. Warsaw: Wydawnictwo Wyższej Szkoły Humanistyczno-Ekonomicznej.

Klimczak, B. (2006). *Etyka gospodarcza*. Wrocław: Wydawnictwo Akademii Ekonomicznej im. Oskara Langego we Wrocławiu.

Kohl, M. (2007). Corporate cultural responsibility: Das kulturelle engagement österreichischer unternehmen. *SWS-Rundschau*, 47(3): 343–362.

Kotler. P. (1967). *Marketing Management*, 1st edition. Englewood Cliffs, NJ: Prentice-Hall.

Kotler, P. (1989). From Mass Marketing to Mass Customization. *Planning Review*, 17(5): 1–47.

Kotler, P., Armstrong, G. (1989). *Principles of Marketing*. London: Prentice Hall International.

Kotler, P., Keller, K. (2006). *Marketing Management*. Englewood Cliffs, NJ: Prentice Hall.

Kotler, P., Armstrong, G., Saunders, J., Wong, V. (2001). *Principles of Marketing*. Third European Edition. Englewood Cliffs, NJ: Prentice Hall, Pearson Education Limited.

Kotler, P., Armstrong, D., Saunders, J., Wong, V. (2002). *Marketing. Podręcznik europejski*. Warsaw: PWE.

Koufteros, X., Vonderembse, M., Jayaram, J. (2005). Internal and External Integration for Product Development: The Contingency Effects of Uncertainty, Equivocality, and Platform Strategy. *Decision Sciences*, 36(1): 97–133.

Kracher, B., Corritore, C.L. (2004). Is There a Special E-Commerce Ethics? *Business Ethics Quarterly*, 14(1): 71–94.

Kramer, M.R., Pfitzer, M. (2017). Ekosystem wartości wspólnej. *Harvard Business Review Polska*, 170.

Kulawczuk, P., Bąk, M., Bednarz, P., Kulawczuk, T., Szcześniak, A. (2007). Analiza korzyści ekonomicznych ze stosowania zasad społecznej odpowiedzialności biznesu w polskich przedsiębiorstwach. In: Kulawczuk, P., Poszewiecki, A. (eds) *Wpływ społecznej odpowiedzialności biznesu i etyki biznesu na zarządzanie przedsiębiorstwami*. Warsaw: IBnDiPP, EQUAL: 55–112.

Kurz, W., Többens, T. (2012). Global Pricing Survey. Managing Global Pricing Excellence. Deloitte & Touche GmbH, https://www2.deloitte.com/content/dam/Deloitte/de/Documents/strategy/C-studie-b2b-pricing_122012.pdf.

Lacy, P., Cooper, T., Hayward, R., Neuberger, L. (2010). A New Era of Sustainability, UN Global Compact and Accenture, http://web2.fit.edu/sustainability/documents/UNGC%20&%20Accenture.%202010.%20CEO%20study.pdf (12.05.2018).

Langtry, B. (1994). Stakeholders and the moral responsibilities of business. *Business Ethics Quarterly*, 4(4): 431–443.

Łapa, M., Gruszecka-Tieśluk, A. (2018). *Raport. Odpowiedzialny biznes w Polsce. Dobre praktyki 1918–1939*. Warsaw: Responsible Business Forum.

Laufer, W.S. (2003). Social Accountability and Corporate Greenwashing. *Journal of Business Ethics*, 43(3): 253–261.

Lee, S.M., Olson, D.L., Trimi, S. (2012). Co-innovation: Convergenomics, Collaboration, and Co-creation for Organizational Values. *Management Decision*, 50(5): 817–831.

Leś, E. (2001). *Zarys historii dobroczynności i filantropii w Polsce*. Warsaw: Wydawnictwo Prószyński i S-ka.

Lewandowska, A., Witczak, J., Kurczewski, P. (2017). Green Marketing Today – A Mix of Trust, Consumer Participation and Life Cycle Thinking. *Management*, 21(2): 28–48.

Lewicka-Strzałecka, A. (1999). *Etyczne standardy firm i pracowników*. Warsaw: IFiS PAN.

Lewicka-Strzałecka, A. (2006). *Odpowiedzialność moralna w życiu gospodarczym*. Warsaw: IFiS PAN.

Lewicka-Strzałecka, A. (2012). Konsumenci: prawa i obowiązki. In: Gasparski, W. (ed) *Biznes, etyka, odpowiedzialność*. Warsaw: PWN: 259–268.

Li, Y. (2010). The Case Analysis of the Scandal of Enron. *International Journal of Business and Management*, 5(10): s. 37–41.

Lichtenstein, D.R., Drumwright, M.E., Braig, B.M. (2004). The effects of corporate social responsibility on customer donations to corporate-supported nonprofits. *Journal of Marketing*, 68(4): 16–32.

Liozu, S.M., Hinterhuber, A. (2013). Pricing Orientation, Pricing Capabilities, and Firm Performance. *Management Decision*, 51(3): 594–614.

Lipowski, M. (2016). Kanał komunikacji a kanał dystrybucji – zanikanie różnic i ich konsekwencje. *Studia Ekonomiczne. Zeszyty Naukowe. Uniwersytetu Ekonomicznego w Katowicach*, 254: 99–107.

Lloyd, S. (2002) Branding from the Inside Out. *Business Review Weekly*, 24(10): 64–66.

Low, S.M. (1988). Cultural Aspects of Design: An Introduction to the Field. *Architecture and Behavior*, 4(3): 187–196.

Low, J., Kalafut, P.C. (2004). *Niematerialna wartość firmy. Ukryte źródła przewagi konkurencyjnej*. Cracow: Oficyna Ekonomiczna.

Lozano, J.M. (2002). Towards the Relational Corporation: From Managing Stakeholder Relations to Building Stakeholder Relationships (Waiting for Copernicus). *Corporate Governance*, 5(2): 60–77.

Luo, X., Bhattacharya, C. B. (2006). Corporate social responsibility, customer satisfaction, and market value. *Journal of Marketing*, 70(4): 1–18.

Lusch, R.F., Vargo, S.L. (2006). Service-Dominant Logic: Reactions, Reflections, and Refinements. *Marketing Theory*, 6(3): 281–288.

Lyke, B., Jickling, M. (2002). *WorldCom: The Accounting Scandal*. CRS Report for Congress.

Lyon, T.P., Maxwell, J.W. (2004). Astroturf: Interest Group Lobbying and Corporate Strategy. *Journal of Economics and Management Strategy*, 13(4): 561–597.

Lyon, T.P., Maxwell, J.W. (2006). Greenwash: Corporate Environmental Disclosure under Threat of Audit. Ross School of Business Working Paper Series: Working Paper No. 1055. Social Sciences Research Network Electronic Paper Collection, http://ssrn.com/abstract=938988.

Mackey, A., Mackey, T.B., Barney, J.B. (2007). Corporate Social Responsibility and Firm Performance: Investor Preferences and Corporate Strategies. *Academy of Management Review*, 32(3): 817–835.

Maignan, I., Ferrell, O.C. (2000). Measuring Corporate Citizenship in Two Countries: The Case of the United States and France. *Journal of Business Ethics*, 23(3): 283–297.

Majkut, R., Wójcik, D. (2015). Społeczna odpowiedzialność biznesu spółek Skarbu Państwa. In: Uziębło, A. (ed) Społeczna odpowiedzialność biznesu, podatki, inwestycje. Wybrane aspekty. Prace Naukowe Wyższej Szkoły Bankowej w Gdańsku, 38: 17–43.

Makuch, Ł. (2010). *Instytucje rynku CSR w Polsce 2010. Przewodnik po kluczowych organizacjach, mediach oraz inicjatywach promujących i edukujących w zakresie Społecznej Odpowiedzialności Biznesu w Polsce*. Warsaw: Instytut Odpowiedzialnego Biznesu.

Malara, Z. (2006). *Przedsiębiorstwo w globalnej gospodarce. Wyzwania współczesności*. Warsaw: PWN.

Maon, F., Lindgreen, A. (2014). Reclaiming the Child Left Behind: The Case for Corporate Cultural Responsibility. *Journal of Business Ethics*, 4(130): 755–766.

Marcoux, A.M. (2003). Snipers, Stalkers, and Nibblers: Online Auction Business Ethics. *Journal of Business Ethics*, 46(2): 163–173.

Margolis, J., Walsh, J. (2003). Misery Loves Companies: Rethinking Social Initiatives by Business. *Administrative Science Quarterly*, 48(2): 268–305.

Maspex rozwiązał umowę z agencją odpowiedzialną za aferę „powstańczą" (2017), https://wadowiceonline.pl/biznes/10216-maspex-rozwiazal-umowe-z-agencja-odpowiedzialna-za-afere-powstancza.

Matten, D., Crane, A. (2005). Corporate Citizenship: Toward an Extended Theoretical Conceptualization. *Academy of Management Review*, 30(1): 166–179.

Matten, D., Crane, A., Chapple, W. (2003). Behind the Mask: Revealing the True Face of Corporate Citizenship. *Journal of Business Ethics*, 45(1/2): 109–120.

Mayo, E. (1933). *The Human Problems of an Industrial Civilization*. New York, NY: McMillan Co.

Mazurowska, M. (2014). Rachunkowość na rzecz zrównoważonego rozwoju. Gospodarka – etyka – środowisko. In: Dziawgo, D., Borys, G. (eds) *Prace Naukowe Uniwersytetu Ekonomicznego we Wrocławiu*, 329: 225–231.

McCarthy, E.J. (1960). *Basic Marketing: A Managerial Approach*. Irwin, IL: Homewood.

McWilliams, A., Siegel, D. (2001). Corporate Social Responsibility: A Theory of the Firm Perspective. *Academy of Management Review*, 26(1): 117–127.

Menon, S., Kahn, B.E. (2003).Corporate Sponsorships of Philanthropic Activities: When Do They Impact Perception of Sponsor Brand? *Journal of Consumer Psychology*, 13(3): 316–327.

Meta (2021). Sustainability Report, https://sustainability.fb.com/2021-sustainability-report/.

Miles, R.A. (1987). *Managing the Corporate Social Environment*. Englewood Cliffs, NJ: Prentice Hall.

Mitchell, R.K., Agle, B.R., Wood, D.J. (1997). Toward a Theory of Stakeholder Identification and Salience: Defining the Principle of Who and What Really Counts. *Academy of Management Review,* 22(4): 853–886.

Möller, K. (2006). The Marketing Mix Revisited: Towards the 21st Century Marketing by E. Constantinides. *Journal of Marketing Management*, 22(3–4): 439–450.

Morgan, R. Hunt, S. (1994). The Commitment-Trust Theory of Relationship Marketing. *Journal of Marketing*, 58(3): 20–38.

Mroziewski, M. (2010). *Styl zarządzania jako instytucjonalny czynnik kreowania kapitału przedsiębiorczości organizacyjnej. Koncepcja ewolucyjno-normatywna*. Gdańsk: Wydawnictwo Uniwersytetu Gdańskiego.

Murphy, P.E. (1999). Character and Virtue Ethics in International Marketing: An Agenda for Managers, Researchers, and Educators. *Journal of Business Ethics*, 18(1): 107–124.

Murphy, P.E., Laczniak, G.R., Bowie, N.E., Klein, T.A. (2005). *Ethical Marketing: Basic Ethics in Action*. Upper Saddle River, NJ: Prentice Hall.

Myśliwiec, G. (2013). *Etyka gospodarcza i zawodowa*. Warsaw: Almamer.

Nagar, Y., Boer, P.M., Garcia, A.C. (2016). Accelerating the Review of Complex Intellectual Artifacts in Crowdsourced Innovation Challenges. In: Thirty Seventh International Conference on Information Systems, Dublin 2016, 11 December 2016–14 December 2016.

Nakonieczna, J. (2008). *Społeczna odpowiedzialność przedsiębiorstw międzynarodowych*. Warsaw: Difin.

Näsi, J. (1995). What is stakeholder thinking? A snapshot of a social theory of the firm. In: Näsi, J. (ed), *Understanding stakeholder thinking*. Helsinki: LSR-Julkaisut Oy: 19–32.

Ness, M.R. (1992). Corporate Social Responsibility. *British Food Journal*, 94: 38–44.

Nike Inc. (2020). FY20 NIKE, Inc. Impact Report. Executive Summary, https://purpose-cms-preprod01.s3.amazonaws.com/wp-content/uploads/2021/03/30191535/FY20-NIKE-Inc.-Impact-Report_Executive-Summary1.pdf.

Nogalski, B., Śniadecki, J. (2001). *Etyka zarzadzania przedsiębiorstwem*. Bydgoszcz: Oficyna Wydawnicza Ośrodka Postępu Organizacyjnego Sp. z o.o.

Normann, R., Ramirez, R. (1993). From Value Chain to Value Constellation: Designing Interactive Strategy. *Harvard Business Review*, 71(4): 65–77.

New Universal Encyclopedia (1988). T 3. Warsaw: PWN.

New Universal Encyclopedia PWN (1995). T. 2. Warsaw: PWN.

New Universal Encyclopedia PWN (1995). T. 3. Warsaw: PWN.

New Universal Encyclopedia PWN (1995). T. 4. Warsaw: PWN.

Nurse, K. (2006). *Culture as the fourth pillar of sustainable development*. Paper prepared for Commonwealth Secretariat, London, UK, https://pdfs.semanticscholar.org/92da/e4886a02f1fb27dd4131db5912aae6b7074f.pdf, accessed on September.

O'Malley, L., Patterson, M. (1998). Vanishing Point: The Mix Management Paradigm Reviewed. *Journal of Marketing Management*, 14(8): 829–851.

O'Neill Jr, G.D., Hershauer, J.C., Golden, J.S. (2006). The Cultural Context of Sustainability Entrepreneurship. *Greener Management International*, 55: 33–46.

Oakland, J.S. (1992). *Total Quality Management*. Oxford: Butterworth-Heinemann.

Obłój, K. (1997). *Strategia sukcesu firmy*. Warsaw: PWE.

Otto, J. (2004). *Marketing relacji. Koncepcja i stosowanie*. Warsaw: C.H. Beck.

Paliwoda-Matiolańska, A. (2014). *Odpowiedzialność społeczna w zarządzaniu przedsiębiorstwem*. Warsaw: C.H. Beck.

Pantano, A., Treuer, J., Baki, Y.S. (2022). The UCI Math Circle: Building an Online Community of Young Math Researchers. *Journal of Math Circles*, 2(2): 66–120.

Parasuraman, A., Zeithaml, V.A., Berry, L.L. (1988). Servqual: A Multiple Item Scale for Measuring Consumers' Perceptions of Service Quality. *Journal of Retailing*, 64(1): 12–40.

Payne, A., Frow, P. (2005). A Strategic Framework for Customer Relationship Management. *Journal of Marketing*, 69(4): 167–176.

Payne, A.F., Storbacka, K., Frow, P. (2008). Managing the Co-creation of Value. *Journal of the Academy of Marketing Science*, 36(1): 83–96.

Peattie, K., Crane, A. (2005). Green Marketing: Legend, Myth, Farce or Prophesy? *Qualitative Market Research: An International Journal*, 8(4): 357–370.

Piller, F., West, J. (2014). Firms, Users, and Innovation: An Interactive Model of Coupled Open Innovation. In: Chesbrough, H., Vanhaverbeke, W., West, J. (eds) *New Frontiers in Open Innovation*. Oxford: Oxford University Press: 29–49.

Pinkston, T.S., Carroll, A.B. (1996). A Retrospective Examination of CSR Orientations: Have They Changed? *Journal of Business Ethics*, 15(2): 199–206.

Piontek, B. (2002). *Koncepcja rozwoju zrównoważonego i trwałego Polski*. Warsaw: PWN.

PN-ISO 8402:1996. *Zarządzanie jakością i zapewnienie jakości – Terminologia*. Warsaw: PKN.

Polska Agencja Rozwoju Przedsiębiorczości (2018). *Zwiększenie konkurencyjności regionów poprzez społeczną odpowiedzialność biznesu (CSR)*, https://www.parp.gov.pl/csr.

Popovic, D. (2006). Modelling the Marketing of High-Tech Start-ups. *Journal of Targeting, Measurement and Analysis for Marketing*, 14(3): 260–276.

Porter, M.E. (1980). *Competitive Strategy: Techniques for Analyzing Industries and Competitors*. New York, NY: Free Press.

Porter, M.E. (1987). From Competitive Advantage to Corporate Strategy. *Harvard Business Review*, 65(3-May–June): 43–59.

Porter, M.E., Kramer, M.R. (2002). The Competitive Advantage of Corporate Philanthropy. *Harvard Business Review*, 80(12): 56–69.

Porter, M.E., Kramer, M.R. (2003). *Filantropia przedsiębiorstwa jako źródło przewagi konkurencyjnej*. Warsaw: Harvard Business Review Polska.

Porter, M.E., Kramer, M.R. (2006). Strategy & Society: The Link Between Competitive Advantage and Corporate Social Responsibility. *Harvard Business Review*, 84(12), 78–92.

Porter, M.E., Kramer, M.R. (2011). Creating Shared Value. *Harvard Business Review*, 89(1–2): 62–77.

Porter, M.E., Kramer, M.R. (2011a). Creating Shared Value. How to Reinvent Capitalism – and Unleash a Wave of Innovation and Growth. *Harvard Business Review*, 89 (1–2): 1–17.

Porter, M.E., van der Linde, C. (1995). Green and Competitive: Ending the Stalemate. *Harvard Business Review*, 73(5): 120–134.

Post, J.E., Frederick, W.C., Lawrence, A.T., Weber, J. (1996). *Business and Society. Corporate Strategy, Public Policy, Ethics*. New York, NY: McGraw-Hill.

Post, J.E., Preston, L.E., Sachs, S. (2002). *Redefining the Corporation: Stakeholder Management and Organizational Wealth*. Stanford, CA: Stanford University Press.

Potocki, A. (2000). *Współczesne tendencje w zarządzaniu – teoria i praktyka*. Chrzanów: Wyższa Szkoła Przedsiębiorczości i Marketingu w Chrzanowie.

Prahalad, C.K., Krishnan, M.S. (2010). *Nowa era innowacji*. Warsaw: PWN.

Prahalad, C.K., Ramaswamy, V. (2000). Co-opting Customer Competence. *Harvard Business Review*, 78(1), 79–87.

Prahalad, C.K., Ramaswamy, V. (2004). *The Future of Competition. Co-creating Unique Value with Customers*. Boston, MA: Harvard Business School Press.

Prahalad, C.K., Ramaswamy, V. (2004a). Co-creating Unique Value with Customers. *Strategy & Leadership*, 32(3): 4–9.

Pratley, P. (1998). *Etyka w biznesie*. Warsaw: Gebethner i Ska.

Preston, L.E., Post, J.E. (1975). *Private Management and Public Policy: The Principle of Public Responsibility*.Englewood Cliffs, NJ: Prentice-Hall.

Prothero, A. (1990). Green Consumerism and the Societal Marketing Concept: Marketing Strategies for the 1990s. *Journal of Marketing Management*, 6(2): 87–103.

Przybyłowski, K., Hartley, S.W., Kerin, R.A., Rudelius, W. (1998). *Marketing*. Warsaw: Dom Wydawniczy ABC.

Public Eye on Davos, https://en.wikipedia.org/wiki/Public_Eye_on_Davos.

Rafiq, M., Ahmed, P. (1995). Using the 7Ps as a Generic Marketing Mix: An Exploratory Survey of UK and European Marketing Academics. *Marketing Intelligence and Planning*, 13(9): 4–15.

Rana, S. (2008). From Making Money Without Doing Evil to Doing Good Without Handouts: The Google.Org Experiment in Philanthropy. *Journal of Business & Technology Law*, 3(1): 87–96.

*Raport: Odpowiedzialności Społecznej i Środowiskowej 2006–2009*. Danone, www.danone.pl/news?newsId=8841.

*Raport: Odpowiedzialny biznes w Polsce 2010. Dobre praktyki* (2011). Warsaw: Responsible Business Forum.

*Raport: Odpowiedzialny biznes w Polsce 2015. Dobre praktyki* (2016). Warsaw: Responsible Business Forum.

*Raport: Odpowiedzialny biznes w Polsce 2017. Dobre praktyki* (2018). Warsaw: Responsible Business Forum.

*Raport: Rynek Sponsoringu Sportowego 2018* (2018). Sponsoring Insight. Research & Consulting, http://www.sportbizforum.com/images/pdf/Raport-Rynek-sponsoringu-sportowego-2018.pdf.

Rawls, J. (2009). *Teoria sprawiedliwości*. Warsaw: PWN.

Reale, G. (2004). *Historia filozofii starożytnej*. T. III. Lublin: RW KUL.

Reilly, B.J., Kyj, M. (1994). Corporate Citizenship. *Review of Business*, 16: 37–43.

Reinhardt, F.L., Stavins, R.N., Vietor, R.H.K. (2008). *Corporate Social Responsibility Through an Economic Lens. Resources for the Future*. RFF-DP 08–12, 1616 P St. NW Washington, DC 20036, 202-328-5000, www.rff.org.

Rhenman, E. (1964). *Foeretagsdemokrati och foeretagsorganisation*. Stockholm: Thule.

Rieder, K., Voss, G. (2010). The Working Customer – an Emerging New Type of Consumer. *Psychology of Everyday Activity*, 3(2): 2–10.

Ritzer, G. (1997). *Makdonaldyzacja społeczeństwa*. Przeł. Stawowy, L. Warsaw: Warszawskie Wydawnictwo Literackie Muza S.A.

Rok, B. (ed) (2001). *Więcej niż zysk czyli Odpowiedzialny biznes: programy, strategie, standardy*. Warsaw: Responsible Business Forum.

Rok, B. (2004). *Odpowiedzialny biznes w nieodpowiedzialnym świecie*. Warsaw: Akademia Rozwoju Filantropii w Polsce Forum Odpowiedzialnego Biznesu.

Rok, B. (2013). *Podstawy odpowiedzialności społecznej w zarządzaniu*. Warsaw: Poltext.

Rok, B., Stolorz, S., Stanny, D. (2003). *Menedżerowie 500 i odpowiedzialny biznes. Wiedza – podstawy – praktyka*. Warsaw: Bank Światowy, Responsible Business Forum.

Roper Organization (1990). *The Environment: Public Attitudes and Individual Behaviour*. New York, NY: Roper Organization and SC Johnson & Son.

Rozporządzenie Ministra Pracy i Polityki Socjalnej z dnia 26 września 1997 r. w sprawie ogólnych przepisów bezpieczeństwa i higieny pracy (Dz.U./Journal of Laws 1997 Nr/No 129, poz./item 844).

Runes, D.D. (1964). *Dictionary of Philosophy*. Patterson, NJ: Littlefields Adams and Co.

Rybak, M. (2004). *Etyka menedżera – społeczna odpowiedzialność przedsiębiorstwa*. Warsaw: PWN.

Saiia, D.H. (2001). Philanthropy and Corporate Citizenship: Strategic Philanthropy is Good Corporate Citizenship. *Journal of Corporate Citizenship*, 2: 57–74.

Saiia, D.H., Carroll, A.B., Buchholtz, A.K. (2003). Philanthropy as Strategy: When Corporate Charity "Begins at Home". *Business and Society*, 42(2): 169–201.

Savage, G.T., Nix, T.H., Whitehead, C.J., Blair, J.D. (1991). Strategies for assessing and managing organizational stakeholders. *Academy of Management Executive*, 5(2): 61–75. https://doi.org/10.5465/ame.1991.4274682

Schlegelmilch, B.B., Öberseder, M. (2010). Half a Century of Marketing Ethics: Shifting Perspectives and Emerging Trends. *Journal of Business Ethics*, 93(1): 1–19.

Schlusberg, M.D. (1969). Corporate Legitimacy and Social Responsibility: The Role of Law. *California Management Review*, 12(1): 65–76.

Schwartz, M.S., Carroll, A.B. (2003). Corporate Social Responsibility: A Three-Domain Approach. *Business Ethics Quarterly*, 13(4): 503–530.

Seiffert, B., Morris, S., Bartkus, B. (2003). Comparing Big Givers and Small Givers: Financial Correlates of Corporate Philanthropy. *Journal of Business Ethics*, 45(3): 195–211.

Sen, S., Bhattacharya, C.B. (2001). Does Doing Good Always Lead to Doing Better? Consumer Reactions to Corporate Social Responsibility. *Journal of Marketing Research*, 38(2): 225–243.

Sen, S., Bhattacharya, C.B., Korschun, D. (2006). The Role of Corporate Social Responsibility in Strengthening Multiple Stakeholder Relationships. *Journal of the Academy of Marketing Science*, 34(2): 158–166.

Sethi, S.P. (1975). Dimension of Corporate Social Responsibility An Analytical Framework. *Califoria Management Review*, 17(3): 58–64.

Shaw, R. (2001). *Nowe spojrzenie na marketing*. Warsaw: Wydawnictwo Studio EMKA.

Sheth, J., Parvatiyar, A. (1995). The Evolution of Relationship Marketing. *International Business Review*, 4(4): 397–418.

Sikorska-Kowalska, M. (2010). Kierunki i formy działalności dobroczynnej na rzecz kobiet w wielkich miastach Królestwa Polskiego. Od dobroczynności do wsparcia, In: Przeniosło, M. i M. (eds) *Dobroczynność i pomoc społeczna na ziemiach polskich w XIX, XX i na początku XXI wieku*. T. 2, Kielce.

Simon, F. (1995). Global Corporate Philanthropy: A Strategic Framework. *International Marketing Review*, 12(4): 20–37.

Skiba, Ł. (2013). Różne tradycje rozumienia obowiązku: deontologia jako inspiracja. In: Oleksyn, T. (ed) *Filozofia a zarządzanie*. Warsaw: Wolters Kluwer Polska: 179–212.

Skrzypek, E. (2000). *Jakość i efektywność*. Lublin: Wydawnictwo Uniwersytetu M. Curie-Skłodowskiej.

Smith, N.C. (1994). The new corporate philanthropy. *Harvard Business Review*, 72, 105–114.

Smith, N.C., Lenssen, G. (2009). *Odpowiedzialność biznesu. Teoria i praktyka*. Warsaw: Wydawnictwo Studio EMKA.

Snider, J., Hill, R.P., Martin, D. (2003). Corporate Social Responsibility in the 21st Century: A View from the World's Most Successful Firms. *Journal of Business Ethics*, 48(2): 175–187.

Solomon, R.C. (1993). *Ethics and Excellence. Cooperation and Integrity in Business*. Oxford: Oxford University Press.

Srinivasan, D. (2019). The Antitrust Case Against Facebook. *Berkeley Business Law Journal*, 16(1): 39–101.

Środa, M. (1999). Przedmowa do wydania polskiego. In: Jackson, J. (ed) *Biznes i moralność*. Warsaw: PWN.

Stanford Research Institute (1963), *Internal note* (unpublished). Menlo Park, CA: Stanford Research Institute.

Starik, M. (1994). The Toronto conference: Reflections on stakeholder theory. *Business & Society*, 33(1): 82–131.

Stelzner, M. (2010). *2010 Social Media Marketing Industry Report. How Marketers Are Using Social Media to Grow Their Businesses*, http://www.socialmediaexaminer.com/social-media-marketing-industry-report-2010/.

Stelzner, M. (2018). *2018 Social Media Marketing Industry Report. How Marketers Are Using Social Media to Grow Their Businesses*, https://www.socialmediaexaminer.com/report2018/.

Sternberg, E. (1998). *Czysty biznes. Etyka biznesu w działaniu*. Warsaw: PWN.

Stoner, J.A., Freeman, R.E., Gilbert, D.R. (1998). *Kierowanie*. Warsaw: PWE.

Sułkowski, Ł. (2013). Dylematy etyczne z perspektywy krytycznego nurtu zarządzania. In: Sułkowski, Ł., Ignatowski, G. (eds) *Etyka w służbie biznesu*. Studia i Monografie No 44, Łódź: Wyd. Społecznej Akademii Nauk w Łodzi: 43–59.

Swanson, D.L. (1995). Addressing a Theoretical Problem by Reorienting the Corporate Social Performance Model. *Academy of Management Review*, 20(1): 43–64.

Świerk, J. (2016). Koncepcja interesariuszy w zarządzaniu strategią – analiza przypadku gminy Inowrocław. *Acta Universitatis Lodziensis. Folia Oeconomica*, 6(326): 31–32.

Swink, M., Nair, A. (2007). Capturing the Competitive Advantages of AMT: Design Manufacturing Integration as a Complementary Asset. *Journal of Operations Management*, 25(3), 736–754.

Swink, M., Narasimhan, R., Wang, C. (2007). Managing Beyond the Factory Walls: Effects of Four Types of Strategic Integration on Manufacturing Plant Performance. *Journal of Operations Management*, 25(1): 148–164.

Sztompka, P. (2016). *Kapitał społeczny. Teoria przestrzeni międzyludzkiej*. Cracow: Wydawnictwo Znak.

Teisl, M., Roe, B., Hicks, R.L. (2002). Can Eco-labels Tune a Market? Evidence from Dolphin-Safe Labeling. *Journal of Environmental Economics and Management*, 43(3): 339–359.

The Coca-Cola Company (TCCC) (2020). 2019 Business & Sustainability Report, https://www.coca-colacompany.com/reports/business-sustainability-report-2019.

The Coca-Cola Company (TCCC) (2022). The Coca-Cola Company's Responsible Marketing Policy, https://www.coca-colacompany.com/policies-and-practices/responsible-marketing-policy.

The Good Company. A survey of corporate social responsibility. The Economist 22 January 2005.

Thompson, J.K., Wartick, S.L., Smith, H.L. (1991). Integrating corporate social performance and stakeholder management: Implications for a research agenda in small business. *Research in Corporate Social Performance and Policy*, 12: 207–230.

Toffler, A. (1980). *The Third Wave: The Classic Study of Tomorrow*. New York, NY: William Morrow.

Trattner, C., Kappe, F. (2013). Social Stream Marketing on Facebook: A Case Study. *International Journal of Social and Humanistic Computing*, 2(1–2): 86–103.

Trevino, L.K. (1992). Moral Reasoning and Business Ethics: Implications for Research, Education and Management. *Journal of Business Ethics*, 11(5): 445–459.

Turban, D.B., Greening, D.W. (1997). Corporate Social Performance and Organizational Attractiveness to Prospective Employees. *Academy of Management Journal*, 40(3): 658–672.

UN Global Compact-Accenture CEO Study 2010. Accenture Sustainability Services: 20, https://www.fit.edu/sustainability/academics-and-research/research/.

UNESCO (2002). *Universal declaration on cultural diversity: A vision, a conceptual platform, a pool of ideas for implementation, a new paradigm*. Paris: United Nations Educational, Scientific and Cultural Organization.

United Nations Development Program in Poland 2007 (2007). *Społeczna odpowiedzialność w biznesie w Polsce. Wstępna analiza*. Warsaw: CeDeWu.

United Nations Global Contact, The Ten Principles of the UN Global Compact (2020), https://www.unglobalcompact.org/what-is-gc/mission/principles.

Ustawa z dnia 23 maja 1991 r. o związkach zawodowych (Dz.U./Journal of Laws 1991 Nr/No 55, poz./item 234).

Ustawa z dnia 26 czerwca 1974 r. Kodeks pracy (Dz. U./Journal of Laws 1974 Nr/No 24, poz./item141). Art. 11.

Ustawa z dnia 27 kwietnia 2001 r. o odpadach. (Dz.U./Journal of Laws 2001 Nr/No 62, poz./item 628).

Ustawa z dnia 29 września 1994 r. o rachunkowości (Dz.U./Journal of Laws 1994 Nr/No 121, poz./item 591), wraz z późn. zm.

Ustawa z dnia 7 kwietnia 2006 r. o informowaniu pracowników i przeprowadzaniu z nimi konsultacji (Dz.U./Journal of Laws 2006 Nr/No 79, poz./item 550).

Valasquez, M. (1983). Why Corporation are Not Morally Responsible for Anything They Do? *Business and Professional Ethics Journal*, 2(3): 1–18.

Valasquez, M. (2003). Debunking Corporate Moral Responsibility. *Business Ethics Quarterly*, 13(4): 531–562.

Valentine, S., Fleischman, G. (2008). Ethics Programs, Perceived Corporate Social Responsibility and Job Satisfaction. *Journal of Business Ethics*, 77(2): 159–172.

Valor, C. (2005). Corporate Social Responsibility and Corporate Citizenship: Towards Corporate Accountability. *Business and Society Review*, 110(2): 191–213.

Van Luijk, H.J. (2001). Business Ethics in Europe: A Tale of Two Efforts. In: Lang, R. (ed) *Wirtschaftsethik in Mittel und Osteuropa*. Munich: Rainer Ham: 9–18.

Vandermerwe, S., Oliff, M. (1990). Customers Drive Corporations Green. *Long Range Planning*, 23(6): 10–16.

Vargo, S.L., Lusch, R.F. (2004). Evolving to a New Dominant Logic for Marketing. *Journal of Marketing*, 68(1): 1–17.

Velazquez, M.G. (1988). *Business Ethics: Concept and Cases*. Engelwood Cliffs, NJ: Prentince Hall.

Vilanova, M., Lozano, J., Arenas, D. (2009). Exploring the Nature of the Relationship between CSR and Competitiveness. *Journal of Business Ethics*, 87(1): 57–69.

Visser, W. (2010). The Evolution and Revolution of Corporate Social Responsibility. In: Pohl, W.M., Tolhurst, N. (eds) *Responsible Business: How to Manage a CSR Strategy Successfully*. West Sussex: Wiley Online Library: 311–328.

Visser, W. (2012). The Future of CSR: Towards Transformative CSR, or CSR 2.0, Kaleidoscope Futures Paper Series, 1.

Vitell, S.J. Jr. (1986). *Marketing Ethics: Conceptual and Empirical Foundations of a Positive Theory of Decision Making in Marketing Situations Having Ethical Content*, Dysertacja, Texas Tech University.

Von Hippel, E. (2001). Innovation by User Communities. Learning from Open-Source Sofware. *Sloan Management Review*, 42(4): 82–86.

Waddock, S. (2000). The Multiple Bottom Lines of Corporate Citizenship: Social Investing, Reputation, and Responsibility Audits. *Business & Society Review*, 105(3): 323–346.

Waddock, S., Bodwell, C. (2004). Managing Responsibility: What can be Learnt from the Quality Movement? *California Management Review*, 47(1): 25–37.

Walton, C. (1967). *Corporate Social Responsibilities*. Belmont, TN: Wadsworth Publishing.

Wartick, S.L., Cochran, P.L. (1985). The Evolution of the Corporate Social Performance Model. *Academy of Management Review*, 10(4): 758–769.

Webley, S., More, E. (2003). *Does Business Ethics Plays? Ethics and Financial Performance*. London: Institute of Business Ethics.

Webster, F. (1992). The Changing Role of Marketing in the Corporation. *Journal of Marketing*, 56(4): 1–17.

Webster, F. (1998). Interactivity and Marketing Paradigm Shifts. *Journal of Interactive Marketing*, 12(1): 54–55

Węgrzecki, A. (2012). Aksjologiczne podstawy gospodarowania i etyki biznesu. In: Gasparski, W. (ed) *Biznes, etyka, odpowiedzialność*. Warsaw: PWN: 17–28.

Wells, H. (2002). The Cycles of Corporate Social Responsibility: An Historical Retrospective for the Twenty-first Century. *University of Kansas Law Review*, 51: 77–140.

Wicks, A.C., Gilbert, D.R., & Freeman, R.E. (1994). A Feminist Reinterpretation of the Stakeholder Concept. *Business Ethics Quarterly*, 4, 475–497.

Wiktor, J. (2016). System komunikacji marketingowej w perspektywie produktu systemowego. *Studia Ekonomiczne. Zeszyty Naukowe. Uniwersytetu Ekonomicznego w Katowicach*, 262: 47–56.

Williams, R. (1981) *Culture*. Glasgow: Fontana Paperbacks.

Williams, R., Barrett, J. (2000). Corporate Philanthropy, Criminal Activity, and Firm Reputation: Is there a Link? *Journal of Business Ethics*, 26(4): 341–350.

Windsor, D. (2001). The Future of Corporate Social Responsibility. *The International Journal of Organizational Analysis*, 9(3): 225–256.

Wood, D.J. (1991). Corporate Social Performance Revisited. *The Academy of Management Review*, 16(4-Oct): 691–718.

World Business Council for Sustainable Development (1999). *Meeting Changing Expectations. Corporate Social Responsibility*. New York, NY: WBCSD.

Wytyczne OECD dla przedsiębiorstw wielonarodowych, 10 Zasad ONZ Global Compact, Wytyczne ONZ dotyczące biznesu i praw człowieka, https://www.miir.gov.pl/strony/zadania/wsparcie-przedsiebiorczosci/spoleczna-odpowiedzialnosc-przedsiebiorstw-csr/raportowanie-spoleczne/.

Xie, Ch., Bagozzi, R.P., Troye, S.V. (2008). Trying to Prosume: Toward a Theory of Consumers as Co-creators of Value. *Journal of the Academy of Marketing Science*, 36: 109–122.

Yudelson, J. (1999). Adapting McCarthy's Four P's for the Twenty-first Century. *Journal of Marketing Education*, 21(1): 60–67.

Żabiński, L. (2002). *Marketing globalny i jego strategie*. Katowice: Wydawnictwo Akademii Ekonomicznej im. Karola Adamieckiego w Katowicach.

Zadek, S. (2001). *The Civil Corporation: The New Economy of Corporate Citizenship*. London: Earthscan.

Zbiegień-Maciąg, L. (1991). *Etyka w zarządzaniu*. Warsaw: PWN.

*Zdrowiej i po stronie natury. Raport wkładu firmy Żywiec Zdrój S.A. w rozwój Polski i regionów* (2018) Warsaw: Żywiec Zdrój S.A.

Żemigała, M. (2007). *Społeczna odpowiedzialność przedsiębiorstwa: budowanie zdrowej, efektywnej organizacji*. Warsaw: Wolters Kluwer Polska.

Żemigała, M. (2016). Społeczna odpowiedzialność biznesu. In: Klincewicz, K. (ed) *Zarządzanie, organizacje i organizowanie – przegląd perspektyw teoretycznych*. Warsaw: Wydawnictwo Naukowe Wydziału Zarządzania Uniwersytetu Warszawskiego: 226–235.

Zineldin, M., Philipson, S. (2007). Kotler and Borden are not dead: myth of relationship marketing and truth of the 4Ps. *Journal of Consumer Marketing*, 24(4): 229–241.

Zmuda, N. (2022). Ukraine: How Google is helping, https://www.thinkwithgoogle.com/collections/how-google-is-supporting-ukraine/.

Zu, L., Song, L. (2008). *Determinants of Managerial Values on Corporate Social Responsibility: Evidence from China*, IZA Discussion Paper No. 3449, Forschungsinstitut, zur Zukunft der Arbeit, Institute for the Study of Labor, https://www.econstor.eu/bitstream/10419/34845/1/564785873.pdf.

ZWIA (2018). *Zero Waste Planning Group*, http://zwia.org/standards/zw-definition/.

# Index

Note: **Bold** page numbers refer to tables; *Italic* page numbers refer to figures and page numbers followed by "n" denote endnotes.